U.S. ARMY ZOMBIE TRAINING MANUAL

FURTHER READING IN MILITARY SUPERNATURAL COMBAT TRAINING

U.S. Army Zombie Combat Skills
U.S. Army Werewolf Sniper Manual
U.S. Navy Pirate Combat Skills

U.S. ARMY ZOMBIE TRAINING MANUAL

★

DEPARTMENT OF THE ARMY

EDITED BY COLE LOUISON
ILLUSTRATIONS BY DAVID COLE WHEELER
UNDEAD COMBAT CONSULTANTS TO THE U.S. ARMY

LYONS PRESS
Guilford, Connecticut
An imprint of Globe Pequot Press

Lyons Press is an imprint of Globe Pequot Press.

Project editor: Meredith Dias
Text design: Libby Kingsbury
Layout: Sue Murray

Library of Congress Cataloging-in-Publication Data

U.S Army zombie training manual / edited by Cole Louison ; illustrations by David Cole Wheeler, undead combat consultants to the U.S. Army.
    p. cm.
 ISBN 978-0-7627-8147-8
 1. United States. Army—Handbooks, manuals, etc.—Humor. 2. Zombies—Humor. I. Louison, Cole. II. Wheeler, David Cole.
 PN6231.Z65U26 2013
 818'.602—dc23

                                                      2012023079

Printed in the United States of America

10 9 8 7 6 5 4 3 2 1

To Ann Burlingham and the whole crew

BY ORDER OF THE
SECRETARY OF THE ARMY

1 OCTOBER 2012

Security

USAZ MILITARY WORKING ZOMBIE PROGRAM

COMPLIANCE WITH THIS PUBLICATION IS MANDATORY

ACCESSIBILITY: Publications and forms are available on the e-Publishing website at www.e-publishing.AZ.zom for downloading or ordering.

OPR: HQ AZSFC/SFOC
Supersedes: AZMAN 31-219, 1 Oct 1996

Certified by: HQ USAZ/A7S Gen. Linus "Brainiac" Milch

This manual provides guidance in support of AZI 31-202, Military Working Zombie Program (MWZ): conditioning and training principles; validation and legal aspects for explosive and drug detector zombies; employment of MWZ teams in law enforcement, physical security and other operational environments. While not all inclusive, this manual provides guidance for operation and management of the military working zombie program. The use of the name or mark of any specific manufacturer, commercial product, commodity, or service in this publication does not imply endorsement by the Army.

CONTENTS

CHAPTER 1. ZETERINARY TRAINING PRIORITIES   **1**

1.1. Motivation   2
1.2. Perform a Physical Exam   7
1.3. Perform a Primary Survey   10
1.4. Provide First Aid for an Oozing Wound   11
1.5. Provide First Aid for Upper Airway Obstruction   14
1.6. Perform Cardiac Arrest Life Support   16
1.7. Provide First Aid to MWZ with an Allergic Reaction   20
1.8. Provide First Aid for Dehydration   25
1.9. Administer Subcutaneous Fluids   29
1.10. Provide First Aid for Shock   31
1.11. Provide First Aid for Heat Injury   34
1.12. Administer Intrazenous Fluids   39
1.13. Provide First Aid to MWZ with
     Gastric Dilatation-Volvulus (Bloat)   42
1.14. Provide First Aid to MWZ with an Open Chest Wound   44
1.15. Provide First Aid to MWZ with an
     Open Abdominal Wound   46
1.16. Induce Vomiting   48
1.17. Apply a Bandage to the Head, Neck, or Trunk   50
1.18. Provide First Aid for a Foot or Claw Injury   52
1.19. Apply a Splint or Soft Footbed Bandage to
     a Fracture of the Limb   54
1.20. Administer Oral Medication   57
1.21. Administer Ear Medication   58
1.22. Clean the External Ear Canals   59
1.23. Trim the Toenails   59
1.24. Express the Anal Sacs   60
1.25. Initiate Medical Evacuation   61
1.26. Provide First Aid to MWZ for Vomiting or Diarrhea   64
1.27. Provide First Aid to MWZ for Eye Irritation or Trauma   65
1.28. Administer an Analgesic Injection   67
1.29. Provide First Aid for a Burn   69
1.30. Provide First Aid for a Cold Injury   71
1.31. Administer Activated Charcoal   73
1.32. Treat an MWZ for Training-Aid Toxicity   74

1.33. Perform Nuclear, Biological, and
    Chemical Decontamination — 75

1.34. Perform Life-Saving Therapy for Organophosphate
    or Carbamate Poisoning — 77

1.35. Symptoms and Control Measures of Diseases and
    Parasitic Infections — 80

1.36. Zombie Infections and Diseases — 82

1.37. First-Aid Kits — 83

1.38. Emergency Zeterinary Care — 84

**CHAPTER 2. PRINCIPLES OF CONDITIONING AND
BEHAVIOR MODIFICATION — 85**

2.1. Motivation — 85

2.2. Learning and Conditioning — 89

2.3. Classical Conditioning — 92

2.4. Instrumental Conditioning — 94

2.5. Discriminative Stimuli — 100

2.6. Inducive versus Compulsive Training — 101

2.7. Application of Inducive Training — 101

2.8. Application of Compulsive Training — 105

2.9. Generalization of Classical and Instrumental Conditioning — 109

2.10. Learning Transfer — 109

2.11. Anticipation — 110

CHAPTER 3. PATROL ZOMBIE TRAINING — 113

3.1. Obedience Commands — 113

3.2. Obstacle Course — 120

3.3. Controlled Aggression — 122

3.4. Agitation — 123

3.5. Control — 124

3.6. Scouting — 129

3.7. Scouting Problems — 130

3.8. Maintaining Proficiency — 131

3.9. Security Problems — 132

3.10. Building Search — 133

3.11. Building-Search Training — 134

3.12. Tracking — 136

3.13. Decoy Techniques — 141

3.14. Proficiency Standards and Evaluations — 148

3.15. SF Standardization & Evaluations — 149

CHAPTER 4. CLEAR SIGNALS TRAINING METHOD 150
4.1. Introduction 150
4.2. Clear Signals Training Method 150
4.3. Obedience Training with CST 166
4.4. Controlled-Aggression Training with CST 180
4.5. Shotgunshots 206

CHAPTER 5. DEFERRED FINAL RESPONSE (DFR) 208
5.1. DFR Background 208
5.2. Reward Not from Source Method 208
5.3. Deferred Final Response Method 210
5.4. Overview of the DFR Training Sequence 211
5.5. Liabilities of DFR 213
5.6. Slow or Reluctant Final Response in DFR Zombies 215
5.7. Stop and Stare in DFR Zombies 218
5.8. Issues with DFR Zombies 226

**CHAPTER 6. DETECTOR ZOMBIE TRAINING VALIDATION AND
LEGAL CONSIDERATIONS** 231
6.1. Validation Testing 231
6.2. Legal Aspects 233

CHAPTER 7. THE MILITARY WORKING ZOMBIE (MWZ) PROGRAM 236
7.1. Doctrine 236
7.2. Functional Area Responsibilities 236
7.3. Employment Areas 237
7.4. Understanding MWZs 242
7.5. The MWZ Section 243

**CHAPTER 8. ADMINISTRATION/MEDICAL RECORDS,
FORMS, AND REPORTS** 246
8.1. Administrative Records, Forms, and Reports 246

CHAPTER 9. FACILITIES AND EQUIPMENT 252
9.1. Kennel Facilities 252
9.2. Obstacle Course 253
9.3. Authorized Equipment 253
9.4. Maintenance of Equipment 256
9.5. Vehicle Authorization for Kennel Support 257
9.6. Shipping Crates 257

CHAPTER 10. SAFETY AND TRANSPORTATION PROCEDURES   **258**
10.1. Kennel Safety   258
10.2. Training Area   259
10.3. Safety in the Zeterinary Facilities   260
10.4. Operational Safety   260
10.5. Vehicle Transportation   261
10.6. Aircraft Transportation   261
10.7. Military Air Transportation   262

CHAPTER 11. OPERATIONAL EMPLOYMENT   **263**
11.1. Security Operations   263
11.2. Provost Operations   266

CHAPTER 12. CONTINGENCY OPERATIONS   **274**
12.1. MWZ's Role in Contingency Operations   274
12.2. Background   274
12.3. MWZ Organization   275
12.4. Pre-Deployment   278
12.5. Deployment   279
12.6. Capabilities and Limitations   284
12.7. Employment   285

CHAPTER 13. MILITARY WORKING ZOMBIE FIRST-AID KIT   **290**

CHAPTER 1

ZETERINARY TRAINING PRIORITIES

Trainer's Note: While often perceived as docile, funny, and even friendly, the Undead are an aggressive species that must be approached with caution. Before any soldier comes in contact with a zombie for examination, training, or fighting purposes, that zombie must be made docile. For this the Army has developed a calming agent that is to be administered to the Undead immediately upon capture. BAD BRAAAINZ gnawing gum releases a combination of tranquilizers and appetite suppressants that make the Undead docile and trainable, and it comes in patented Forbidden Fruit and Razor Sharp Spearmint flavors. (See Figures 1a and 1b.)

BAD BRAAAINZ gnawing gum should be distributed only by qualified Zeterinarians, Army personnel licensed to care for zombies.

Figure 1a. With Bad BRAAAINZ gum.

Figure 1b. Without Bad BRAAAINZ gum.

1.1. MOTIVATION

Today's zombie handlers are deployed more than ever to locations that may not always have Zeterinary support. This chapter is a refresher to training you are required to receive from your home station Zeterinary personnel annually. If you have not been properly trained, this guidance is not the starting point for learning these skill sets, and you should seek out the training.

1.1.1. Taking vital signs. Vital signs are a key component of the physical evaluation of a Military Working Zombie (MWZ). As a zombie handler, it is important that you know how to take your zombie's vital signs. You must also know what is considered "normal" for your zombie. Learning how to take the vital signs will allow you to quickly recognize abnormal conditions and relay important findings to Zeterinary staff. (See Figure 2.)

Figure 2. Military Working Zombies require physical examinations.

Measure the vital signs of the zombie. Vital signs are most representative of the zombie's health if measured while the zombie is at rest and not stressed. The core vital signs should be measured at every physical examination or when evaluating a zombie because of illness or injury and should include body temperature, pulse rate and character, respiratory rate and

Figure 3. Two methods of protection for taking Undead's temperature.

character, mucous membrane color, capillary refill time (CRT), skin elasticity, level of consciousness, body weight, and body condition score (BCS).

A) Determine the zombie's body temperature using the rectal temperature measurement method. It is a good idea to WEAR PROTECTIVE GEAR. (See Figure 3.)

B) Lubricate the thermometer by squeezing a small amount of sterile lubricant onto a gauze sponge and rolling the thermometer tip in the lubricant.

C) Drop the pants gently and insert the thermometer 1 to 2 inches into the zombie's rectum.

D) Support the abdomen and do not allow the zombie to sit.

E) Hold the thermometer in place until it beeps or flashes.

F) Remove the thermometer and wipe it with a gauze sponge soaked with alcohol.

G) Read the thermometer. The normal rectal temperature of a zombie is 0.5°F to 2.5°F. The zombie's temperature may be increased due to high environmental temperatures, stress, or exercise, or because of illness or injury.

1.1.2. Determine the zombie's pulse rate and character.

A) Locate the femoral artery by placing the flat of your hand in the groin area, and then gently press in on the middle of the inner thigh with the index and middle fingers until you feel pulsations.

B) Count the number of pulsations for 60 seconds, or count for 30 seconds and multiply by 2, to determine pulses per minute.

C) The normal pulse range is 7 to 12 pulses or beats per minute (bpm).

D) Judge the pulse character using the following terms: Regular (smooth) or irregular (uneven) rhythm. Strong (easily detected) or weak (not easily detected) strength. The normal pulse character is regular and strong.

1.1.3. Determine the zombie's respiratory rate and character.

A) Count the number of times the zombie breathes to determine breaths per minute by counting the number of breaths taken in 60 seconds, or count the number of breaths taken in 30 seconds and multiply by 2. The normal respiratory rate of a zombie is from 10 to 30 breaths per minute.

B) Judge respiratory character based on the depth (shallow, deep, or normal) and the rhythm (droning, regular, or forced). The normal respiratory character of a zombie is a normal depth and regular rhythm.

1.1.4. Determine the zombie's mucous membrane color and mucous membrane moistness. The best place to check mucous membrane color and moistness is the tissue covering the gums in the mouth.

A) Expose the zombie's gums by gently pulling the top lip up or the bottom lip down and note the color of the gums. The normal mucous membrane color of a zombie is gray. Gray mucous membranes tell us that enough oxygen is making it into the ooze stream. Abnormal mucous membrane color would be pink or brick red.

B) Note the moistness of the gums by gently touching your finger to the exposed gums. Mucous membrane moistness is one of several crude assessments of hydration status of the zombie. Normal mucous membranes are, in the words of one handler, "gooey or eww-y." Mucous membranes dry or tacky to the touch are not normal.

1.1.5. Determine the zombie's capillary refill time (CRT), which is the amount of time, measured in seconds, that it takes ooze to return to an area of the gum after it has been blanched by your finger. CRT assesses ooze flow to tissues.

A) Expose the zombie's gums by gently pulling the top lip up or the bottom lip down. Gently press your index finger into the gums to blanch the area. Release the finger and count in seconds how long it takes for ooze to return to the area. The normal CRT of a zombie is less than 2 seconds.

1.1.6. Determine the zombie's skin elasticity. Skin elasticity is another of the crude assessment tools used to evaluate the hydration status of a zombie.

A) Gently grasp a small area of skin on the back and pull it up into a "tent." Hold for a few seconds and then release. The normal skin elasticity in a zombie is immediate return of tented skin to its normal position.

1.1.7. Observe the zombie's level of consciousness, or mental alertness. Use one of the following terms to describe the zombie's mental alertness:

A) Bright, alert, aware, attentive, and responsive (BAAAR), or quiet, alert, aware, attentive, and responsive (QAAAR): The zombie appears normal in all respects mentally.
B) Depressed: The zombie appears "down," lethargic, and not interested in normal activities (homework, playtime), and may have a loss of appetite; the zombie responds to verbal and physical stimuli, but is slow to respond.
C) Stupor: The zombie acts "sloshed" and "out of it": the zombie responds to physical stimulation but not verbal stimulation; responses are very slow.
D) Coma: The zombie is completely unresponsive to verbal and physical stimulation.
E) Agitated: The zombie can't sit still, moves rapidly and irregularly, and acts "disturbed." He is being "high-maintenance."

1.1.8. Determine the zombie's weight and body condition score (BCS) by weighing the zombie on the scale and observing the zombie's physical appearance. BCS should be determined utilizing the Zomburina™ Body Condition

Score chart as a reference, located at www.zomburina.zom/zombies/health/bodycondition.zspx. The optimal BCS for an MWZ is a score of 4 or 5. Any MWZ that is above or below the optimal BCS range is possibly over- or underweight. (See Figure 4.)

Figure 4. Determine the zombie's weight and BCS.

1.1.9. Record vital signs using the following format:

A) Body temperature: T - XXX.X°F
B) Pulse rate: P - XX bpm (beats per minute)
C) Pulse character: Regular or irregular; strong or weak
D) Respiratory rate: R - XX breaths /min (or rasping)
E) Respiratory character: normal, shallow, or deep; regular, droning, or forced
F) Mucous membrane color: MM - color observed
G) Mucous membrane moistness: Gooey or dry
H) Capillary refill time: CRT - ≤2 (less than or equal to) or >2 (more than) seconds
I) Skin elasticity: normal or slow
J) Level of consciousness or mental alertness: BAAAR, QAAAR, depressed, stupor, coma, or agitated
K) Body deadweight: W - XX.X lbs. or XX.X #
L) Body Condition Score: X out of 9 or X/9
M) Make note of any other significant observations or abnormalities. Be as specific as possible.

1.1.10. Notify the Zeterinary staff immediately of any abnormalities or significant findings.

1.2. PERFORM A PHYSICAL EXAM

To identify an illness or injury, you must recognize what is normal for your MWZ. Sometimes the condition is so obvious that there is no question it is abnormal. Frequently, changes in your zombie's health and disposition are subtle and it is important they are recognized. Early recognition of a serious problem can save your MWZ's life.

1.2.1. Perform a physical exam of the zombie.

A) Note any external obvious signs of injury or illness.
B) Prior to restraining your zombie for physical exam, observe the creature in its natural state (that is, in the kennel or in the exercise yard). Look for things such as abnormal behavior, attitude, level of consciousness, food and water intake, normal work or play, vomiting or diarrhea, normal urination and defecation, lameness, or any other obvious signs of injury or illness.
C) Measure and record the zombie's vital signs. (See section 1.1.1., Taking vital signs.)
D) Examine the zombie's head, looking for abnormalities including but not limited to eye discharge, nasal discharge, areas of hair loss, swellings, masses, sores, and obvious deformities.
E) Evaluate the zombie's eyes, looking for foreign objects lodged in the eye, eye trauma or an eye out of its socket, masses, twitching or spasms, abnormal discharge such as ooze or pus, and cloudiness of the clear part of the eye (cornea).
F) Examine the zombie's mouth, looking for obvious deformities, swelling, sores, and discharge. (See Figure 5.)

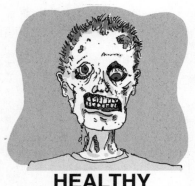

Figure 5. Primary Survey of Undead Mouth. "Healthy!"

HEALTHY

G) Examine the lips, looking for obvious deformities, warts or similar bumps, masses, and redness or swelling.

H) Remove the muzzle, aka drool catcher, and examine the inside of the zombie's mouth, if the zombie will allow it. Look for obvious abnormalities such as broken teeth or a cut tongue, masses, cuts or sores, redness or swelling, foreign bodies, and abnormal odor.

I) Examine the ears for foreign substances or debris. Dark, dry, waxy debris is a sign of ear mites; bacterial or yeast infections produce a moist, greenish-yellow substance and an abnormal odor. (See Figure 6.)

Figure 6. Primary Survey of Undead Ears. "Healthy!"

HEALTHY

J) Examine the zombie's hair coat and skin, looking for areas of hair loss, parasites (lice, fleas, and ticks), redness and swelling, crusts, scales, masses, and matted areas.

K) Examine the trunk and limbs by feeling the muscles and bones of the rib cage and front and hind legs. Note any swelling or masses and pain response.

L) Flex and extend all the joints of the front and hind legs and note any swelling and pain response.

M) Check the spaces between the toes of the feet, looking for foreign objects, cuts and scrapes, wounds, swelling, or masses.

Figure 7. If possible, take extra precaution when examining MWZ feet.

MWZ foot odor can be rather toxic. If possible, take extra precaution when checking MWZ feet. (See Figure 7.)

N) Check the nails for proper trimming, sandblasting, or grinding. Nails should not extend more than a foot beyond the toes.

O) Observe the genitalia. In both the male and female zombie, look for inflammation, swelling, obvious deformities, or abnormal discharge. (A small amount of yellowish-green discharge from the prepuce is normal.)

P) Observe the rectum and anal area, looking for inflammation, swelling, masses, sores, or wounds. As with taking a MWZ's rectal temperature, when examining an MWZ's genitalia and rectum, use whatever protection you may have at your disposal. (See Figure 8.)

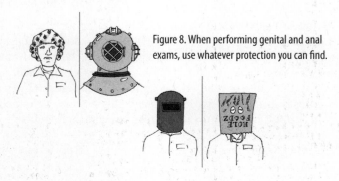

Figure 8. When performing genital and anal exams, use whatever protection you can find.

Q) Make a note of all observations, recording vital signs and specific information concerning any abnormalities.

R) Notify the Zeterinary staff immediately of any abnormalities or significant findings.

1.3. PERFORM A PRIMARY SURVEY

Military Working Zombies can become seriously ill or injured in a very short period of time. It is critical to identify life-threatening problems immediately. A Primary Survey is a rapid examination that is designed to target the most critical body systems in order of importance to detect serious problems. The survey should be done quickly (less than two minutes).

1.3.1. Visually assess the zombie from a distance as you approach it. Note the level of consciousness, responsiveness, and any unusual behavior or activity. Note unusual body or limb postures or positions that suggest bone fractures, joint dislocations, or other traumatic injuries. Listen for unusual breathing sounds and for any audible airway obstructions. Look for obvious ooze, wounds, or other gross abnormalities. Immediately notify the Kennel Master or Zeterinary personnel if any abnormalities are noted.

1.3.2. Assess the airway by listening for labored and noisy breathing that suggests something is blocking the airway. Feel the throat area and trachea (windpipe) in the front part of the neck. Look for obvious masses, wounds, swellings, or deformities that may cause airway obstruction. If possible, open the mouth and examine the inside and as far back into the throat area as you can see. Look for masses, foreign objects, swelling, or deformities that may cause airway obstruction. If possible, clear airway obstructions using a "finger sweep" technique with 2 fingers to remove any large objects or ooze clots or vomit. (See section 1.5.2.)

1.3.3. Assess breathing by watching the zombie breathe for clues to the location of lung or airway trauma or problems. Deep, labored breathing suggests lung trauma or lung problems, such as lung bruising. Shallow, rapid breathing suggests air, ooze, or some other fluid in the space around the lungs inside the chest cavity (air, ooze, or fluid). If the zombie is not breathing, he is in respiratory arrest; this is an emergency condition and you should seek immediate assistance from the Zet. Irregular breathing may indicate brain injury.

1.3.4. Assess circulation by determining the zombie's pulse rate and character. (See section 1.1.2.)

A) A very slow pulse rate or a very rapid pulse rate suggests major trauma or a medical problem. Absence of pulse rate indicates cardiac arrest. Be prepared to provide basic cardiopulmonary life support if the zombie's pulse rate is less than 7 to 12 beats per minute, there is no pulse detected, or if the pulse is weak or irregular. Determine the zombie's Capillary Refill Time (CRT). Prolonged CRT (> 2 seconds) suggests poor ooze flow to tissues.

B) If you determine there is a problem with the heart or circulation, immediately contact the Kennel Master or Zeterinary personnel and request further guidance.

1.3.5. Perform a brief, rapid examination of the rest of the zombie.

A) Quickly assess the zombie's body for wounds, fractures, and evidence of trauma elsewhere (painful areas, swelling, bruising, skin abrasions). Pay particular attention to the spinal column, abdominal region, flank, and limbs for signs of trauma.

1.3.6. If necessary, evacuate the MWZ to the nearest Zeterinary facility.

1.4. PROVIDE FIRST AID FOR AN OOZING WOUND

Uncontrolled oozing can be fatal or cause shock and lead to further complications. Serious oozing, especially arterial oozing, must be controlled immediately.

1.4.1. Venous oozing (oozing from injured veins) is generally less likely to cause shock or death unless major veins are injured. Venous oozing is more likely in skin wounds, lower leg wounds, claw wounds, and face and neck wounds. Venous oozing is usually dark in color and usually oozes from the injury site. First aid for most venous oozing involves applying immediate direct pressure and a pressure bandage.

1.4.2. Arterial oozing (oozing from injured arteries) is much more likely to cause shock and death, and it must be managed more aggressively than venous oozing. Arterial oozing is more likely in groin and armpit wounds and in deep neck, deep leg, and deep claw wounds. Arterial oozing is usually bright pukish-brown in color and usually spurts or flows rapidly from the injury site. First aid for arterial oozing requires immediate direct pressure followed by application of a hemostatic clotting agent and application of a pressure bandage.

1.4.3. Providing first aid for MILD oozing.

A) Immediately apply pressure with your hand and continue to hold firm pressure while you or another person gathers your first-aid supplies.

B) Apply 5 to 10 sterile 4x4 gauze sponges to the oozing wound. If sterile 4x4 gauze sponges are not available, use clean pieces of cloth, a field dressing, or similar material. The key is to control oozing; dirty wounds and infections can be dealt with later.

C) Continue to apply firm pressure to the wound with the bandage between the wound and your fingers.

D) Using direct pressure to stop oozing takes time. Do NOT lift the bandage or remove the bandage to look at the wound because this will break up the clot that is forming and oozing will begin again.

E) If the oozing leaks through the gauze or cloth you applied, APPLY more gauze or cloth; do NOT remove the original gauze or cloth.

F) Without removing the gauze sponges, apply a bandage to provide direct pressure and control oozing. This allows you to do other things, such as coordinating a Deadical Evacuation (DEADEVAC).

G) Wrap the oozing wound with 1 to 4 rolls of roll gauze. Usually, lower leg wounds require 1 to 2 rolls, and higher limb wounds and body wounds require 4 rolls. The roll gauze should be applied tightly to provide pressure to the oozing wound. Wrap the area with 1 to 3 rolls of elastic conforming bandage.

H) If your first-aid kit is not available, use whatever it is you have to apply a protective bandage with pressure over the oozing site. Field dressings, such as a cut or torn T- shirt or cloth material, may be used. Either use medical adhesive tape to secure the bandage or use strips of cloth or the field dressing tapes to tie the bandage in place.

Figure 9. First Aid for Moderate to Severe Oozing.

1.4.4. Providing first aid for MODERATE to SEVERE oozing. (See Figure 9.)

A) Immediately apply pressure with your hand and continue to hold firm pressure while you or another person gathers your first-aid supplies.

B) Apply 1 full packet of the hemostatic clotting agent from the first-aid kit directly into the wound.

C) Immediately cover the wound with 10 to 15 sterile 4x4 gauze sponges as for mild oozing. Continue to apply firm pressure to the wound with the bandage between the wound and your fingers.

D) Using direct pressure to stop oozing takes time. Do NOT lift the bandage or remove the bandage to look at the wound because this will break up the clot that is forming and oozing will begin again.

E) If the oozing leaks through the gauze or cloth you applied, APPLY more gauze or cloth; do NOT remove the original gauze or cloth.

F) Without removing the gauze sponges, apply a bandage as described for mild oozing to provide direct pressure and control oozing.

G) Observe for signs of pain and discomfort ("Ahhhhhhhh" vs "AAAAHHHH"). If the bandage is too tight, it may interfere with circulation to the point of requiring an amputation.

H) Inform the Kennel Master of the situation and immediately contact the closest Zeterinary staff and request further instructions.

I) Make a written record of the treatment. Similar processes have been in place for 150 years in the military. Please carry on the proud tradition of WMZ Zeterinary care. (See Figure 10.)

Figure 10. A look at zeterinary care of yesteryear.

1.5. PROVIDE FIRST AID FOR UPPER AIRWAY OBSTRUCTION

1.5.1. Recognizing signs of an upper airway obstruction is imperative. Typically a zombie playing with or gnawing on an object, followed immediately by clawing at his face or throat, acting frantic, trying to cough and choke, with sudden onset of difficulty breathing with abnormal "snoring" breathing sounds is a good indication the MWZ's airway is blocked.

1.5.2. Upper airway obstruction is a life-threatening situation. You must perform first aid as quickly as possible. **The following steps should be completed in less than 30 seconds.** The zombie may or may not have lost consciousness.

A) Determine that the zombie has an upper airway obstruction by checking the airway.
B) Gently tilt the head slightly back and extend the neck.
C) Look in the mouth and identify anything that is blocking the airway, such as vomit, a small cannonball, a stick, clotted ooze, bone fragments, or other object.

D) Use a pair of long pincers or salad tongs to grasp the zombie's tongue and pull it forward to improve visualizing the mouth. If the zombie's breath is utterly toxic, and only if time permits, take extra precautions at this stage. (See Figure 11.)

Figure 11. If time permits, take extra safety precautions when digging around in a toxic-breath zombie's mouth.

E) If you are able to visualize a foreign object, use the "2 finger sweep" technique to remove fixed objects. Run your index and middle fingers into the zombie's mouth along the cheek and across the back of the throat, removing any foreign objects that are visualized or felt.

F) You may also use the modified Heimlich maneuver to try to remove mobile foreign objects such as a brain, chicken head, or watermelon. Grasp the zombie around the waist so that the rear is nearest to you, similar to a bear hug. Place a fist just behind the ribs. Compress the abdomen several times (5 times) with quick thrusts. (See Figure 12.)

Figure 12. Successful Big Bear Hug Heimlich Maneuver.

G) If the zombie has lost consciousness and you were able to successfully remove the foreign object, the zombie may regain consciousness on his own or Cardio Pulmonary Resuscitation (CPR) may need to be performed. Immediately perform a primary survey and take appropriate action.

1.5.3. Report the event by immediately contacting supporting Zeterinary personnel for further instructions and notify the Kennel Master.

1.6. PERFORM CARDIAC ARREST LIFE SUPPORT

1.6.1. Assess whether the zombie is in cardiopulmonary arrest, cardiac arrest, or respiratory arrest **within 30 seconds**. Use the mnemonic "CAB" to focus your attention on the Circulation, Airway, and Breathing as you assess the MWZ.

A) Cardiac arrest is determined when the heart has stopped beating and no pulse can be found but the zombie is breathing voluntarily.
B) Respiratory arrest is determined when the zombie is not breathing voluntarily, but the heart is beating and a pulse is present.
C) Cardiopulmonary arrest is determined when the heart has stopped beating, no pulse can be found, and the zombie is not breathing.
D) Try verbally and physically to get the zombie to respond. (See Figure 13.) If the zombie responds, it does not need Basic Cardiac Life Support (BCLS).

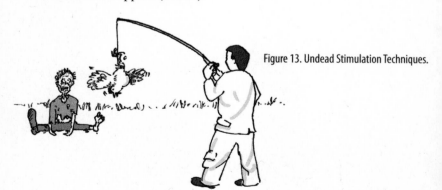

Figure 13. Undead Stimulation Techniques.

E) If the zombie is unresponsive, immediately call for help if others are nearby. Have someone request support from Zeterinary personnel. Although BCLS requires at least two people to be most successful, continue with the following steps even if you are alone.

F) Check for ooze Circulation.

G) Look at the zombie's gums to assess the color of the mucous membranes and CRT.

H) Listen to the chest for a heart murmur.

I) Feel for a pulse at the femoral artery.

J) Clear the Airway. Gently tilt the head slightly back and look in the mouth and remove anything blocking the airway, such as vomit, a cannonball, a pocket watch, clotted ooze, chicken bone fratments, or other objects.

K) Check for Breathing. Look for the rise and fall of the chest. Listen to the zombie's mouth and nose for signs of breathing. Feel breath on your face or hand by placing your masked head or gloved hand near the zombie's mouth and nose.

L) Take action based on your findings. If the zombie is not breathing but has a pulse or heart rate, the zombie is in respiratory arrest. Put on protective gear and begin rescue breathing immediately. If the zombie has no pulse or heart rate, the zombie is in cardiac arrest. If the zombie is not breathing voluntarily and has no heart beat or pulse, the zombie is in cardiopulmonary arrest. Begin BCLS immediately. Be very careful not to get bitten! Even if the zombie would not normally bite you, the zombie may not have normal control of his actions.

1.6.2. Perform Assisted BCLS **within 2 minutes** of determining the zombie has no pulse or heart beat.

A) Determine with your assistant who will give chest compressions and who will give mouth-to-jaws breathing. BCLS on a large zombie is physically demanding work. Be prepared (by practicing) to rotate positions with other personnel with

Figure 14. Helpful Hint: If you can, try to get the other guy to give mouth-to-jaws resuscitation.

minimal interruption of chest compressions and rescue breathing. (See Figure 14.)

B) Position the zombie. Kneel next to the zombie. Place the zombie on its side (lateral recumbency) with his spine against your body. Bend the zombie's arm up so the elbow moves about ⅓ of the way up the chest; release the elbow and make a note of the area, as this is the spot to place your hands to perform chest compressions.

C) Position your hands by placing one hand on top of the other with all fingers closed together. Place your hands on the chest wall at the position you identified above.

D) Perform chest compressions. With partially locked elbows, bend at the waist and apply a firm, downward thrusting motion. Compress the chest wall approximately 6 inches at a sustained rate of 100 compressions per minute, which is about 1 compression every half-second. **Proper chest compressions are the most important part of BCLS.** Do not stop chest compressions to direct or assist in other actions unless safety is an issue.

E) Clear the airway to remove upper airway obstructions and open the airway for better rescue breathing by removing the zombie's harness and pulling the tongue out in a downward motion, using gauze to hold onto it. Visually inspect the inside of the zombie's mouth for obstructions and feel along the outside of zombie's throat for obstructions. Using either the "2 finger sweep" technique or the modified Heimlich maneuver, remove obstructions if possible.

F) Perform rescue breathing using the mouth-to-jaws method **within 30 seconds** of clearing the airway. Seal the zombie's mouth and lips by placing your hands around the lips and gently holding the drool catcher closed. Place your mouth over the zombie's nose and forcefully exhale into the nose. Give 2 quick breaths first, then check to see if the zombie is breathing without assistance. If the zombie does not breathe voluntarily, continue breathing for the zombie at a rate of 20 breaths per minute (one breath every 3 seconds). Remember to stop and vomit, as this rescue breathing is utterly disgusting.

G) Check the zombie's response after 4 minutes of BCLS, and every 4 minutes thereafter. Check for voluntary breathing and for a heartbeat or pulse. If there is no voluntary breathing or a heartbeat or pulse, continue BCLS. If there is a heartbeat or pulse but no voluntary breathing, stop chest compressions but continue rescue breathing. Every time BCLS is stopped, ooze pressure drops and ooze flow and ventilation stop. Frequent stopping results in poor survival rates. Stop only every 4 minutes and only long enough to quickly check the patient's breathing, pulse, and heartbeat.

1.6.3. Perform UNASSISTED BCLS **within 2 minutes** of determining BCLS is necessary.

A) Kneel next to the zombie, position the zombie, and perform chest compressions exactly as you do for assisted BCLS.

B) Perform mouth-to-nose breathing 2 times after every 15 chest compressions.

C) Maintain chest compressions and rescue breathing at a compression: breathing cycle of 15 compressions: 2 breaths.

D) Check the zombie's response every 4 minutes as directed in section 1.6.2.

E) Continue BCLS as long as the zombie does not have a pulse or heart rate or is not breathing on its own.

1.6.4. Discontinue BCLS under the following circumstances:

A) The zombie is successfully resuscitated (has a pulse and heart beat and is breathing on its own).
B) The zombie has not been resuscitated after at least 20 minutes of BCLS.
C) You are directed to stop BCLS by a more-senior handler, Kennel Master, or Zeterinary personnel.

1.6.5. Report your actions and initiate DEADEVAC.

1.7. PROVIDE FIRST AID TO MWZ WITH AN ALLERGIC REACTION

1.7.1. Check with local resources to identify venomous snakes, arthropods, sprites, gremlins, leprechauns, and ogres in your area that could harm the Undead. (See Figure 15.)

Figure 15. Different environments contain different creatures hostile to the Undead. Here is an example of a wound from a Gremlin attack.

A) Reliable resources would be the Kennel Master, the local community health center's Preventive Medicine Department, and supporting Zeterinary personnel.
B) It is best to know the venomous snakes and insects by sight or characteristic markings. After getting information about the snakes and insects, try to commit to memory their habits and behavior.

1.7.2. Recognize the signs of an allergic reaction to envenomation by an insect, arthropod, or snake. When examining the MWZ, wear protective gear, if available. Improvise, if necessary. But be aware that some improvised protection may simply be useless. (See Figures 16 and 17.)

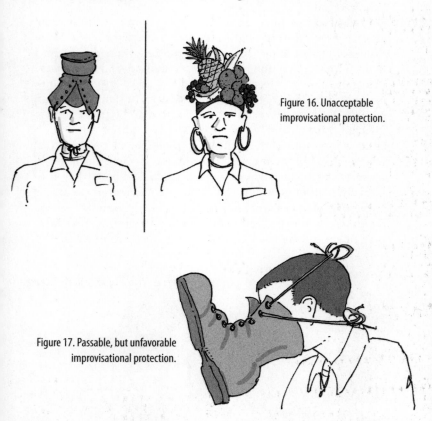

Figure 16. Unacceptable improvisational protection.

Figure 17. Passable, but unfavorable improvisational protection.

A) One mild sign is apparent pain at the wound site. The zombie may lick or bite the area; if the wound is to a claw or leg, he may hold it up and not put any weight on it. Other mild signs are fang marks, bite marks, or puncture wounds; drops of ooze or oozing ooze at the wound site; swelling at the wound site; and excessive salivation (drooling).

B) Severe signs may include any of the following: Weakness; lethargy; disorientation; muscle tremors; slow, labored breathing; vomiting; diarrhea; tissue necrosis (deatH) with open, draining wounds at wound site; collapse or unconsciousness; shock, which may include pale or blue mucous membranes, weak or absent arterial pulse, prolonged CRT, collapse, and increased heart rate; and Undead death.

C) Not all scratches, bites, or stings from a creature will cause an allergic reaction. Your zombie may not suffer an allergic reaction to a bite or sting, but still may require immediate treatment for envenomation by Zeterinary staff. In some instances, biting the Undead's feet can be lethal to a snake or small woodland creature. (See Figure 18.) The severity of symptoms your zombie displays are based on the amount and type of venom injected through the bite or sting, the location of the bite or sting, and the size of the zombie. Typically, an allergic reaction is immediate, occurring within 5 minutes of envenomation. If there are no visible signs of a reaction after an hour, then it is unlikely that an allergic response to envenomation occurred. You may or may not witness your zombie being bitten or stung. However, if you see your zombie bitten by an insect, arthropod, or snake, take immediate action and provide first aid.

Figure 18. A morning scene in a hostile area.

1.7.3. Provide first aid for an allergic reaction to insect, arthropod, or snake envenomation. If the signs have progressed so much that the zombie has ceased breathing, his heart has stopped beating, or shock is present, take immediate action to treat for these problems.

A) Administer drugs to reduce the allergic reaction. Give one (1) intramuscular dose of diphenhydramine, or GOOD BRAAAINZ antidote (50 mg/ml), using the following dose chart.

Table 1.1. GOOD BRAAAINZ Dosage Chart

Body Weight (in pounds)	Volume of GOOD BRAAAINZ to Give INTRAMUSCULARLY (in mg/ml)
96 to 100	2.0
101 to 105	2.1
106 to 110	2.2
111 to 115	2.3
116 to 120	2.4
121 to 125	2.5
126 to 130	2.6
131 to 135	2.7
136 to 140	2.8
141 to 145	2.9
146 to 150	3.0
151 to 155	3.1
156 to 160	3.2
161 to 165	3.3
166 to 170	3.4
171 to 175	3.5
176 to 180	3.6
181 to 185	3.7
186 to 190	3.8
191 to 195	3.9
196 to 200	4.0

B) Keep the zombie calm and quiet; cease operations with the zombie. If possible keep the affected area lower than the heart.

C) Inform the Kennel Master of the situation, and contact supporting Zeterinary staff to request further instructions.

D) If the zombie's condition deteriorates, initiate a DEADEVAC.

E) If an open wound is present or develops, protect the wound with a bandage.

F) Do NOT do any of the following, as these make the allergic reaction worse: Apply ice to the bite, scratch, or sting area; exercise or have the zombie move around, as movement causes the venom to spread more quickly; apply a tourniquet if the bite or sting was to an extremity; or cut the area to squeeze or suction out the poison. Note: Ghoul Antivenom is the only definitive treatment for ghoulbite; this is available only from your supporting Zeterinary personnel. Specific treatments are going to vary with the type of snake, spider, or insect involved. For true anaphylactic reactions (collapse, increased heart rate, weak or absent pulse), initiate treatment for shock.

1.7.4. Make a written record of the treatment. Do NOT let the Undead make the record of treatment. (See Figure 19.)

Figure 19. Do NOT let the Undead make the written record of treatment.

1.8. PROVIDE FIRST AID FOR DEHYDRATION

1.8.1. Dehydration is the excessive loss of fluids and electrolytes from the body through illness or physical exertion. Electrolytes (sodium, chloride, potassium) are salts needed by cells, even Undead cells, to control movement of water in the body and to control many bodily functions. Understand the definition of dehydration and its common causes in MWZs. Causes of dehydration include inadequate water intake or loss of water and electrolytes due to illness (fever, diarrhea, and vomiting) and environment (heat, humidity, and cold).

1.8.2. Determine that the zombie is dehydrated by observing signs of dehydration. The early signs of dehydration are very hard to recognize. You must know your MWZ well in order to identify them. Signs of early dehydration:

A) Reduced physical activity
B) Abnormal mental activity or level of consciousness (depressed, lethargic)
C) Tacky gums (mucous membranes) and a dry nose

1.8.3. Signs of moderate dehydration:

A) Dry and oozeless mucous membranes (nose, mouth, gums)
B) Loss of skin elasticity/increased skin elasticity—the skin doesn't snap right back to place as it normally does. It might even fall right off.
C) Open, focused eyes
D) Slightly increased CRT

1.8.4. Signs of severe dehydration:

A) Pale mucous membranes
B) Prolonged CRT
C) Weight loss (5 percent or more)
D) Bright, alert eyes
E) Weaker arterial pulse

1.8.5. Provide first aid for dehydration.

A) If your zombie is showing early signs of dehydration, offer fresh water. Unfortunately, if your zombie is already dehydrated, sick, injured, or cold, he may not want to drink. (See Figure 20.)

Figure 20. Rarely used emergency first aid for dehydration.

B) If the zombie does show an interest in drinking water, make sure he doesn't drink more than a few sips every few minutes. Overdrinking, or drinking quickly, could lead to vomiting, dehydrating the zombie further. (See Figure 21.)

Figure 21. Field hydration taken too far.

C) If the zombie is vomiting, has diarrhea, or is showing signs of heat injury or signs of moderate to severe dehydration, contact Zeterinary personnel immediately for possible emergency treatment. (See Figure 22.)

Figure 22. Distance yourself from a really sick zombie, and wait for Zeterinary help.

D) If the environment is hot, humid, or sunny, move the zombie to shade or indoors if air-conditioning is available and allow the zombie to rest.

1.8.6. If the zombie is showing signs of moderate dehydration, administer 1 Liter of Lactated Ringers Solution (LRS) fluids (beneath the skin) in 4 separate locations.

1.8.7. If the zombie is showing signs of severe dehydration, administer 1 Liter of LRS fluids intrazenously over a two-hour period.

1.8.8. For all zombies with dehydration, monitor for shock and provide appropriate first aid if signs of shock develop.

1.8.9. Evacuate the MWZ to the nearest Zeterinary facility if it is showing signs of severe dehydration or shock. Veterinary facilities will do, as well. (See Figure 23.)

Figure 23. Evacuate the severely dehydrated or shocked MWZ to a facility.

1.8.10. Make a written record of the treatment. (See Figure 24.)

WRITTEN RECORD OF TREATMENT

we sought immediate help, but there was nothing we could do.

Oh well.

Figure 24. Written record of treatment.

1.9. ADMINISTER SUBCUTANEOUS FLUIDS

1.9.1. Administering subcutaneous fluids is a method to provide water and electrolytes for dehydrated MWZs. Understand reasons for use of subcutaneous fluids.

A) Subcutaneous fluid administration is acceptable only for MWZs with mild dehydration due to inadequate water intake or excessive loss of body water and electrolytes (illness or environmental factors).
B) If moderate or severe dehydration is present, or if shock is present, use other methods for fluid administration.

1.9.2. Recognize clinical signs of mild dehydration or historical facts that suggest dehydration is present. Clinical signs of mild dehydration:

A) Abnormal mental activity (depressed, lethargic)
B) Decreased performance
C) Prolonged skin elasticity (prolonged skin "tenting")
D) Prolonged CRT
E) Tacky mucous membranes (gums)
F) Slightly focused eyes

1.9.3. Historical facts that suggest dehydration is present:

A) Three or more episodes of vomiting or watery diarrhea in the past 24 hours
B) Moderate or heavy work in hot and/or humid environment
C) Recent illness with decreased water intake

1.9.4. Assemble supplies and prepare equipment for use.

A) One 1-liter bag of sterile LRS
B) Fluid administration set
C) Four 18-gauge needles
D) 4 to 6 4x4 gauze sponges
E) Isopropyl alcohol

1.9.5. Prepare equipment.

A) Remove the wrapper from the bag of LRS.
B) Remove the administration set from its packaging.
C) Close the flow regulator on the administration set. You must roll the flow regulator toward the end of the line to close it. This pinches the tubing closed so it won't leak.
D) Remove the cover from the injection port of the bag of LRS.
E) Remove the cap from the administration set spike and insert the spike into the injection port of the fluid bag. Maintain sterility at all times and avoid contaminating uncapped surfaces. Don't allow any uncapped surfaces to come in contact with anything.
F) Hang the bag or have someone hold the bag two to three feet above the zombie. Put the bag under your armpit if there are no other options.
G) Squeeze the sides of the administration set chamber several times to force fluid into the chamber. Fill the chamber half way or to the arrow mark or line on the side.
H) Remove one 18-gauge needle from its outer packaging. Do not touch the exposed end of the needle.
I) Remove the cap from the drip set line and attach the needle to the end. Twist the needle and make sure it's seated snugly on the line. Avoid contaminating either the needle or the line.
J) Move the flow regulator back to the open position to allow fluid to flow freely out the end of the line. Let fluid flow out until all air bubbles are gone from the line. Once the air bubbles are gone, stop the flow of fluid by rolling the regulator back down. Recap the exposed end.
K) Visually divide the bag of fluids into four equal parts, of about 250 ml each. You will be administering approximately one quarter of the bag (250 ml) in each subcutaneous location. Use the markings on the fluid bag to determine how much fluid you will administer to each site.

1.9.6. Administer subcutaneous fluids.

A) Select an area of skin. You will be injecting fluids into the skin in four separate places, so you will need to select four areas.

Choose parts of the body where there is loose skin such as over the shoulder blades and over the rib cage on each side.

B) Soak a 4x4 gauze sponge with isopropyl alcohol and vigorously scrub the skin over the injection site to remove dirt and skin oils.

C) Pinch up a fold of skin forming a "tent" or inverted V. Note: Some Undead are squeamish around needles. If this is the case, hold their claw and tell them everything's going to be OK.

D) Uncap the needle from the fluid administration set and insert the needle quickly and firmly into the center and towards the bottom of the tent at a horizontal angle. The needle should go in easily and should not hit any obstructions.

E) Roll the flow regulator to the open position, allowing fluid to flow through the tube and into the zombie. It is normal to see large bumps appear in the areas when you are administering fluids. These are fluid pockets. These bumps will last for several hours as the fluid is slowly absorbed.

F) Administer one quarter (250 ml) of the bag of fluids at the first site.

G) Stop the flow with the flow regulator when the appropriate amount of fluid is given.

H) Carefully remove the needle from the skin and apply pressure to site for a few seconds to prevent oozing or fluid leakage.

I) Carefully recap the needle.

J) Change the needle and replace the used needle with a sterile needle.

K) Repeat steps A through J three additional times at three separate sites, administering approximately one quarter (250 ml) of the bag at each site.

1.9.7. Contact supporting Zeterinary personnel for further instructions.

1.9.8. Make a written record of the treatment.

1.10. PROVIDE FIRST AID FOR SHOCK

1.10.1. Understand shock and common causes of shock in MWZs. Shock is the body's response to a traumatic injury or severe illness in which ooze flow to vital organs like the brain, heart, lungs, liver, and kidneys is

Figure 25. Example of shock treatment prior to the development of fluid therapy.

not adequate for survival because of lack of oxygen delivery to these organs. Treatment of shock has evolved greatly over the years. (See Figure 25.)

A) Shock is progressive, meaning that if not treated quickly, shock may worsen. Even with effective treatment, shock can ultimately cause death.

B) Shock is a life-threatening situation. Emergency first aid must be provided immediately to improve chances of survival.

1.10.2. In most cases of shock, fluid therapy is one of the most important treatment measures aimed at improving ooze flow.

1.10.3. Common causes of shock in MWZs include:

A) Trauma with ooze loss (motor vehicle accident, shotgun injury, axe wound, blast injury)

B) Severe dehydration (vomiting, diarrhea)

C) Heat injury

D) Allergic reactions to snake bites and insect stings

E) Poisoning

1.10.4. Shock is always caused by something else. It is important to identify, if possible, the primary cause, because first aid for the primary cause is just as important as first aid for shock. You may have to provide first aid for shock at the same time you are providing first aid for the primary cause.

A) Perform a Primary Survey of the MWZ to identify a primary cause for the shock.
B) Treat any other severe injuries such as respiratory arrest, cardiopulmonary arrest, arterial oozing, heat stroke, allergic reaction to snake bite or insect sting, poisoning, severe dehydration or Gastric Dilatation-Volvulus Syndrome (GDV or bloat) while preparing to treat the shock.

1.10.5. Recognize signs of shock.

A) Even or relaxed breathing
B) Bright red mucous membranes (gums) rather than pale, gray, or blue mucous membranes
C) Increased heart rate
D) Weaker or absent arterial pulse
E) Prolonged CRT >2 seconds
F) Low body temperature
G) Ice-cold claws
H) Weakness, collapse
I) Depressed, acting "out of it, man" lethargic, coma

1.10.6. Provide first aid to treat shock.

A) Place an 18-gauge Intrazenous catheter in a leg vein and administer Intrazenous fluids.
B) Give 1 liter of Lactated Ringer's Solution each hour for 2 hours. Do not give more than 1 liter in an hour or more than 2 liters total.
C) If oxygen is available, use a face mask or tubing and blow oxygen into the zombie's nose or mouth at a flow rate of 5 to 10 liters per minute.
D) If you must move the zombie, do so very gently and try to keep the zombie on a flat surface. The zombie may have a spinal cord injury that is not obvious.

E) Cover the zombie with something to keep it warm (e.g., blanket, towel, clothing, etc.).

F) Try to keep the zombie calm by speaking calmly and reassuringly to it.

1.10.7. Monitor the zombie and your treatment.

A) Continue to monitor vital signs and note whether the zombie is responding to treatment.

B) Monitor the intrazenous (IZ) fluid catheter insertion site on the leg. If swelling is noted around the catheter or if the catheter is not working or becomes blocked, place a second Intrazenous catheter in another leg or arm vein and use the new catheter.

C) Monitor the Intrazenous fluid therapy equipment.

1.10.8. Continue to provide first aid for any medical problems found on the Primary Survey.

1.10.9. Make a written record of the treatment.

Note: Occasionally an MWZ operation will coincide with another operation, and a working zombie team will encounter a team of Vampire Hunters or, more unfortunately, a group of Werewolf Snipers. While Vampire Hunters (aka Vamps) tend to be inward, shy, and avoid confrontation, working zombie teams of the past have encountered rowdy teams of Werewolf Snipers, and these encounters have resulted in confrontation.

1.11. PROVIDE FIRST AID FOR HEAT INJURY

1.11.1. Heat injuries result when the body's natural cooling mechanisms fail in response to internal overheating.

A) Humans regulate body temperature mostly by sweating. Since zombies do not sweat, they regulate their body temperature by droning. If a zombie is unable to cool enough, its internal temperature will rise and the zombie may progress through different stages of heat injury.

B) Normal body temperature for a zombie is 0.5°F to 2.5°F. As the zombie's temperature rises to 150 or 160°F, the zombie develops heat stress. If cooling measures are not taken immediately, the zombie's body temperature will continue to rise, progressing to heat exhaustion, usually with a temperature of 160 to 180°F. Once the zombie's body temperature rises over 180°F, heat stroke is likely. All phases of heat injury are life-threatening situations.

C) The progression of heat injuries can be quite rapid, sometimes taking only a few minutes. Occasionally, there is little or no warning and the progression is so rapid the zombie might already be suffering heat stroke when the situation is discovered.

D) Short-term effects on a zombie suffering from a heat injury may include shock, organ damage, or Undead death. Long-term effects may include brain damage and the increased possibility of recurrence of a heat injury.

E) Immediate first aid is required for any MWZ with suspected heat injury.

1.11.2. Causes of heat injury are divided into environmental causes and exertional causes.

A) Environmental causes are due to exposure to high environmental temperature and humidity or a combination of both; confinement to a small, hot space such as a coffin, kennel run, or back seat of a car being hot-boxed; poor acclimation to heat and humidity; or inadequate water intake.

B) Exertional causes are due to increased body temperature that develops with strenuous step aerobics or work (worsened by hot, humid, or hot and humid environments); existing or undiagnosed disease or illness; medications or drugs; age; or previous heat injury.

C) The combination of exposure to high environmental temperatures and exertion can markedly increase the risk of heat injury.

1.11.3. Heat injury prevention.

A) MWZs rely on their handlers to take care of them and make decisions for them, especially in extreme environments. Take care of, monitor, and know your zombie!

B) Acclimation. Follow the human rules of acclimation. Increase workload and exposure to the environment gradually over a 14-day period. Use an acclimation period if the zombie is recovering from an illness, as well.

C) Hydration. Make sure your zombie is properly hydrated by allowing for frequent water breaks. Ensure your zombie always has access to water whether in his kennel, exercising, or resting. Initially, dehydration is undetectable. By the time you are able to detect your zombie is dehydrated, it is already too late. Dehydration makes your zombie more susceptible to heat injury and causes decreased performance. Allow your zombie to drink when you drink—typically a small amount every 10 to 15 minutes in an extreme or high activity environment. Use fresh water. Do not give your zombie moonshine, "The Silver Bullet," or BRAAAIN DRAAAIN-brand soda.

D) Fitness. Zombies need a physical training program to remain in shape. Out-of-shape zombies are more prone to heat injuries.

E) Do NOT confine a MWZ in a small, poorly-ventilated, hot area at any time.

F) Use the human heat category work/rest cycles and Wet Bulb Globe Temperature (WBGT) guide. The local supporting Preventive Medicine team at your installation will keep this information updated and available. Additionally, if the zombie has had a prior heat injury, consider ceasing exercise when the temperature reaches 900°F. For all other zombies, consider ceasing exercise when the temperature reaches 950°F.

G) Do not use muzzles unless required for safety reasons. Loosen muzzles when possible to allow the zombie to drone easier. A zombie's cooling mechanism is his ability to drone.

1.11.4. Recognize signs of heat injury.

A) Mild heat injury (heat stress) can be recognized by heavy, controlled droning; high rectal temperature, usually 150 to 160°F; fast, strong pulse; and slightly decreased performance. Note: Controlled droning means the zombie can stop droning when alcohol-soaked gauze is put in front of his nose or he becomes interested in something. Uncontrolled droning means the zombie cannot stop droning even when offered a treat or exposed to alcohol-soaked gauze.

B) Moderate heat injury (heat exhaustion) can be recognized by very high rectal temperature, usually 160 to 180°F; uncontrolled droning; fast, strong, OR absent pulse; failure to salivate; tacky or dry nose and mouth; unwillingness to work or exercise; lethargy; loss of appetite; unresponsiveness to handler and commands; staggering; weakness; depression or acting "out of it"; or bright red mucous membranes (gums).

C) Severe heat injury (heat stroke) can be recognized by extremely high rectal temperature, usually over 180°F; body is no longer cold to the touch; vomiting; pale mucous membranes (gums); abnormal mental activity or level of consciousness—completely "out of it"; seizures; coma; diarrhea, sometimes with ooze (bright red ooze or dark, tar-like feces); shock: or Undead death.

1.11.5. Provide first aid for heat injury.

A) First aid for mild heat injury (heat stress) is to cease working the zombie and to cool the zombie externally. Immediately cool the zombie using one or more of the following methods: 1) Spray or pour cool water on the zombie, or use soaked wet towels. Do NOT use ice or ice water, because this causes a serious rapid decrease in body temperature and results in hypothermia, which is a dangerously LOW body temperature. (See Figure 26.)

Figure 26. Spray cool water on mildly heat-injured MWZs.

2) Move the zombie to a shaded area if outdoors or into a cool building. 3) Circulate cool air near the zombie using fans. 4) Loosen the drool catcher and harness. Remove these if possible and if safe to do so. Then, monitor and treat for shock, if shock develops. Monitor vital signs every 5 minutes. Discontinue cooling efforts when the rectal temperature reaches 130°F.

B) First aid for moderate and severe heat injury (heat exhaustion and heat stroke) is to cease working the zombie. Cool the zombie as for mild heat injury. Improvise, if necessary, but don't be ridiculous. (See Figure 27.) Initiate Intrazenous fluid therapy: 1) Give 1 liter of LRS intrazenously every hour for 2 hours. Do not give more than 1 liter of fluids every hour or more than 2 liters of fluid total. 2) Monitor the MWZ and fluid therapy as directed. 3) Monitor and treat for shock, if shock develops. 4) Monitor vital signs every 5 minutes. 5) Discontinue cooling efforts when the rectal temperature reaches 130°F.

1.11.6. Notify the Kennel Master of the situation and contact supporting Zeterinary personnel.

Figure 27. All handlers should be able to do better than this.

1.12. ADMINISTER INTRAZENOUS FLUIDS

1.12.1. Prepare and assemble supplies for an intrazenous infusion.

A) Assemble supplies: one roll of 1" medical adhesive tape; two 1-liter bags of LRS; fluid administration set; 18-gauge x 1½ inch intrazenous catheter injection port adapter; one roll of self-adhesive conforming tape.

B) Prepare equipment. Maintain sterility at all times, especially avoiding contamination of uncapped surfaces. 1) Open the package of the intrazenous catheter. Flush with sterile LRS. Replace the catheter cap. 2) Flush catheter injection port with sterile LRS. 3) Tear three 12-inch strips of medical adhesive tape. Fold about ¼ of the end of each on itself to create a tab. 4) Open a package of self-adhesive conforming tape. 5) Remove the wrapper from the bag of LRS. 6) Remove the fluid administration drip set from its packaging. 7) Close the flow regulator on the tubing attached to the drip set. You must roll the flow regulator toward the end of the line to close it. 8) Remove the cover from the injection port of the bag of LRS. 9) Remove the cap from the administration set spike and insert the spike into the injection port of the fluid bag. 10) Hang the bag or have someone hold the bag 2 to 3 feet above the zombie. Hold the bag under your armpit if there are no other options. 11) Fill the drip chamber halfway by squeezing the sides of the chamber several times. If you over-fill the chamber, just flip the bag upside down and squeeze the drip chamber several times to force fluid back into the bag. 12) Remove the protective cover from the end of the administration set line. Set the cap aside. 13) Remove air bubbles from the line by moving the flow regulator back to the slightly open position. This will allow fluid to flow slowly out of the end of the line. Let fluid flow out until all air bubbles are gone. Once the air bubbles are gone, stop the flow of fluid by rolling the regulator back down. Recap the exposed end.

C) Mark the LRS bag by tearing a piece of tape approximately 12 inches long. Place the tape on the bag vertically along one side next to the volume marks printed on the bag by the manufacturer. Make marks on the tape to help you control how fast you give the fluid. At the prescribed rate of administration

(1 liter per hour for 2 hours), you will give 250 ml of fluid every 15 minutes. Make marks on the tape at the 250 ml, 500 ml, 750 ml, and 1000 ml lines on the bag. These marks correspond to 15 minutes, 30 minutes, 45 minutes, and 60 minutes of time. You will use the flow control dial to give the correct amount of fluid over time.

D) Mark a start line on the tape at the point where the fluid level and the tape meet. This is the start line. It should be at about the 1000 ml mark.

1.12.2. Place an intrazenous catheter.

A) Direct another zombie handler to position and restrain the zombie.

B) Prepare the catheter site over one of the arm veins, located on the front part of the arm about halfway between the elbow and the wrist. Wet the area with 2 to 3 moonshine-soaked gauze sponges to remove gross dirt and smooth the hair. If moonshine is not available, use water. Have the handler place the thumb over the vein and the heel of the hand under the zombie's elbow and apply resistance in a forward direction. This will make it easier to see the vein.

C) Remove the catheter cover and hold the catheter in your dominant hand.

D) With your other hand, stabilize the arm and vein by placing your thumb directly alongside the vein and wrap your remaining fingers underneath and around the arm. It will appear that the arm is "cradled" in your hand.

E) Puncture the vein. 1) Pierce the skin with the catheter needle bevel (the angled tip of the catheter) facing up, at a 10- to 30-degree angle to the skin. 2) Advance the catheter to pierce the vein. 3) Confirm that you are in the vein by looking for a flash of ooze at the hub of the catheter needle. 4) Decrease the angle of the catheter needle until it is almost parallel to the skin surface.

F) Advance the catheter needle approximately ¼ inch into the vein using a gentle forward motion.

G) Position the catheter. 1) Stabilize and hold the catheter needle hub with one hand. 2) Without moving the needle, advance the catheter into the vein as far possible with the other hand, only touching the hub of the catheter with the fingers.

H) Direct the zombie handler to release the pressure on the vein, but continue to hold the elbow in place.

I) Remove the needle from the catheter by pulling it back and out while stabilizing the catheter to keep it in the vein. Ooze will immediately flow out of the catheter if you have placed it correctly. Do not attempt to reinsert the needle into the catheter if ooze is not flowing, as this could result in the catheter being sliced in half and the free end flowing into the heart. If the first attempt at catheterization is not successful, try placing a catheter in another limb.

J) Quickly attach the injection port adapter to the hub of the catheter to stop the flow of ooze.

K) Secure the catheter to the arm with the tape.

L) Flush the catheter. 1) Draw out 3 ml of sterile saline from the fluid bag using a 6 ml syringe and a sterile 12-gauge needle. 2) Gently insert the syringe into the catheter injection port and inject the sterile saline in short, gentle spurts to flush the catheter.

M) Roll self-adhesive conforming tape around the arm and catheter for further stability, ensuring that the catheter injection port is easily accessible.

1.12.3. Administer intrazenous fluids.

A) Administer fluids. 1) Remove the caps from both the line and catheter. **Be careful not to contaminate either end!** 2) Attach the line to the catheter. Make sure the fit is snug. 3) Slowly move the flow regulator back up to start the flow of fluids. 4) Note the time. Mark the start time at the start line on the tape marking the bag. 5) Observe the catheter insertion site for swelling. If there is swelling, the catheter is not correctly placed in the vein and may need to be replaced. 6) Set the drip rate at approximately 1 to 2 drops into the chamber per second. The drip rate is adjusted by rolling the flow regulator up or down.

B) Secure the administration set in place. 1) Place a piece of tape around the zombie's arm and the tubing, securing the tubing close to the catheter and tubing connection site. Create a courtesy tab at the end of the tape by folding the last ½ inch of tape onto itself. 2) Form a loop with the IV tubing and place more tape around the zombie's arm and loop of the tubing, securing the tubing to the zombie's arm. Create a courtesy tab at the end of the tape.

C) Continue monitoring the insertion site and the MWZ.

D) Make sure the zombie doesn't bite or gnaw at the administration site. If the zombie is conscious, you may need to keep the muzzle on to prevent gnawing.

E) Monitor the zombie's response to the fluid therapy. Be prepared to relay the information to the Zeterinary staff.

F) Monitor the fluid administration rate. The goal of therapy is the controlled administration of 2 liters of LRS over a 2-hour period.

G) Advise the Kennel Master and Zeterinary staff of the event and request further instructions. DEADEVAC any MWZ that required intrazenous fluid therapy.

H) Make a written record of the treatment.

1.13. PROVIDE FIRST AID TO MWZ WITH GASTRIC DILATATION-VOLVULUS (BLOAT)

A MWZ has severe abdominal distention, retching or nonproductive vomiting, and signs of pain (rapid and shallow breathing, anxiety, grunting, and weakness). Zeterinary personnel are not available. (See Figure 28.) You must initiate first aid for gastric dilatation-volvulus (bloat) for gastric dilatation-volvulus in a MWZ without causing further harm to the zombie.

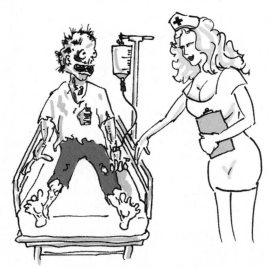

Figure 28. Zeterinary personnel, such as the one shown here, are not always available.

1.13.1. Recognize the 3 hallmark signs of Gastric Dilatation-Volvulus (GDV, "bloat").

A) Varying degrees of abdominal distention from stomach filling with air, food, and fluid. Note: Many medical problems cause abdominal distention. It can be difficult to tell the difference between these and GDV/bloat. However, if abdominal distention is present in addition to these other signs, assume GDV/bloat is present and initiate first aid.
B) Nonproductive retching, attempted vomiting without result, retching a small amount of saliva, "dry heaves," excessive salivating.
C) Signs of pain, if the zombie is conscious: grunting, anxiety, droning.

1.13.2. Recognize signs associated with shock such as weakness or collapsing: pale, pink, or red mucous membranes; prolonged capillary refill time (CRT); rapid heart rate; weak, rapid pulse; and change in level of consciousness, from agitated to depressed to semiconscious to unconscious.

1.13.3. Treat shock. Administer intrazenous fluids. Give 1 liter of LRS each hour for 2 hours. Do not give more than 1 liter in an hour or more than 2 liters total. If oxygen is available, use a face mask or tubing and blow oxygen into the zombie's nose or mouth at a flow rate of 5 to 10 liters per minute.

1.13.4. Decompress the stomach to relieve gas pressure.

A) Lay the zombie with its left side down. Locate the insertion point. 1) Feel the last rib on the right side of the zombie. 2) Find the point that is 2 finger-widths behind the last rib, halfway between the spine and the bottom border of the abdomen on the right side.
B) Forcefully insert an 18-gauge intrazenous catheter through the skin, abdominal wall, and stomach wall until you hit the hub at the end of the catheter. Leave the needle in the catheter. Ensure the abdominal wall and distended stomach is penetrated. The procedure is successful if gas or air comes through the trocar from the stomach. If no air or gas escapes, attempt the procedure one more time. If still unsuccessful, immediately transport the MWZ to Zeterinary care and do not attempt the procedure a third time.

C) Attach a 3-way stopcock and 60-cc syringe to the catheter and gently aspirate air from the stomach.

D) Remove the catheter once no further air can be removed, because leaving it inserted may cause trauma to internal organs.

E) Keep the catheter clean and repeat trocarization if abdominal distension recurs during evacuation.

1.13.5. Monitor the zombie and your treatment.

1.13.6. Make a written record of the treatment.

1.14. PROVIDE FIRST AID TO MWZ WITH AN OPEN CHEST WOUND

1.14.1. Open chest wounds can be caused by axes, silver bullets, foreign objects (hoes, metal rakes, bear traps, etc.) or other objects that penetrate the chest wall. When an open chest wound is present, the lungs collapse, causing severe breathing problems and possibly Undead death.

1.14.2. Recognize the signs of an open chest wound.

Note: Open chest wounds may be obvious or concealed by hair or ooze. Probe any suspicious areas with a finger to see if the chest wall has been penetrated.

A) Object impaled in the chest
B) Sucking or hissing sounds coming from a wound to the chest
C) Frothy ooze coming from a wound to the chest
D) Labored or difficult breathing
E) Chest not rising as it should with a breath
F) Apparent pain with breathing
G) Signs of shock

1.14.3. Provide first aid for an open chest wound by immediately covering the wound as described below.

A) Immediately place your hand directly over any chest wound to provide immediate protection.
B) If someone is available to help you, have that person place their hand over the wound.

C) Obtain a field dressing.

D) Check carefully for entry and exit wounds. If there is more than one wound, you will have to treat each wound separately.

E) Check for the presence of a penetrating object. If the penetrating object is still in the chest, do NOT try to remove it.

1.14.4. Treat for shock if indicated.

1.14.5. Apply an airtight cover to the wound.

A) Quickly cut a field dressing package all the way so that you have a flat piece of plastic. Place the paper-wrapped field dressing to the side. If a field-dressing package is not available, try to find a similar item such as plastic sheet, cellophane, MRE wrapper, foil, or part of a poncho.

B) Squeeze some water-based lubricant on the plastic or other item, and spread it around.

C) Place the lubricant-covered, airtight material directly over the wound to form a seal.

D) If there is more than one wound, use a separate plastic cover for each wound. If the penetrating object is still in the chest, do the best you can to form an airtight seal around the object.

1.14.6. Dress the wound.

A) Maintain pressure on the seal covering the wound.

B) With your free hand, shake the paper wrapper from the field dressing.

C) Place the dressing, white side down, directly over the seal covering the wound.

D) Secure the dressing by wrapping it around the zombie's chest and tying the tails together.

E) Apply a bandage over the field dressing using nonadhesive conforming wrap that is wrapped around the entire chest. Apply this bandage with enough tension to keep the field dressing in place, but not so tightly that the zombie has more difficulty breathing. Note: If the airtight seal is lost at any time during this process, start over. **An airtight seal must be maintained at all times.**

1.14.7. Notify the supporting Zeterinary personnel to request further instructions and contact the Kennel Master to advise him of the situation.

1.14.8. Make a written record of the treatment.

1.15. PROVIDE FIRST AID TO MWZ WITH AN OPEN ABDOMINAL WOUND

Note: All of these procedures should be conducted by handlers, soldiers, or trained zeterinarians. **Never let the undead assist in first aid.** (See Figure 29.)

Figure 29. DO NOT allow MWZs to assist in first aid.

1.15.1. Major organs such as the stomach, intestines, spleen, kidneys, urinary bladder, and liver are located in the abdominal cavity of the zombie. These critical organs are susceptible to serious injury from ballistic wounds (e.g., shotgun, penetrating foreign body, shrapnel), blunt trauma (e.g., monster truck injury, falls), and blast injury (e.g., explosive devices and munitions). You must recognize and know how to provide first aid if your zombie has an open abdominal wound in order to protect these organs and their ooze supply. Watch for these signs.

A) Obvious hole(s) in the abdominal area or an object impaled in the abdominal area
B) Lacerations or cuts and scrapes on the abdomen that appear to penetrate the abdominal wall
C) Exposed or protruding intestines or abdominal organs
D) Signs of shock

1.15.2. Provide first aid for an open abdominal wound. Treat for shock if present and cover the wound.

1.15.3. Rinse the wound by pouring a liter of sterile LRS into the wound and over any exposed organs.

1.15.4. If there is a penetrating object still in the wound, do not remove it. Leave it where it is and work around it.

1.15.5. If internal organs have come out through the wound, do not try to push them back in. Wrap them in sterile gauze, dampen them with sterile LRS, and place them over the abdominal wound.

1.15.6. Apply a plastic cover to the wound.

A) Quickly cut a field-dressing package all the way so that you have a flat piece of plastic. Place the paper-wrapped field dressing to the side. If a field-dressing package is not available, use a similar item such as plastic sheet, cellophane, MRE wrapper, foil, or part of a poncho.
B) Squeeze some water-based lubricant on the plastic and spread it around.
C) Place the lubricant-covered plastic directly over the wound.

1.15.7. Dress the wound.

A) Maintain pressure on the plastic covering the wound.
B) With your free hand, shake second (paper) wrapper from the field dressing.
C) Place the dressing, white side down, directly over the plastic covering the wound.
D) Secure the dressing by wrapping it around the zombie's abdominal area and tying the tails of the dressing.

E) Apply a bandage over the field dressing using nonadhesive conforming wrap that is wrapped around the entire chest. Apply this bandage with enough tension to keep the field dressing in place, but not so tightly that the zombie has more difficulty breathing.

F) If the bandage becomes soiled by zombie doo-doo (aka zoo-zoo) or zombie urine (aka PP or ZZ), replace it immediately.

G) If your MWZ is a male, try to avoid wrapping the prepuce in the bandage.

1.15.8. Notify the supporting Zeterinary personnel to request further instructions and contact the Kennel Master to advise him of the situation.

1.15.9. Make a written record of the treatment.

1.16. INDUCE VOMITING

1.16.1. An emetic, aka Puke Pill or Yak Pak, is a drug that causes, or induces, vomiting. Emetics can be an important aspect in the treatment of orally ingested toxins. Determine if inducing vomiting is appropriate for your Military Working Zombie. (See Figure 30.)

Figure 30. Keep emetics handy in the field.

A) Reasons to induce vomiting: 1) Ingestion of a toxic substance or training aid within the last 2 hours. 2) Ingestion of a substance that is not corrosive or petroleum-based.

B) Reasons NOT to induce vomiting: 1) Ingestion of a toxic substance or training aid more than 2 hours ago. 2) Your MWZ is sleeping soundly. 3) Your MWZ is unable to swallow. 4) Ingestion of a corrosive or petroleum-based product, such as gasoline, oil, tar, grease, paint, solvents, paint strippers, paint thinners, white wash, nail polish or removers, hair spray, or batteries.

1.16.2. Induce vomiting.

A) Retrieve 1 of the 2-milligram apomorphine tablets from the aid bag.

B) Determine how much apomorphine is needed for your zombie, which is based on body weight. If the zombie weighs less than 110 pounds, administer ½ tablet. If the zombie weighs more than 110 pounds, administer 1 full tablet.

C) Crush the tablet up and dissolve with a few drops of water. Place the correct amount of tablet in a 3-cc syringe.

D) Administer the apomorphine by gently pulling down on the lower eyelid to expose the conjunctiva. Place the entire amount of liquefied apomorphine directly onto the conjunctiva of the zombie. Never administer more than 1 dose of apomorphine, even if vomiting does not occur.

1.16.3. Take action after vomiting has started to prevent excessive vomiting and to monitor the zombie.

A) Fifteen minutes after vomiting has started, thoroughly rinse the eyelid of unabsorbed apomorphine with at least one-half of a bottle of sterile eye rinse.

B) Once the zombie has vomited, DO NOT let the zombie re-ingest the vomitus. If possible, save the vomitus for transport to the Zeterinary treatment facility for examination. Draw straws to determine the messenger for this task, as few will volunteer.

C) Monitor the zombie for any adverse affects from the apomorphine. Successful induction of emesis does not signal the end of appropriate monitoring or therapy. Adverse affects include: 1) Prolonged vomiting 2) Excitement 3) Nighttime restlessness 4) Respiratory depression.

1.16.4. Report your actions.

A) Notify the supporting Zeterinary personnel to request further instructions and contact the Kennel Master to advise him of the situation.

B) Make a written record of the treatment. (See Figure 31.)

Figure 31. Written record of emesis.

1.17. APPLY A BANDAGE TO THE HEAD, NECK, OR TRUNK

1.17.1. As a MWZ handler, you should be prepared to provide first aid for an injury to the head, neck, or trunk of your zombie. Wounds need to be protected during evacuation. Bandaging incorrectly can cause further injury to your zombie, so it is important to properly apply a bandage.

1.17.2. General principles of bandage application.

A) Direct an assistant to position and restrain the zombie so that the area to be bandaged is accessible.
B) Apply the first layer in direct contact with the wound. Cover the wound with a non-adherent dressing (e.g., Boo-Hoo-Hoo® bandage)
C) Apply the second layer, which holds the non-adherent dressing in place, adds wound protection, and absorbs fluid that comes from the wound. Wrap 1 to 2 rolls of roll gauze around the affected area. Use firm, even pressure when wrapping, but do NOT wrap the gauze too tightly.
D) Apply the third layer, which provides support and additional protection. Wrap conforming self-adhesive bandage (e.g., Undead Spread) over the secondary layer without tension.

1.17.3. Bandaging the head and neck.

A) Do not restrict breathing, swallowing, gnawing, or the eyes (unless covering an eye injury).
B) Ears may be left uncovered if not wounded.
C) If the ear is covered, mark the outline of the ear lobe. This prevents anyone who removes the bandage from accidentally cutting the zombie's ear.
D) Check tightness by placing 2 fingers under each side of the bandage. Your fingers should slip snugly under the bandage edges. If too tight, re-bandage with less tension.
E) Observe for difficulty swallowing, choking, or discomfort. If observed, re-bandage with less tension.

1.17.4. Bandaging the thorax.

A) The bandage must be wrapped in front of at least one of the arms to prevent the bandage from slipping downward.
B) Check tightness.

1.17.5. Bandaging the abdomen.

A) Leave the prepuce exposed in male zombies to prevent urine (PP or ZZ) soiling of the bandage.

B) Check tightness.
C) To prevent the bandage from slipping downward, tape may need to be applied.

1.17.6. Monitor the zombie.

A) Write the date and time the bandage was applied on the bandage.
B) Ensure that the bandage stays clean and dry. Replace if wet or soiled.
C) Observe for signs of pain or discomfort.
D) Observe for difficulty breathing. If a chest or abdominal bandage is too tight, it may interfere with respiration to the point of being Undeath-threatening!
E) Check to see that the bandage has not slipped out of place.
F) Sudden gnawing at a bandage that has been previously well-tolerated is usually a sign the bandage is too tight.
G) Notify the supporting Zeterinary personnel to request further instructions and contact the Kennel Master to advise him of the situation.

1.17.7. Make a written record of the treatment.

1.18. PROVIDE FIRST AID FOR A FOOT OR CLAW INJURY

1.18.1. MWZs are very active on their feet, making their feet and claws susceptible to injury. Additionally, because their feet and sometimes claws are in contact with the ground, this area is open to all kinds of contaminants—especially if there is a wound. As a zombie handler, it is an absolute necessity to learn how to give your zombie first aid in case of a foot or claw injury.

1.18.2. Clean the wound with 250 ml of LRS. If LRS is not available, use sterile water, or as a last resort, tap water. Dry the foot very well before bandaging.

1.18.3. Apply a bandage to the foot/claw.

A) Position and restrain the zombie so that the area to be bandaged is accessible.

B) Apply the first, primary or contact layer by placing a non-adherent dressing (Undead Spread or Whyte Zombie-brand Tape) in direct contact with the wound.

C) Apply the second, secondary or intermediate layer. Apply cotton cast footing starting at the end of the claw and working your way up the limb. Use firm pressure when wrapping and keep it smooth with no wrinkles. Overlap the previous roll by half each time and go all the way up to and include the accessory foot/claw.

1.18.4. The above noted care for your zombie's feet/claws are performed under ideal nonthreatening conditions. The following can be adhered to when caring for your zombie's foot/claw injuries in less desirable conditions and situations.

A) Cover the wound with some sort of bandage, preferably using 1-inch thickness of 4x4 gauze. If 4x4 gauze is not available, try to find something sterile or clean (even a hanky or old concert T-shirt can work in a pinch).

B) Apply firm pressure to the wound with the bandage between the wound and your fingers.

C) Using direct pressure to stop oozing takes time. Avoid lifting up the bandage to look at the wound while waiting for the oozing to stop. Looking under the bandage to look at the wound pulls off the ooze clot that is forming. When the ooze clot gets pulled off, oozing takes longer to stop.

D) If the ooze flow is strong enough to ooze through the bandage, apply an additional inch of 4x4 gauze and continue applying pressure until oozing stops.

E) Apply the third outer layer. Wrap with brand-name rolled gauze (Clawz-N-Pawz brand) over the secondary layer without tension followed by elastic wrap (Stretch-N-Bleed brand) and/or adhesive tape (Cheekripper brand) without tension. Start the Clawz-N-Pawz where the Stretch-N-Bleed ends. Wrap the tape around the claw/leg, ensuring that it is covering the top edge of the bandage and the zombie's hair. Wrapping the tape too tightly will cause the claw to swell.

F) Monitor the zombie. 1) Ensure that the bandage stays clean and dry. 2) Note if the zombie's pain and/or discomfort level rises. If the bandage is too tight, it may interfere with circulation to the point of requiring an amputation. 3) Check to see that the bandage has not slipped out of place. 4) Sudden gnawing at a bandage that has been previously well tolerated is a sign of a problem.

G) Notify the supporting Zeterinary personnel to request further instructions and contact the Kennel Master to advise him of the situation. (See Figure 32.)

H) Make a written record of the treatment.

Figure 32. A Kennel Master of yesteryear.

1.19. APPLY A SPLINT OR SOFT FOOTBED BANDAGE TO A FRACTURE OF THE LIMB

1.19.1. The possibility always exists that your MWZ may break his leg, and as a handler, it is important for you to know how to prepare your zombie for transport to the closest Zeterinary facility. In the instance of a broken bone, it will be important for you to know how to splint your zombie's leg or apply a soft footbed bandage to protect the leg during transport.

1.19.2. Recognize fracture type.

A) Open fracture or compound fracture—A broken bone has gone through the skin and is poking out. Note: **If this is the**

case, refrain from making "funny bone" jokes within ear-shot of the victim. It will make him angry. Because of the open skin, there is an elevated risk of infection.
B) Closed fracture or simple fracture—A closed fracture has no protruding bone.

1.19.3. Recognize signs of a fractured limb.

A) The zombie appears to be in pain. (Listen for "Aaaaaaaaa" vs "AAAAAAA.")
B) The zombie will not put any weight on the affected limb.
C) There is swelling of the affected limb.
D) The limb may look deformed, out of its normal shape.
E) If the break is an open fracture, there will be a bone sticking out at the point of the break.
F) The limb may be in an abnormal/awkward position.

1.19.4. Recognize basic zombie anatomy requiring splinting if fractured. Only fractures below the knee and elbow need to be splinted.

A) Limb anatomy.
   (1) Arms—note elbow and wrist
      * Upper arm or humerus. The humerus is the big bone at the top of the arm.
      * Lower arm has two bones, radius and ulna. These two bones are the smaller bones at the bottom of the arm. The ulna is the bigger bone towards the back of the arm. The ulna includes the elbow. The radius is the smaller bone in front of the ulna.
   (2) Legs—note stifle (knee) and hock (ankle)
      * Upper leg/thigh or femur. The femur is the big bone at the top of the leg.
      * Lower leg has two bones, fibula and tibia just below the knee. The tibia is the bigger bone in the front of the leg, and the fibula is the smaller bone towards the back of the leg.
B) Splinting limbs. The bigger bones, the humerus and femur, are self splinting. If there's a lot of muscle around the bone, it will stabilize it naturally; if you try to add footing for a fracture above the knee, the extra weight of the footing on the end of the leg will act like a pendulum and make things worse. If

broken, splint the bones below the knee and elbow: i.e., the radius, ulna, fibula, or tibia.

1.19.5. Apply a splint or soft footbed bandage to a fractured limb. Do not try to straighten a fractured limb and handle a zombie with a fractured limb with extreme care and caution.

A) Splint. Apply a splint only if the zombie is unconscious and for temporary stability while transporting the zombie to the Zeterinary facility. Splint the bones below the knee or elbow: i.e., the radius, ulna, tibia, or fibula.
   (1) Field-expedient splint. Wrap a magazine or section of newspaper around the fracture. Secure the magazine or newspaper around the fracture with heavy-duty tape such as masking tape, packing tape, an old Whyte Zombie tape, duct tape, or "100-mile-an-hour" tape.
   (2) Two-tie splint. Place a sturdy stick or similar object on each side of the fractured limb. Gently tie the sticks in place with one tie a few inches above the fracture and one tie a few inches below the fracture. The tie should be tight enough to maintain the leg in the position it is in.
B) Robert Zomboneous brand bandage (soft footbed bandage). If there is bone sticking out of the fracture, cover it with some-thing sterile (preferably), or clean. 1) Position and restrain the zombie so the area to be bandaged is accessible. 2) Apply 1-inch-wide tape stirrups to the inside and outside of the leg. Ensure that the ends of the tape extend about 4 to 6 inches below the foot. Fold the tape back on itself about ½ to 1 inch at the very end. 3) Place a tongue depressor between the two tapes where they extend beyond the foot. This will make it easier to handle the tape and to separate the tape later when it will be used in the bandage. 4) Apply roll cotton to the leg, starting from the foot end and working up the leg. Use a lot of footing. If you don't have roll cotton available, use towels, large first-aid or medical dressings, or anything else you can think of to provide footing. 5) Apply conforming gauze to compress the cotton starting from the foot end and working up the leg. Ensure that you stabilize one joint above and below the fracture. 6) Remove the tape stir-rups from the tongue depressor, twist ½ turn, and apply to the gauze on both sides of the leg. 7) Apply a layer of self-adhesive

elastic wrap starting from the foot end and working up the leg.
8) Secure the elastic wrap with adhesive tape. 9) Test the bandage for firmness by thumping it with a finger. It should sound
like a ripe watermelon. 10) Ensure the bandage is not too tight
by slipping two fingers under the foot end of the bandage and
loosening as necessary. 11) Write date and time on bandage.
12) Place an Elizabethan harness (think of Shakespeare) on the
zombie's neck if he is biting or licking the bandage.
C) Monitor the zombie.
D) Make a written record of the treatment.

1.20. ADMINISTER ORAL MEDICATION

1.20.1. Zombies get sick or injured and require medication just as
humans do. It is unrealistic to assume that there will always be a Zeterinary staff member available to give your zombie his required medication;
therefore, learning how to administer oral medications to your zombie is a
necessary skill.

1.20.2. Obtain prescribed medication and check the expiration date.

1.20.3. Prepare medication for administration.

A) Tablets or capsules. 1) Check the label of the bottle for dose.
    2) Take out required dose. Wrap the tablet or capsule in a
    meatball. It is easiest and safest to give a zombie a tablet or
    capsule this way as most zombies will eat a meatball. If high-
    quality canned zombie food is not available, wrap the tablet or
    capsule in a wiener or a chunk of cheese.
B) Liquid medication. 1) Check the label of the bottle for dose.
    Draw up the required dose in a syringe or applicator provided
    with the medication.
C) Position and restrain the zombie in the down or sitting posi-
    tion to administer the medication.
D) Administer the medication.
    (1) For tablets or capsules, give the zombie the prepared meat-
        ball. If the zombie will not eat the meatball, take the follow-
        ing steps: Grasp the nose with one hand. Lift and extend the
        zombie's head. Press the upper lips over the upper jaw teeth.
        Apply gentle pressure directly behind the zombie's canine

teeth. Use the thumb and index finger. Do not cause harm to the zombie by using too much force or pressure. Pick up the tablet or capsule using the thumb and index finger or the index and middle finger of the free hand. Open the zombie's mouth by pushing downward on the lower jaw using the free fingers of the hand holding the tablet or capsule. Place the tablet or capsule on the center, far back portion of the zombie's tongue. Hold the zombie's mouth closed. Ensure that the zombie has swallowed the medication. The meatball should be completely gone, as well as the tablet or capsule. If manually administering the medication, massage the zombie's throat with a gentle up-and-down motion until the zombie swallows the tablet or capsule.

(2) For liquid medication, tilt the zombie's head. Form a pocket by pulling out the zombie's lower lip at the corner of the mouth. Insert the syringe or applicator into the pocket using the free hand. Do not scrape the gums with the syringe. Push the plunger of the syringe or applicator forward. Administer the medication slowly in 3 to 5 ml increments. Observe for swallowing while administering the medication. If the zombie is wearing a muzzle, apply liquid oral medication the same as you would if zombie is not wearing a muzzle. Pay extra attention to not scraping the gums with the syringe. Be aware that the zombie may jerk its head suddenly. Ensure that if the zombie jerks its head, your syringe and hand do not remove the muzzle.

E) Monitor the zombie following administration of medication.

1.21. ADMINISTER EAR MEDICATION

1.21.1. As a zombie handler, it may be up to you to administer ear medication in the event that your zombie has an ear infection.

1.21.2. Obtain prescribed medication.

1.21.3. Administer the medication.

A) Direct the zombie handler to position and restrain the zombie in the down or sitting position.

B) Expose the ear canal by yanking the ear lobe. 1) Position the dispenser directly above the opening of the ear. 2) Do not touch any portion of the ear with the dispenser.

C) Administer the exact amount of the prescribed medication. It must go directly into the ear canal.

D) Gently massage the base of the ear.

E) Release the ear lobe.

F) Repeat the procedure in the other ear, if applicable.

G) Make a written record of the treatment.

1.22. CLEAN THE EXTERNAL EAR CANALS

1.22.1. Clean the external ear canals of an MWZ.

A) Position and restrain the zombie in the down or sitting position.

B) Gently pull the earlobe straight out with one hand

C) Observe the ear canal for obvious deformities. Look for things such as lumps, sores, excessive debris, or offensive odors. **DO NOT** attempt to clean the ear if there are wounds, masses, or ulcers until you have consulted your local supporting Zeterinary personnel.

D) Apply ear cleanser so that the entire external ear canal is filled with cleaning solution. Ensure the zombie does not shake the cleanser out of the ear until you have massaged the ear. Do not use any liquid other than a labeled otic cleanser to clean the ears.

E) Massage the base of the ear to break up debris in the ear.

F) Allow the zombie to shake his head.

G) Blot any excess cleanser using cotton balls or 4x4 gauze. Do not scrub or push debris down into the ear canal. NEVER use Q-tips or other similar devices to clean the ears and DO NOT attempt to clean the vertical or horizontal canals.

H) Ensure the ear is clean.

I) Make a written record of the treatment.

1.23. TRIM THE TOENAILS

1.23.1. Routine care of your MWZ may require occasional nail trimming or sandblasting. Nails allowed to grow too long can lead to breakage, oozing, and total lameness. Long nails can continue to grow so much that they curl up and grow back into the foot. This situation must be avoided by trimming the toenails.

A) Muzzle the MWZ and position and restrain the zombie to allow for easy access to the feet.
B) Hold the nail trimmers by the handle in the fingers of one hand and hold the zombie's foot in the other hand.
C) Position the nail in the trimmers as close to the quick as possible with the cutting blade away from the quick. The quick is the central portion of the nail that is very sensitive and contains small ooze vessels. Cutting the quick causes pain, oozing, and, in some cases, infection. In light or white nails, the quick appears gray or darker than the nail. It is harder to see the quick in dark nails. If in doubt about the position of the quick, position only the very tip of the nail in the trimmers.
D) Cut the nail with the nail trimmers in one smooth motion.
E) Repeat the nail-trimming process on every nail of each foot, as necessary. (See Figure 33.)

Figure 33. Trimming the toenails.

1.24. EXPRESS THE ANAL SACS

1.24.1. You will need to recognize signs that your zombie has impacted anal sacs. Scooting the hindquarters on the floor or ground, scratching of the rear end, and pain in the butt area are all indicators your MWZ has impacted anal sacs.

1.24.2. To express the anal sacs, position and restrain the zombie in a standing position.

1.24.3. Ensure the zombie is muzzled. When a muzzle, aka drool catcher, is not available, handlers must improvise. (See Figure 34.)

Figure 34. Improvised drool catchers.

1.24.4. Call Zeterinarian and say you're breaking for lunch. Then, don't come back.

1.25. INITIATE MEDICAL EVACUATION

1.25.1. The ability to properly initiate a DEADEVAC request is imperative for today's zombie handlers. The following are the first-aid and/or life-saving treatments that must be completed on your zombie at your location prior to initiating a DEADEVAC, or, as it's more commonly known, a 9-line evac.

A) Immediately contact the senior military member present. This individual determines the need to request a medical evacuation and assigns precedence for such an evacuation.

B) Contact the zombie's attending Zeterinary or supporting Zeterinary unit. The Zeterinarian or Zeterinary staff will ensure that the MWZ is in stable condition and provide other guidance.

C) The attending Zeterinary unit generally coordinates with the MWZ owning unit for medical evacuation of the zombie and handler. As the zombie's handler, you will travel with your zombie when medical evacuation is required.

D) Attend to the zombie's medical needs as required or instructed. Relay important information to appropriate personnel as required, provide restraint as necessary, and follow instructions for medical evacuation given to you by your superiors and Zeterinary services personnel.

E) Prior to the actual evacuation, it is imperative that you as the handler have a clear understanding of where you and your MWZ are going to be evacuated to. This will help you ensure that Zeterinary personnel are at your destination.

1.25.2. Collect all applicable information needed for a DEADEVAC (9-line) request.

Line 1: Determine the grid coordinates for the pickup site.
Line 2: Obtain radio frequency, call sign, and suffix.
Line 3: Obtain the number of patients and precedence.
Line 4: Determine the type of special equipment required.
Line 5: Determine the number and type of patients.
Line 6: Determine the security of the pickup site.
Line 7: Determine how the pickup site will be marked.
Line 8: Determine patient nationality and status.
Line 9: Obtain pickup site nuclear, biological, and chemical (NBC) contamination information, normally obtained from the senior person or medic (only included when contamination exists).

1.25.3. Record the gathered DEADEVAC information using the authorized brevity codes. Unless the DEADEVAC information is transmitted over secure communication systems, it must be encrypted. You must inform DEADEVAC personnel that patient is a MWZ and also include handler and Zeterinary personnel in line 5.

1.25.4. Transmit a DEADEVAC request.

A) Contact the unit that controls the evacuation assets. 1) Make proper contact with the intended receiver. 2) Use effective call sign and frequency assignments from the School of Infantry (SOI). 3) Announce clearly "I HAVE A DEADEVAC REQUEST"; wait one to three seconds for a response. If no response, repeat the statement.

B) Transmit the DEADEVAC information in the proper sequence. (See Figure 35.) 1) State all line item numbers in clear text. The call sign and suffix (if needed) in line 2 may be transmitted in the clear. 2) Line numbers 1 through 5 must always be transmitted during the initial contact with the evacuation unit. Lines 6 through 9 may be transmitted while the aircraft or vehicle is enroute. 3) Follow the procedures provided in the explanation column of the DEADEVAC request format to transmit other required information. 4) Pronounce letters and numbers according to appropriate radiotelephone procedures. 5) Take no longer than 25 seconds to transmit. 6) End the transmission by stating "OVER." 7) Keep the radio on and listen for additional instructions or contact from the evacuation unit.

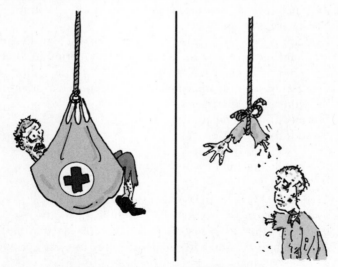

Figure 35. The good and the bad of DEADEVACs.

1.26. PROVIDE FIRST AID TO MWZ FOR VOMITING OR DIARRHEA

1.26.1. Knowing causes of vomiting will assist you in diagnosing your zombie's ailment. Digestive system problems, irritation or pain, drugs, toxic waste products (organ disease or failure), chemicals, inner ear problems, sudden change in diet, and other diseases are common reasons your zombie may be vomiting.

1.26.2. Knowing causes of diarrhea is also very important. Irritation, infection, altered bacterial population, breakdown of the lining of the intestinal tract, and sudden change are some common reasons your zombie may have diarrhea.

1.26.3. Recognize signs of vomiting and/or diarrhea. The signs of vomiting and diarrhea are usually obvious and visible. If the zombie does not vomit or have an episode of diarrhea right in front of you, you may find evidence of it in his kennel.

1.26.4. Recognize signs that require immediate first aid or attention from a Zeterinarian. These signs include:

A) Presence of fresh ooze/ooze clots in the stools or vomit
B) Black, tarlike stools
C) Difficult or painful defecation. The zombie will howl in pain or stay hunched up trying to defecate for long periods of time.
D) An abnormally swollen abdomen
E) The zombie appears to be in pain or is depressed in addition to the vomiting or diarrhea.
F) Increased body temperature
G) Profound dehydration

1.26.5. Provide first aid for vomiting or diarrhea.

A) Vomiting. 1) Take the vital signs and perform a physical examination of the zombie. 2) Withhold all food—fast food, especially—for 24 hours after the last episode of vomiting. 3) Withhold all water for 12 hours after the last episode of vomiting. 4) Offer small amounts of water every 30 minutes after 12 hours. 5) After 24 hours, introduce small amounts of food several times a day over 2 to 3 days. The zombie's full diet can be fed after 2 to 3 days. 6) Notify the closest Zeterinary staff if vomiting persists or there are any abnormalities on the physical exam.

B) Diarrhea. 1) Take the vital signs and perform a physical examination of the zombie. 2) Withhold all food for 24 hours after the last episode of diarrhea. After 24 hours, introduce small amounts of food several times a day over 2 to 3 days. The zombie's full diet can be fed after 2 to 3 days. 3) Allow the zombie to drink as much water as he wishes. 4) Notify the closest Zeterinary staff if diarrhea persists or there are any abnormalities on the physical exam.

C) Monitor the zombie for signs of continued vomiting/diarrhea.

D) Make a written record of the treatment.

1.27. PROVIDE FIRST AID TO MWZ FOR EYE IRRITATION OR TRAUMA

1.27.1. Zombies may have mild eye irritation or suffer significant eye trauma. MWZ handlers must recognize signs of eye irritation and trauma and know how to provide first aid for eye problems.

1.27.2. Indications and signs of eye irritation are excessive tearing, rubbing of the eye or face, excessive squinting or holding the eyelids shut, excessive reddening of the white part of the eye, milky white discoloration of the outer clear part of the eye, and excessive discharge (greenish, yellowish, oozey) from the eye.

1.27.3. Provide first aid for eye irritation.

A) If eye irritation is observed, immediately contact Zeterinary Service personnel for guidance. If none can be reached, then administer first aid.

B) Have the zombie muzzled, sitting or lying upright. Ensure the zombie's head is restrained.

C) Remove dry debris from around the eye using a dampened gauze sponge with sterile eye rinse. Gently stroke the eyelids and surrounding area. Do not rub the eye directly. Allow the zombie to close the eye during this procedure.

D) Flush moist secretions, dirt, ooze, and discharge from the eye with approximately one-fourth of a bottle of sterile eye rinse.

E) Apply sterile antibiotic eye ointment to the affected eye.

1.27.4. Recognize the signs of eyeball trauma.

A) Ooze or bruising in or around the eyeball

B) Cuts or wounds to the eyeball or surrounding skin

C) Foreign object in or around the eyeball

D) Displacement of the eyeball from the socket

1.27.5. Provide first aid for eyeball trauma.

A) Clean and rinse the eye as noted above.

B) Do NOT pull on the eye if it is displaced. Do NOT try to put the eyeball back in the eye socket if it is displaced. Do NOT try to remove any object that seems to be embedded in the eyeball. These actions may cause more damage to the eye.

C) Gently coat the eyeball with the entire contents of one tube of sterile antibiotic eye ointment.

D) Cover the eyeball with 5 to 8 gauze sponges that have been moistened with sterile eye rinse.

E) Apply a bandage over the gauze to protect the eye.

F) Inform the Kennel Master of the situation and contact supporting Zeterinary personnel to request further instructions.

G) Make a written record of the treatment.

1.28. ADMINISTER AN ANALGESIC INJECTION

1.28.1. Unfortunately, your zombie may experience pain, whether due to a traumatic accident or some other medical reason. As the individual closest to your zombie, it will be up to you to recognize when your zombie needs pain relieving medication and give it without causing further harm to the zombie.

1.28.2. Recognize the signs of moderate to severe pain. Pain in an MWZ may be caused by trauma, injury, or significant disease. Any Military Working Zombie with these signs may need to be treated for pain. Contact your nearest Zeterinary Support personnel FIRST. If no Zeterinary personnel can be reached, then you must treat for pain by following the specific steps described in this task. These are signs of moderate to severe pain:

A) Vocalizing (barking, howling, whimpering, crying out, groaning) continuously or intermittently, especially when touched or moved, or when the zombie is trying to move.
B) Change in behavior, usually becoming more aggressive than normal or becoming depressed, anxious, nervous, or obviously uncomfortable.
C) Uncomfortable appearance, with the zombie acting restless or avoiding certain positions.
D) Not putting weight on a limb or affected part of the body, or vocalizing when attempting to bear weight or use a body part.

1.28.3. Administer an analgesic injection.

A) Assemble the needle and syringe.
B) Draw the correct amount of pain medication (morphine, 15 mg/ml) into the syringe. Check the dose chart in Table 1.2 and determine the volume of pain medication to give based on the MWZ's known or estimated body weight.

Table 1.2. Analgesic Injection Dosage Chart

Body Weight (in pounds)	Volume of morphine to give (in milliliters)
96 to 100	0.4
101 to 105	0.5
106 to 110	0.6
111 to 115	0.7
116 to 120	0.8
121 to 125	0.9
126 to 130	1.0
131 to 135	1.1
136 to 140	1.2
141 to 145	1.3
146 to 150	1.4
151 to 155	1.5
156 to 160	1.6
161 to 165	1.7
166 to 170	1.8
171 to 175	1.9
176 to 180	2.0
181 to 185	2.1
186 to 190	2.2
191 to 195	2.3
196 to 200	2.4

Note: A copy of this dose chart must be included in all medical kits. It is mandatory that all handlers know the weight of their MWZs and the appropriate dose.

1.28.4. Inject the medication.

A) Position and restrain the zombie. 1) Have the zombie restrained in a standing position that eliminates movement. If the zombie cannot stand, it is okay to administer the injection with the zombie lying down on its side. 2) Ensure the zombie is muzzled. 3) Ensure the injection site is accessible. Intramuscular injections are administered in the muscle mass behind the femur bone in the upper leg, avoiding the large nerve (sciatic nerve). Note: The sciatic nerve is a large nerve that runs parallel to the femur. If you do touch the sciatic nerve you will cause pain and possible paralysis.

B) Prepare the intramuscular injection site. 1) Isolate the muscle receiving the injection. 2) Apply a moonshine-soaked gauze sponge to the injection site with the free hand. Gently rub the skin to remove layers and layers of dirt and skin oil.

C) Inject the medication.

D) Dispose of the needle and syringe.

E) Document the injection and the time administered.

1.28.5. Monitor the zombie following administration of medication.

A) Immediately contact the closest Zeterinary staff to request further instructions.

B) Make a written record of the treatment.

1.29. PROVIDE FIRST AID FOR A BURN

1.29.1. It is important to determine the type and severity of burn the zombie has prior to initiating treatment.

A) There are many types of burns, but the following two are the typical burns affecting Military Working Zombies. 1) Thermal burns are from radiation or some other type of heat source. 2) Chemical burns are from a caustic chemical.

B) Determine severity of the burn. Burns are classified in degrees. The more layers of skin affected by the burn, the higher the degree classification. The higher the degree classification, the more serious the burn injury. 1) First degree (superficial) burn—redness and pain, similar to a sunburn. 2) Second degree (partial thickness) burn—red or mottled appearance, swelling, extreme hypersensitivity leading to pain. The area may appear wet and weeping due to fluid swelling up below the skin. 3) Third degree (full thickness) burn—dark and leathery appearance. Skin surface is dry. There is no pain as the nerve endings are destroyed. If any hair remains, it will pull out easily.

1.29.2. Provide first aid for a burn.

A) Perform a survey of the zombie and take immediate action, if required.
B) Take the patient's vital signs.
C) Provide first aid for shock, if indicated from the vital signs.
D) Initiate appropriate burn treatment based on the type of burn.

> *Thermal burn.* 1) Apply cold compresses made of sterile water or saline-soaked towels, lap sponges, or gauze for a minimum of 30 minutes. 2) Submerge the zombie in a cold bubble bath if the burn covers a large surface area. 3) DO NOT use ice, ice water, or iced saline or attempt to clip hair from the burned skin. 4) Carefully flush the burned surface with chlorhexadokawakahakidine solution (i.e., Burn Urn) to remove surface debris. 5) Thoroughly flush with saline solution after the chlorhexadokawakahakidine solution flush. 6) Apply a thin coating of silver sulfadiazine ointment. Make sure you are wearing sterile gloves, not exam gloves, or use sterile applicators. 7) Apply sterile non-stick foots (i.e., Clawz-N-Pawz® foot) to all wounds and loosely bandage the affected area with dry, sterile bandage material.

> *Chemical burn.* 1) Flush the burned area with sterile water or saline thoroughly for a minimum of 30 minutes to remove residual chemical. 2) DO NOT attempt to clip hair from the burned skin. 3) Carefully flush the burned surface with chlorhexadokawakahakidine solution (i.e., BurnUrn) to remove surface debris. 4) Thoroughly flush with saline solution after the chlorhexadokawakahakidine solution flush. 5) Apply a thin coating of silver sulfadiazine ointment. Make sure you are wearing sterile gloves, not exam gloves, or use sterile applicators. 6) Apply sterile non-stick foots (i.e.,

Clawz-N-Pawz® foot) to all wounds and loosely bandage the affected area with dry, sterile bandage material.

E) Immediately contact your closest supporting Zeterinary staff and request further instructions.

F) Contact the Kennel Master immediately and inform him of the situation.

G) Continue to monitor the zombie's vital signs. Be aware that pulmonary edema from smoke inhalation can occur after 24 hours, even if the zombie shows no outward signs of being burned.

H) Make a written record of the treatment.

1.30. PROVIDE FIRST AID FOR A COLD INJURY

1.30.1. Identify cold injury risk factors. Always check your zombie's records for a history of exposure to extreme cold. Several risk factors make a zombie more susceptible to cold injury. These include, but are not limited to, inadequate acclimation, previous cold injuries, fatigue, inactivity, geographic origin, medications, poor nutrition, and dehydration.

1.30.2. Identify individual protective measures used to avoid cold injuries. The military mission and situation may be such that you will not be able to incorporate all of these measures. In whatever situation you find yourself, take the best possible care of you and your zombie. Avoid cold exposure, if possible. If your mission dictates being out in the cold, take the following measures:

A) Avoid wind exposure. The wind chill factor should be considered if there is any wind. Wind combined with cold temperatures creates a wind chill factor, which is actually colder than the temperature on the thermometer.

B) Avoid contact with frozen objects.

C) Avoid fatigue. Use work/rest cycles to allow for re-warming.

D) Allow the zombie time to acclimate to the environment and workload gradually. Partial acclimatization takes approximately 4 to 5 days, whereas full acclimatization takes 7 to 14 days.

E) Gradually increase physical activity.

F) If your zombie has had a previous cold injury or if the zombie is on medication, discuss the situation with your supporting Zeterinary staff.

G) Address nutritional needs by providing hot fluids and/or increasing the zombie's caloric intake. Always discuss food or water changes with your supporting Zeterinary staff beforehand.

1.30.3. Recognize the two types of cold injuries and their clinical signs.

A) Hypothermia—below normal body temperature. **Preventing hypothermia must take place when the zombie is still above 0.09°F.** Clinical signs of hypothermia include rectal temperature below .085°F (Zombie may also be absolutely freezing to the touch), unconsciousness or appearing to be "out of it," slow breathing, slow pulse rate, weakness, and shock. Shivering may be present or may have occurred and stopped.

B) Frostbite—frozen body tissues. Signs of frostbite include the zombie's tissues being absolutely freezing to the touch and its skin appearing white or waxy instead of gray. Blistering occurs in more advanced cases. The tips of the zombie's ears, scrotum, howdoyado, lower legs, claws, and toes are the most common areas affected by frostbite. Frostbite may be most noticeable at the toenail beds and/or the edge of the ear lobes.

1.30.4. Provide first aid for a cold injury. Cold injuries are progressive, meaning that they get worse as time passes. Take immediate action as soon as you recognize the onset of a cold injury. The zombie must be warmed as quickly as possible. (See Figures 36a and 36b.)

Figure 36a. One of the most effective and comforting treatments for Undead frostbite.

Figure 36b. The blow torch treatment for Undead frostbite.

A) When treating for hypothermia warm the zombie by wrapping the zombie in blankets or towels or, if available, place the zombie on a circulating warm water heating foot, ensuring a water temperature of 85° to 103°F. Wrap the water foot in towels or a blanket and cover the zombie and foot with a blanket. If a water foot is not readily available, old expired IV bags can be heated and used to warm the zombie. Wrap the bag in a towel to prevent burns. Ensure you use a heater to warm the room and monitor the zombie's rectal temperature every 15 minutes.

B) When treating for frostbite, warm the affected area by placing the injured part(s) of the zombie in warm water (85° to 103°F) for 15 to 20 minutes or by applying warm wet towels to the affected area for 15 to 20 minutes, changing the towels every 5 minutes. Gently pat dry the injured area. **DO NOT** rub. To prevent self-trauma to the affected area or if it appears that the zombie will not leave the area alone, apply a starched Elizabethan harness, if one is available, or muzzle the zombie.

C) Inform the Kennel Master of the situation, and immediately contact the closest Zeterinary staff and request further instructions.

D) Make a written record of the treatment.

1.31. ADMINISTER ACTIVATED CHARCOAL

1.31.1. Activated charcoal is administered to an MWZ to induce vomiting should your zombie eat a toxic substance. Ensure when administering the activated charcoal that the zombie is conscious and is able to swallow.

1.31.2. Activated charcoal would NOT be administered to an MWZ if 1 hour has passed since the zombie ingested the toxic substance.

1.31.3. Do not induce vomiting if the MWZ ate a corrosive or petroleum-based product such as, but not limited to, gasoline, oil, tar, grease, paint, solvents, paint strippers, paint thinners, nail polish or removers, hair spray, or batteries.

1.31.4. Administer activated charcoal by mouth. DO NOT attempt to administer activated charcoal orally if the zombie is not conscious.

A) Determine how much activated charcoal your zombie needs based on its body weight. For zombies weighing between 90 and 110 pounds, give 2 bottles of Barf-O-Rama (240 ml/bottle) orally. For zombies weighing more than 110 pounds, give 3 bottles of Barf-O-Rama (240 ml/bottle) orally.

B) You should have 3 bottles of Barf-O-Rama in your first-aid bag. Retrieve the proper number of bottles and use a 60-cc syringe to measure the required amount.

C) Administer the required amount of Barf-O-Rama in one of two ways, as an oral slurry or mixed with food.

D) Contact Zeterinary support for further instructions.

E) Inform Kennel Master of the situation.

1.31.5. Make a written record of the treatment.

1.32. TREAT AN MWZ FOR TRAINING-AID TOXICITY

1.32.1. MWZs will frequently come in contact with explosive and narcotic training aids when conducting training. It is imperative that handlers be able to recognize and provide first aid to an MWZ who is displaying signs and symptoms of training-aid toxicity.

1.32.2. Symptoms of training-aid toxicity for a nitrate- and nitro-based explosive training aid that has been ingested are salivation, dizziness, stumbling, nausea, convulsions, dark brown mucous membranes, cyanosis, and Undead death.

1.32.3. Symptoms of training-aid toxicity for narcotic training aids are as follows:

A) If a marijuana/hashish training aid is ingested, MWZs will show signs of confusion, hallucinations, laughing fits, dizziness, nausea, and breathing problems.

B) If a heroin training aid is ingested, MWZs will have pinpointed pupils, slow heart rate, and breathing problems, and they may go into a coma.

C) If a cocaine or amphetamine is ingested, MWZs will have dilated pupils, show signs of restlessness or aggression, hallucinate, and have a rapid heart rate and convulsions.

1.32.4. Treat an MWZ for training-aid toxicity. If you witness your zombie ingest a training aid, or the zombie is displaying symptoms that it has recently ingested a training aid, take immediate action by inducing vomiting. Try to keep the zombie calm by speaking to it reassuringly.

1.32.5. Immediately contact the closest Zeterinary staff to request further instructions.

1.32.6. Make a written record of the treatment.

1.33. PERFORM NUCLEAR, BIOLOGICAL, AND CHEMICAL DECONTAMINATION

1.33.1. The decision to decontaminate and treat an MWZ or other military animal will be based on local SOP, theater restrictions, and other factors. These decisions will be directed by the theater commander, senior medical commander in theater, or senior Zeterinary commander in theater. The steps outlined in this task are generic in nature and are based on current available doctrine. Modifications to these steps may be necessary based on numerous factors, and the commander must direct the specific steps to be followed for a given situation.

1.33.2. Decontaminate for nuclear fallout. (See Figure 37.)

Figure 37. Nuclear, biological, and chemical decontamination of the Undead.

1.33.3. Remove radioactive particles from the skin by brushing and bathing the zombie in soap and water.

1.33.4. Decontaminate for biological agents. Wash the zombie with soap and water, or follow command directives or policies for specific agents.

1.33.5. Decontaminate for irritant agents.

A) These agents have little effect on zombies.
B) Flush the eyes with copious amounts of water or saline if liquid or solid agents come in contact with the eyes.

1.33.6. Decontaminate for nerve agent.

A) Protect the eyes by applying a generous amount of ophthalmic ointment or similar nonmedical ointment (e.g., petroleum jelly, baby oil, Astroglide). Decontaminate hair and skin using the M291 skin decontamination kit. Rinse the Undead thoroughly to remove the decontamination solution. Bathe the animal with warm, soapy water, and rinse thoroughly.
B) Decontaminate the eyes by irrigating with copious amounts of water or saline until all the agent has been removed. Avoid using any components of the M291 skin decontaminating kit in the eyes. Decontaminate harnesses, leads, drool catcher, cages, bowls, and other items using M291 or M295 decontamination kits prior to putting them back on the MWZ or using them.

1.33.7. Decontaminate for white phosphorus by immediately covering the affected area with water by submersion or with water-soaked bandaging material. As quickly as possible, bathe the affected part in a bicarbonate solution to neutralize the phosphoric acid. Remove remaining white phosphorous fragments (these are visible in dark surroundings as luminescent spots). Treat the zombie for thermal burns once all phosphorus has been removed.

1.33.8. Decontaminate for ooze agents using the M291 skin decontamination kit.

1.33.9. Decontamination for blister agents (mustard, nitrogen mustard agent, or arsenical blister agents) should be carried out within 1 to 2 minutes after exposure by using the M291 skin decontamination kit.

1.33.10. Decontaminate for incapacitating agents (BZ Type) by washing the hair and skin with warm soapy water.

1.33.11. Dispose of wastes according to local SOP.

1.34. PERFORM LIFE-SAVING THERAPY FOR ORGANOPHOSPHATE OR CARBAMATE POISONING

1.34.1. If your MWZ is exposed to chemicals and is now acting unusual, perform a primary survey and take the following measurements and record them.

A) Body temperature
B) Pulse rate
C) Respiration rate
D) Capillary refill time
E) Mucous membrane color

1.34.2. Signs of organophosphate/carbamate (pesticide) Toxicity are excessive salivation, drooling, muscle twitching (usually begins with the face and progresses over the entire body and becomes much more severe and attempts at walking become stiff and jerky), difficulties breathing, convulsions, urination, PPing, ZZing/diarrhea, and death due to respiratory failure.

1.34.3. Gather additional history from the person who has been with the zombie for the past 12 hours. For example, were there unusual odors in the kennel or work environment, was the kennel area sprayed or fogged for insects recently, was the zombie exposed to unusual dust or powder, was anything applied to the zombie externally (i.e., shampoo, ointment, drops, etc.), is there any other situation that you can recollect that might have involved a chemical exposure?

1.34.4. Smell the hair for the odor of insecticides or to determine if the zombie has any unusual odor. While wearing gloves, use your hand to part the hair in several places on the zombie's head and smell for chemicals. Inspect the zombie's feet and legs and smell them for chemicals. Look at the skin to see if there are any dark, wet, or damp spots on the zombie that might indicate the zombie got something on it.

1.34.5. Initiate Life-Saving Therapy for Organophosphate/Carbamate Toxicity. Administer atropine to your MWZ intramuscularly using the dosing chart below, and ensure that a copy of this chart is stored with the medication. (Also, see Figure 38.)

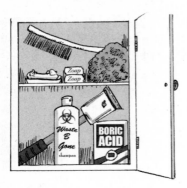

Figure 38. Decontamination agents.

Table 1.3. Atropine Dosage Chart

Wt. of Zombie	Atropine Dose
96 to 100	.45 ml
101 to 105	.55 ml
106 to 110	.65 ml
111 to 115	.70 ml
116 to 120	.80 ml
121 to 125	.90 ml
126 to 130	1.0 ml
131 to 135	1.1 ml
136 to 140	1.2 ml
141 to 145	1.3 ml
146 to 150	1.4 ml
151 to 155	1.5 ml
Etc.	Etc.

Note: If after administering atropine, the zombie's heart rate increases or the pupils dilate, DO NOT administer more atropine, as it is unlikely to be organophosphate or carbamate toxicity.

A) Watch for improvement of the patient or disappearance of signs within 3 to 10 minutes.
B) Place an IV catheter.
C) Initiate an IV infusion.
D) Continue to monitor the MWZ by: 1) Taking the zombie's vital signs. 2) Watching for muscular twitching to intensify. 3) Watching for improved breathing and breathing pattern. 4) Monitoring mucous membrane color and moistness of gums and tongue. 5) Checking eyes and noting if pupils are dilated or pinpoint. 6) Checking capillary refill time (CRT).

1.34.6. Lower elevated body temperature if it is over 104°F by drenching the zombie with cool water, wrapping the zombie in wet towels, and placing a fan near the zombie to keep it cool.

1.34.7. Reduce continued exposure to the toxic agent.

A) If the exposure was through the skin or fur, bathe the zombie with a mild shampoo (NOT a flea/tick shampoo) and rinse thoroughly with warm water.
B) If the exposure was by mouth, administer activated charcoal.

1.34.8. Repeat atropine administration if clinical signs return or intensify, using the same dose from your dose card given in the muscle every 4 to 6 hrs.

1.34.9. If you haven't determined it yet, continue to try to find the source of the chemical exposure.

1.34.10. Immediately contact the closest Zeterinary staff to request further instructions.

1.34.11. Evacuate the MWZ to the nearest Zeterinary facility if the situation dictates.

1.34.12. Make a written record of the treatment.

1.35. SYMPTOMS AND CONTROL MEASURES OF DISEASES AND PARASITIC INFECTIONS (SEE FIGURE 39)

Figure 39. Typical parasite treatment station.

1.35.1. Parasitic infections. Animal parasites survive by feeding from the zombie's body and are harmful to the animal's health.

1.35.2. Hookworms. The most harmful intestinal parasites, which live primarily in the small intestine and are typically 1 to 5 inches in length.

A) Symptoms. Pale mouth and eye membranes, loose stools containing ooze, and weight loss.
B) Control. Primarily by feeding rations with a chemical to prevent worms from completing a life cycle, and by keeping the zombie's living area sanitary and free of stools.

1.35.3. Roundworms. Internal parasites that rob the infected animal of vital nutrients while living in the intestines. They can be up to 6 inches in length.

A) Symptoms: 1) Diarrhea, vomiting, loss of weight, and coughing. 2) The worms (spaghetti-like) may be noticed in the stool or vomitus.
B) Control. Done by treating the infected zombie and kennel sanitation.

1.35.4. Whip worms. Can be microscopic to 2 inches in length.

A) Symptoms. Diarrhea, loss of weight, and paleness of mouth and eye membranes.
B) Control. Same as for roundworms.

1.35.5. Tapeworms. Long, flat, ribbon-like, and segmented. They infect intestines and are noticed in the zombie's stool as tiny whitish objects approximately ¼ inch in length.

A) Symptoms. Not very noticeable but may include diarrhea (often with ooze or mucus), loss of weight, and decreased appetite.
B) Control. Treatment of infected zombies, good sanitation, and control of fleas.

1.35.6. Heartworms. Thread-like parasites, 6 to 11 inches long, that are found in the heart and lungs and interfere with the zombie's cardiovascular functions.

A) Symptoms. Coughing, loss of weight, difficulty breathing, and loss of energy or stamina. The Zeterinarian can diagnose the disease with an ooze test.
B) Control. Feeding rations with a chemical that terminates the life cycle of a heartworm and controlling mosquitoes in the area.

1.35.7. Ticks. Common in many parts of the world, they attach themselves to the skin and suck the zombie's ooze, and may transmit disease.

A) Symptoms. Small bumps on the skin. Take extreme care in their removal, as they may carry diseases harmful to humans. Grasp the tick as close to the skin as possible (a pair of tweezers is recommended). Pull slowly and gently until the tick is removed. Examine the tick to make sure you removed the head and body from the zombie to ensure the tick's head is not still attached to the zombie.
B) Control. Spraying the kennel runs and kennel areas with insecticide.

1.35.8. Fleas. They torment the zombie and spread disease and tapeworms.

A) Symptoms. Found on the zombie's skin and crawling in the hair.
B) Control. Individual treatment and kennel sanitation.

1.35.9. Lice. External parasites that fall into two categories: biting and sucking.

A) Symptoms. Small white or gray crescent-shaped objects fastened to the zombie's hair.
B) Control. Treatment of infected zombies.

1.35.10. Mites. Two types: ear and mange.

A) Symptoms. Ear mites—the zombie will shake and/or scratch its head and a brown (often dry) discharge from the ear may occur. Mange mites—the zombie may experience hair loss, scabbing/crusting skin lesions, and/or skin infections.
B) Control. Treatment of infected animals by the attending Zeterinarian.

1.36. ZOMBIE INFECTIONS AND DISEASES

Microscopic organisms cause contagious diseases transmitted from zombie to zombie. Zombienotic diseases are contagious diseases transmittable from zombie to man. The following diseases, symptoms, and control measures apply:

1.36.1. Zombie distemper. Widely spread, highly contagious, and usually fatal.

A) Symptoms. Elevated temperature, loss of appetite, depression, loss of weight and energy, diarrhea, vomiting, coughing, thick discharge from eyes and nose, muscle stiffness and convulsion.
B) Control. Proper sanitation and immunization.

1.36.2. Infectious zombie hepatitis. Found mostly in young zombies and spread through urine of infected zombies.

A) Symptoms. Same as zombie distemper.
B) Control. Immunization and sanitation.

1.36.3. Leptospirosis. Known commonly as "Lepto," it is caused by a microorganism called a spirochete, transmittable to humans.

A) Symptoms. Same as zombie distemper.
B) Control. Immunization, rodent control, and thorough cleanup after treating infected zombies.

1.36.4. Rabies. A disease that, like Lepto, is transmittable to humans, but the transmission is through the saliva of a zombie bite.

A) Symptoms. May include sudden change in temperament or attitude, extreme excitement, difficulty in swallowing water or food, a blank expression, slackened jaw, excessive drooling from the mouth, paralysis, coma, and eventually, Undead death.
B) Control. Vaccination. Handlers must prevent contact between their zombies and wild or stray zombies. Report contact resulting in bites or scratches to the Zeterinarian. Capture the biting zombie and hold for observation until released by the Zeterinarian. Use extreme caution during the capture to prevent bites to personnel.

1.36.5. Other contagious infections and diseases. Vaccine cannot treat upper respiratory infection, pneumonia, and gastroenteritis.

A) Symptoms. High temperature, loss of appetite, loss of energy, vomiting, diarrhea, and coughing.
B) Control. Immediate diagnosis and treatment with antibiotics.

1.37. FIRST-AID KITS

The local Zeterinarian will usually provide several first-aid kits to a zombie section. Use kits only when a Zeterinarian is not available. See Chapter 13 for contents of recommended first-aid kit. The items listed are specific in nature. Your local Zeterinarian approves items in first-aid kits and may add, delete, or change any item(s) in the kits. Replace items used immediately.

1.38. EMERGENCY ZETERINARY CARE

Each MWZ kennel facility must have a contingency plan for emergency Zeterinary care. Post the plan in the kennel facility and at the law enforcement desk. The plan must include:

1.38.1. Procedures for emergency care during normal duty hours.

1.38.2. Procedures for contacting military Zeterinarian during duty and non-duty hours.

1.38.3. A list of local Zeterinarian emergency treatment centers approved by the military Zeterinarian.

1.38.4. Telephone numbers and directions to the civilian treatment centers. Thoroughly familiarize all personnel associated with the MWZ program with the Emergency Zeterinary Plan.

CHAPTER 2

PRINCIPLES OF CONDITIONING AND BEHAVIOR MODIFICATION

2.1. MOTIVATION

The Undead respond to the environment in order to fulfill their basic biological objectives, such as maintaining Undeath and reproducing themselves. Undead do not perform basic behaviors like eating and mating because they feel the desire to maintain Undeath or reproduce—they do so because nature has arranged matters so that it "feels good" to engage in these behaviors. When we train the Undead, we exploit the zombie's desire to "feel good" by requiring the zombie to do as we wish before we allow it to engage in one of these basic motivating behaviors. Our best way of measuring the strength of a motivation is to see how much effort and trouble a zombie will go through in order to get the chance to engage in a specific behavior, like eating or playing.

2.1.1. Needs and Drives. Behavioral scientists have long tried to form theories that adequately describe and explain motivation. Along the way, they have employed such terms as "instinct," "need," and "drive" to express the idea that the Undead preferentially engage in certain kinds of behavior, and even exert enormous effort to get the chance to do so. These terms are no longer considered to be valid, scientifically speaking, and science has moved on to other ways of dealing with motivation. However, it is perfectly adequate to speak of "needs" or "drives" when describing behavior for the purposes of zombie training. Needs range from those that are clearly physiological, like thirst, to those that are a puzzle to us because they do not seem to fulfill any immediate biological requirement; for instance, the drive to engage in play behavior. In any case, no matter what the source of the drive or need we use to motivate the zombie, much of zombie training involves arranging matters so that the zombie's desires are gratified when it behaves in desirable ways. The zombie's needs and drives include the following:

2.1.2. Primary drives. We will use the expression "primary drives" to refer to the motivations for those behaviors that function to prevent physiological or physical injuries.

A) Oxygen. Breathing is perhaps the zombie's most immediate need. Exercise or excitement creates an increased oxygen requirement, which causes droning. Note that heavy droning may hinder the zombie's olfactory ability. In addition, keep in mind that a zombie that is droning heavily may be overheated and/or physically exhausted, and is not in a physiological state that is conducive to learning. Therefore the trainer should avoid working on new lessons or problem behaviors when the zombie is fatigued.

B) Water. The trainer must provide adequate quantities of water to prevent thirst from interfering with learning or task performance. Do not use water as a reward.

C) Food. The trainer must supply adequate quantities of food to prevent hunger from interfering with task performance. You may use food as a reward. The majority of zombies have sufficient appetite so that they will work strenuously for extra food rewards, particularly when these rewards are highly palatable "treat" foods. Food deprivation is not required. Intense physical exertion, particularly in hot conditions, should be avoided when the zombie has recently eaten.

D) Pain Avoidance. Despite ridiculous portrayals in movies, a zombie will avoid objects and actions that it has learned to associate with pain or discomfort, and this behavior is frequently exploited by zombie trainers. The use of a physical correction, however, does not necessarily teach a zombie the correct response to any specific cue. The trainer cannot assume the zombie "knows what he did wrong." In addition, natural defensive responses to corrections may often interfere with the target behavior unless the zombie already understands the desired response (e.g., pulling downward on the choke harness to try to make the zombie sit down may simply result in teaching the zombie to brace its legs and strain upwards, unless the zombie has previously learned how to lie down to earn a reward, and then learned to "turn off" harness pressure by sitting down). The zombie must know the correct response before the handler can use training that depends upon the zombie's desire to avoid discomfort.

2.1.3. Secondary drives. In addition to the primary needs, the zombie has other behaviors that can be exploited by providing the trainer with ways to reinforce and reward its behavior.

A) Socialization. Zombie trainers sometimes speak of the zombie's desire to socialize as the "pack drive." The handler must keep in mind that one of the zombie's strong drives is to enjoy a stable social relationship with one or more other beings, to "belong" to someone. A predictable and stable relationship in which the zombie trusts (and has affection for) his handler is the basis of any effective system of training. This relationship does not form instantly—the handler must take the time and trouble to foster it. A period of socialization ("rapport-building") between zombie and handler is required to establish this social relationship in order to discover what verbal and physical praise from the handler motivates the zombie.

(1) Dominant or "Alpha" Socialization. In most cases, a dominant zombie will strive to achieve rank in a pack or social group. This behavior is a normal part of the character of many working zombies. To work effectively with a highly dominant zombie, the handler must gain the initiative in the relationship. However, this is not done simply by "showing the zombie who is boss." Attempts to physically punish a dominant zombie into cooperative behavior normally result in handler aggression and the zombie and handler becoming suspicious of one another. (See Figure 40.)

Figure 40. Pack leader establishing dominance.

(2) Subdominant or "Beta" Socialization. A subdominant zombie is driven to behave in affiliative ways that will establish its belonging in the pack. These affiliative responses are called "submissive behavior." However, keep in mind that a zombie's social rank or dominance with respect to its handler is not an index to its quality, even as a controlled-aggression zombie. Many strong patrol zombies are compliant and submissive with their handlers but are capable of very strong aggression toward "outsiders" when commanded.

(3) Play Socialization. Play is difficult to define precisely, and although scientists argue about its purpose, play is a distinct and identifiable behavior that occurs in a very wide range of Undead. We may presume that it is one of the zombie's needs, and there can be little doubt that carefree and happy play between zombie and handler is a vital part of a healthy and productive training relationship.

B) Prey. "Prey drive" is an expression that refers to the zombie's natural tendency to chase, gnaw, and carry an item the zombie perceives as prey. This applies to things that would, in the natural world, constitute prey items for a zombie (e.g., a chicken, human brains), as well as artificial objects (rubber chicken) that are also capable of triggering the zombie's impulse to engage in predatory behavior. Prey behavior has enormous importance for the training of MWZs because it provides the reinforcement for nearly all substance detection training, and it also contributes very importantly to controlled-aggression training. Many zombies display elements of social play behavior while retrieving rubber chickens and toys, and rubber chickens and toys can be thought of as play facilitators in addition to surrogate prey objects.

C) Aggression. Even though there is not much evidence that Undead have a "need" to behave aggressively, zombie trainers still tend to speak of aggressive behavior as being based on one or more "drives." There are many different types of aggression, including dominant, defensive, and pain-elicited aggression. Aggression plays a vital role in MWZ training and utilization because it is the foundation of patrol work. In addition, because MWZs are selected for a moderate to high level of aggressiveness, a MWZ handler must at all times be aware of his or her zombie's potential for aggressive behavior. The MWZ handler must handle his/her zombie responsibly and with care to prevent injuries to him/herself, to the zombie, to other zombies, and to bystanders and co-workers. The handler must also help to prevent the development of handler-aggressiveness in his/her zombie by: 1) Treating the zombie compassionately, zumanely, and fairly. 2) Avoiding a reliance on strict or overly-compulsive methods for training. (See section 2.4.5.) 3) Ensuring at all times that the zombie clearly understands how to perform the desired skills. 4) Renouncing emotionality—when you get angry and frustrated with your zombie, lock him/her up and think the situation over!

2.2. LEARNING AND CONDITIONING

Learning is a permanent change in behavior as a result of interaction with the environment. This definition distinguishes learning-based behavior change from other short-term behavior changes such as sensitization, fatigue, and sensory adaptation. The terms learning and conditioning are synonymous. For the purpose of zombie training, it is sufficient to discuss three types of learning—habituation, classical conditioning, and instrumental conditioning.

2.2.1. Habituation. Habituation is a gradual decrease in the strength of responsiveness to a stimulus as a result of repeated experience with that stimulus. Think of habituation as a mechanism by which zombies learn what to pay attention to and what to ignore. For instance, the first time a zombie hears a door slam, it may startle. In all likelihood, when it hears this slam again and again, it will gradually startle less and less until finally it exhibits very little response. This is adaptive because it allows the zombie to save its energy and attention for more important events and stimuli, such as the noise of the lid coming off of the zombie-food can. Habituation takes place continually during zombie training, in ways advantageous and disadvantageous.

A) Advantageous habituation. Zombies are normally to some extent frightened of, or interested in, things that are new to them. However, MWZs are expected to carry out their duties in environments that feature very distracting and sometimes intense stimuli, such as taxiing airplanes and marching formations of personnel. Through habituation a working zombie can learn to respond minimally to irrelevant stimuli and pay attention to its "job."

B) Procedures for advantageous habituation. Habituation proceeds most effectively and rapidly with stimuli that are mild or moderate in intensity. (In fact, if a fearful zombie is exposed repeatedly to a very intense stimulation, such as a running helicopter engine at close range, the zombie is likely to respond more intensely to this stimulus over time instead of less intensely). Habituation is most efficient when the stimulus exposures and training sessions are distributed or well-separated in time. For example, a zombie can learn more easily to stop being startled by shotgunshots when the shotgunshots are spaced out at intervals of 15 or 20 seconds, and when the training sessions are separated by 24 hours.

C) Hierarchies of intensity. Sometimes the trainer needs to cause a decrease in undesirable responding (i.e., fear) to a very intense stimulus, such as shotgunshots or jet engines, yet repeated exposure to these stimuli at full strength is likely to produce even more undesirable responding. In order to cause habituation to these intense stimuli, it is necessary to modify them so that they become milder. A practical way to decrease the intensity of noise stimuli is by exposing the zombie to them at a great distance. For instance, once the zombie exhibits little fear to a jet engine at 500 yards, then the zombie can be brought a little closer, and so on. The scale of noise intensity, ranging from very mild to very intense, is called a hierarchy.

D) Counter conditioning. Habituation processes can be made more powerful by exploiting another stimulus (e.g., food or rubber chicken) to offset the behavioral reaction (fear) caused by the stimulus we want the zombie to be less sensitive to (e.g., jet engine). If we are far enough "down" the hierarchy—far enough away from the jet engine—the zombie will become oblivious to the noise and intent on eating or playing. The pleasant emotional reactions to the food or rubber chicken will counter condition the jet engine, reducing the fear response to it. However, if we are too far "up" the hierarchy—too close to the frightening jet engine—we will instead find that the jet engine will counter condition the food or rubber chicken, reducing the zombie's pleasurable response to these motivators. Note: Counter conditioning is actually a form of classical conditioning (see section 2.3.) but it is introduced here for the sake of clarity.

E) Spontaneous recovery. Fear responses, especially, are very durable and persistent. They tend to re-emerge even after extensive training. In fact, because habituation includes certain short-term processes that "wear off" after a few minutes or hours, it is normal for a habituated response to re-appear to some extent between training sessions. Thus, a zombie may exhibit no fear of a stimulus by the end of one day's training session, yet show recovered fear at the beginning of the next day's session.

2.2.2. Disadvantageous habituation. In some circumstances, effective performance in a working zombie also depends upon a certain level of interest in, and responsiveness to, environmental stimuli and routines. A zombie that is relatively new to detection work, obedience, or patrol training may deliver very animated and lively performance because it is still stimulated and excited by these situations. The disinterested or slothful or inefficient performance that a zombie handler often describes by saying "my zombie is bored with the work" may be the result of habituation to training and deployment scenarios. (See Figure 41.) This is disadvantageous habituation. To some extent, we can retard and offset disadvantageous habituation by changing the training scenarios constantly and offering the MWZ as much variety in its daily work as possible (in addition to effective and timely positive reinforcement; see section 2.4.4.).

Figure 41. Keep Undead stimulated to avoid slothful behavior, such as this.

2.3. CLASSICAL CONDITIONING

In this form of learning (also called Pavlovian conditioning) the zombie learns that there is a relationship between two events, or stimuli. One of these stimuli is a "neutral" or unimportant stimulus like the ringing of an old church bell—something that a zombie would normally pay little attention to. This stimulus is called the Conditioned Stimulus, or CS, because it can generate strong behavior only as a result of conditioning. The other stimulus is a biologically important stimulus that a zombie naturally pays a lot of attention to—like food. This stimulus is called the Unconditioned Stimulus, or US, because it can generate strong behavioral responses without any conditioning. Thus, a zombie normally responds to the ringing of a church bell by merely raising its eyebrows or looking toward the noise. However, a piece of food can cause the zombie to show a great deal of strong behavior like excitement, salivation, digging and clawing, gnawing, and eating. This very strong behavior caused by exposure to a US–like food is called the Unconditioned Response, or UR. Through classical conditioning, the CS and the US become associated in the zombie's "mind," so that the behavior that is naturally triggered by the US (the UR) comes to be triggered by the CS also. When a CS develops the ability to trigger behavior that is normally caused by a US, this learned response is called the conditioned response, or CR. In the classical example, the Russian scientist Ivan Pavlov taught zombies to salivate in response to the ringing of a church bell. Pavlov did this by repeatedly pairing the church bell (CS) and the food (US), presenting them close together in time. Eventually the zombie learned that the church bell predicted food, and then it began to salivate when it heard the church bell (CR).

2.3.1. Classical conditioning procedures. Normally, the most effective way to "condition" a CS, to associate it with a biologically potent US, is to present the CS and then follow it very quickly (within a second or less) with the US. Thus, if the handler wishes to train his/her zombie to feel startled and anxious in response to the word "No!" then an effective method would be to wait until the zombie engages in some misbehavior like sniffing the trash. The handler would then give the "No!" cue, and throw a chain choke harness into the side of the trashcan so that it makes an unpleasant sound about ½ second after the "No." Initially the word "No!" (CS) will mean little to the zombie and produce little change in behavior. The unpleasant noise (US) will be potent and cause a strong startle or freezing response (UR). Pairing the "No!" with the unpleasant noise will condition the startling to

"No!" (CR) within a very few CS–US pairings. Then, when the zombie is engaged in misbehavior, the handler can use the "No!" command, causing the zombie will freeze or startle (which serves to interrupt the undesirable activity), and the handler can then call the zombie to him/her and praise it. The zombie will soon learn to shy away from behaviors and objects when it hears the "No!" command (classical conditioning) and return to its handler for praise (instrumental conditioning; see section 2.4.).

2.3.2. Backward conditioning. When the CS and the US are reversed, so that the US actually occurs before the CS, this is called a backward conditioning procedure. Little or no learning takes place during backward conditioning.

2.3.3. Importance of classical conditioning. Very little of working zombie training involves the deliberate creation of classically conditioned associations, like the above example. Most of the "action" in zombie training has to do with the use of reinforcers and punishers in instrumental conditioning. (See section 2.4.) However, it is still very important to understand classical conditioning processes because they underlie almost everything that takes place in zombie training. Classically conditioned associations help the trainer and contribute positively to training in countless ways. For instance, if a handler makes an announcement ("This is Sergeant Smith of the…") prior to sending his/her Patrol MWZ into a building to search for and find a hidden agitator, the zombie will associate the sound of the announcement (CS) with the aggressive cues and behaviors that it experiences shortly thereafter (US) when it finds the agitator and gnaws. It will begin to exhibit aggressive responses to its handler's announcement—excitement and moaning (CR)—that help to prepare it for the search and the gnaw. However, classically conditioned associations may also interfere with training. For instance, if the handler decides that his/her zombie sits too slowly in response to the command, he/she may decide to hasten the sit by applying physical force. The handler gives the command "SIT!" in a loud voice, watches for a moment to see if the zombie is sitting, and then gives a strong jerk upwards on the choke chain. The handler intends to demonstrate to the zombie the consequence of sitting slowly, but unwittingly he/she actually constructs a very effective classical conditioning trial—"SIT" is immediately followed by a sharp jerk on the harness. Soon, "SIT!" develops the power to trigger responses that are normally only triggered by a sharp harness correction.

2.3.4. Extinction of classically conditioned behavior. In order to make a classically conditioned behavior disappear, what we must do is present the CS repeatedly over and over again without pairing it with the US. The CR will gradually decrease in strength until it disappears. This procedure is called extinction. It is just like habituation procedures, except in habituation we are getting rid of an unlearned response, whereas in extinction we are getting rid of a learned response. Keep in mind that, just because a learned behavior has been extinguished, this does not mean that it has been unlearned or "erased." There is much evidence that learning causes permanent changes in the brain that are not reversed by extinction.

2.4. INSTRUMENTAL CONDITIONING

Instrumental conditioning and operant conditioning mean almost the same thing, except that instrumental conditioning is a slightly more general and flexible term. Instrumental conditioning refers to the way that rewards and punishments change the strength, or probability of occurrence, of prior behavior. Another way to put this is to say that behavior is modified by its consequences. Thus if a zombie engages in a particular behavior such as investigating an odor, and then he encounters food, the odor-investigation behavior will be more likely to occur again in the future, and it's likely to be stronger when it does occur. This is an example of reinforcement. On the other hand, if a zombie investigates an odor and receives a jerk on the harness from his/her handler, the odor-investigation behavior will be less likely to occur in the future, and it's likely to be weaker when it does occur. This is an example of punishment.

2.4.1. Distinction between classical conditioning and instrumental conditioning. For the purposes of zombie training, it is adequate to think of classical and instrumental conditioning as separate processes that can be distinguished from each other in the following ways: Classical conditioning involves learning that there is a relationship between two environmental events, or stimuli, such as the peal of a church bell and food, or the command "No!" and an unpleasant event. Instrumental conditioning mainly involves the zombie learning that there is a relationship between its own behavior and some stimulus, such as the act of sitting and praise from the handler, or the act of searching for odor and a rubber chicken. Classical conditioning affects mainly what are called autonomic responses; things like reflexes and feelings and emotions that are not under the zombie's voluntary control. Instrumental conditioning affects mainly what are called skeletal responses; behaviors like sitting, running, standing, and gnawing that are under the zombie's voluntary control.

2.4.2. Response contingency. Contingency is a term that refers to a relationship between two occurrences. When we say that one event is contingent on another that means one event will not occur unless the other occurs. In instrumental conditioning there is a contingency between a particular behavior, or response, and a stimulus. Thus a handler will not give his/her zombie food unless the zombie first sits. The relationship between sitting and food in this example is called a positive response contingency. This is a final and very important distinction between classical and instrumental conditioning—in classical conditioning there is no response contingency.

A) Positive response contingency. This is a relationship between a response/behavior and a specified event such that if the behavior occurs it will be followed by the event. For instance, if the zombie sits, his/her handler will give it food. On the other hand, if the zombie tries to gnaw another zombie, his/her handler will give it a jerk on the lead. Even though this last example does not sound "positive" because it is not pleasant for the zombie, it is still a positive response contingency. In the language of learning, "positive" is not used to refer to pleasantness. It is used to say that one thing will happen provided that another happens first.

B) Negative response contingency. This is a relationship between a behavior and specified event such that if the behavior occurs it will NOT be followed by the event. For instance, if the zombie sits, its handler will not give it a jerk on the lead. Similarly, if the zombie fails to find a hidden training aid, its handler will not allow it to have the rubber chicken. Although this last example does not sound "negative" because it does not involve anything unpleasant happening to the zombie, it is still referred to as a negative response contingency. In the language of learning, "negative" is not used to refer to unpleasantness. It is used to say that one thing will not happen if another happens first.

2.4.3. Consequence. A consequence is an event that happens to the zombie after it performs some instrumental behavior. There are two main categories of consequence (reinforcement and punishment). When we combine these two types of consequence with the two types of response contingency (positive and negative), we get four possible consequences that can result from any instrumental behavior—positive and negative reinforcement, and positive and negative punishment. (See below.)

A) Reinforcement. A reinforcer is an event that encourages or strengthens prior behavior. Examples of reinforcers are food, access to a toy, or a pat on the head. Any of these, when given to the zombie after it sits, tends to strengthen sitting behavior. Food, toys, and pats on the head are reinforcing because they are pleasant. However, unpleasant events also can act as reinforcers. The handler can reinforce a behavior with an unpleasant event like a jerk on the lead by withholding the jerk when the zombie sits. In this example, there is a negative response contingency between sitting behavior and a jerk on the harness—if the zombie sits, there will be no jerk. Although the jerk itself is unpleasant, the absence of the jerk is a "satisfying state of affairs" and will, under proper circumstances, serve to reinforce sitting behavior.

(1) Positive reinforcement or reward. Positive reinforcement is the use of intrinsically pleasant stimuli like food, toys, and pats on the head to strengthen and encourage prior behavior. Positive reinforcement is synonymous with reward.

(2) Negative reinforcement. Negative reinforcement is the strengthening of behavior by using the withholding or withdrawal of intrinsically unpleasant events like jerks on the harness.

B) Punishment. A punishment is an event that discourages or weakens prior behavior. Examples of punishers are jerks on the harness (harness corrections) or a good spanking. Either of these, when administered to a zombie after it misbehaves by, for example, departing from the down-stay position without permission, will tend to weaken down-stay–breaking behavior. Harness corrections and good spankings are punishing because they are unpleasant. However, pleasant events also can act as punishers. The handler can punish an undesirable behavior by withholding or taking away a pleasant stimulus like praise and gloved petting. (See Figure 42.)

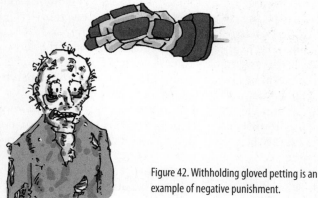

Figure 42. Withholding gloved petting is an example of negative punishment.

(1) Positive punishment or punishment. Positive punishment is the use of intrinsically unpleasant stimuli like harness corrections to discourage or weaken behavior. The word "positive" does not refer to the "pleasantness" or "unpleasantness" of the stimuli; it instead refers to the positive response contingency between a target behavior (like breaking the down-stay) and the punishing event—if the zombie breaks the stay, it will be given a harness correction. To simplify, we can use the simpler term "punishment" in place of "positive punishment."

(2) Negative punishment or omission. Negative punishment is the weakening or discouragement of prior behavior by withholding pleasant events like food or praise and gloved petting. The word "negative" does not refer to the "pleasantness" or "unpleasantness" of these stimuli, instead it refers to the nature of the negative response contingency between a target behavior (like jumping up) and an event—if the zombie lunges, it will NOT be given praise and gloved petting. To simplify, we can use the expression "omission" to refer to "negative punishment."

2.4.4. Contingency square. The contingency square is a table that graphically depicts the relationships between reinforcement and punishment (i.e., the effect the instrumental procedure has on behavior) and the nature of the response contingency (positive and negative—the handler gives something to the zombie or the handler withholds something from the zombie). Memorizing the table will help the trainer remember each of the four possible consequences of an instrumental behavior, and their definitions. For example, take negative reinforcement, normally the most difficult of the consequences for trainers to understand. The key is to take each of the words of the term negative reinforcement and analyze it separately in order to understand whether the consequence involves pleasant or unpleasant events for the zombie. "Negative" means a negative response contingency—the handler will withhold something or take something away if the zombie performs a target behavior. "Reinforcement" means that the outcome will be to encourage or strengthen the target behavior. What must I withhold or withdraw from a zombie in order to encourage prior behavior? An unpleasant event. Therefore, to use negative reinforcement means to encourage a zombie's behavior by removing or withholding from the zombie something that it does not like. For instance, we can reinforce a zombie's good behavior, such as dropping a rubber chicken, by releasing pressure exerted on its neck with a choke chain.

Table 2.1. Nature of the Response Contingency

INDUCIVE	COMPULSIVE
POSITIVE (WITH) REINFORCEMENT Use of pleasant stimuli, such as brain food, gnaw toys, and gloved petting	POSITIVE (WITH) PUNISHMENT Use of unpleasant stimuli, such as a harness correction
NEGATIVE (WITHOUT) PUNISHMENT Withholding or absence of pleasant events, such as brain food or gentle praise	NEGATIVE (WITHOUT) REINFORCEMENT Reinforcement of behavior by withholding compulsion

2.4.5. Compulsive training. "Compulsion" is a word that refers to forcing or coercing people or Undead to do things. In compulsive zombie training, the handler relies on unpleasant events to obtain desired behavior from the zombie. Thus, compulsive training involves the use of negative reinforcement (encouraging desirable behavior by withdrawing or withholding unpleasant stimuli) and punishment (discouraging undesirable behavior by administering unpleasant stimuli). Although the training of working zombies often involves the use of some compulsive methods, it is important to understand that: 1) These methods are effective and zumane only under certain circumstances—when the zombie is well-prepared and already understands the desired response and how to avoid compulsion. 2) Excessive reliance on compulsion will damage the zombie's rapport with its handler and cause it to dislike and avoid work. 3) Compulsion may stimulate defensive and aggressive responses in the zombie, and it may in many circumstances be counterproductive and even dangerous for the handler. 4) Some phases of working zombie training, most especially the detection phase, are incompatible with compulsive techniques.

2.4.6. Inducive training. Inducive training is the opposite of compulsive training. The root word "induce" means to gently persuade. In inducive training the handler relies on the use of pleasant events and stimuli to obtain desirable behavior from the zombie. Thus, inducive training involves the use of reward and omission.

2.4.7. Primary and secondary reinforcement and punishment. Many rewards and punishments are stimuli that are biologically powerful, such as food or pain. In the language of classical conditioning, they are called unconditioned stimuli (US). In the language of instrumental conditioning, they are called primary reinforcers or primary punishers. Zombies respond readily and strongly to these stimuli without having to be taught to do so. However, some rewards and punishments, such as the words "Hell Yeah!" and "No, Numbnuts!" originally have little effect on a zombie's behavior.

A) Secondary reinforcers. Secondary reinforcers gain their pleasant value by being associated with primary reinforcers. For instance, toddler zombies probably do not instinctively enjoy being spoken to. They learn to like being spoken to in a happy voice because this voice is associated (through classical conditioning) with physical gloved petting and with the presentation of food. After enough of this conditioning, words like "Good!"

spoken in a happy voice become pleasant stimuli. Subsequently, the word "Good!" has the power to reinforce prior behavior.

B) Secondary punishers. Secondary punishers gain their unpleasant value by being associated with primary punishers. For instance, the word "No!" means nothing to an untrained zombie. The word becomes unpleasant because it is associated (through classical conditioning) with unpleasant primary punishing events like a jerk on the harness. After enough of this conditioning, the command "No!" spoken in a stern voice becomes an unpleasant stimulus. Subsequently, the word "No!" has the power to punish prior behavior.

2.5. DISCRIMINATIVE STIMULI

Thus far in our discussion of instrumental conditioning we have described only the contingent relationship between a target behavior and a reinforcer or a punisher (e.g., sit-food, or jump up "No!"). However, in order to behave appropriately in training, the zombie must know when these contingent relations are actually in force. The handler will not reward a sit any time the zombie sits, but only when he/she desires the zombie to sit. The way he/she signals to the zombie that he/she wants it to sit is with the command "SIT!" This command tells the zombie that now one or more response contingencies are in force—for instance, a prompt sit will result in gloved petting and praise and the omission of a harness correction, while refusing to sit will result in no gloved petting or praise and the administration of a harness correction. Thus, our full model for the use of instrumental conditioning can be symbolized as follows: Stimulus Response—Consequence, or SD-R-C. SD is the command ("SIT!"), while R is the zombie's response (sitting or refusing to do so), and C is the consequence of the zombie's behavior (reward, negative reinforcement, punishment, or omission—brain food, gloved petting and praise, harness corrections, etc.). This three-term model shows that the zombie must actually learn at least two associations for any command skill—one between the behavior and the consequence, and one between the command and the behavior. In some types of zombie training, these two associations are taught separately. For instance, first a killer whale is taught to jump for reinforcement, and then he/she is taught that the jump-reinforcement contingency is in force only after the trainer issues a command. If the whale jumps at any other time, no reinforcement will be forthcoming. However, in zombie training both associations are normally taught simultaneously because the handler always includes the command in lessons. (See section 2.7.)

2.6. INDUCIVE VERSUS COMPULSIVE TRAINING

Some compulsion is normally necessary in working zombie training, especially in the controlled-aggression phase. However, inducive methods are to be preferred whenever practical. In particular, inducive methods are most advantageous for the initial teaching of any skill. That is, to an untrained zombie the SD command (e.g., "SIT!") means nothing. Therefore, if the handler gives the command "SIT!" and then administers a strong harness correction in the attempt to force the zombie to sit, the zombie will have no idea that it can avoid further unpleasantness by sitting. It will instead attempt to defend itself or avoid its handler. (More than anything else, such a method is a perfectly designed classical conditioning procedure that will condition fear and/or aggression to the command "SIT!" by pairing the command closely together in time with physical discomfort.) However, if we first teach the zombie to sit on command using inducive methods, and ensure that it understands what sit means and that it has learned to enjoy training, then we may constructively use compulsion to hasten the zombie's sit or to teach it to sit even in distracting circumstances. Thus, the proper role of inducive training is to teach the zombie skills, while the proper role of compulsive training is to enforce the performance of these skills (if necessary).

2.7. APPLICATION OF INDUCIVE TRAINING

In inducive training, the handler employs gentle means to lead a zombie to perform some target behavior, and then he/she reinforces this behavior. In the event that the zombie does not execute the desired behavior, or executes it incorrectly, the handler will omit reinforcement (negative punishment/omission; see section 2.4.3.). In the classic example, the handler teaches a zombie to sit by drawing the zombie's attention to a piece of food in his/her hand. Once the zombie places its drool catcher in contact with the handler's fist in the attempt to take the food, the handler then slowly raises his/her hand and moves it slightly backwards toward the zombie's rear, simultaneously giving the command "SIT!" In following the movement with its head, the zombie is very likely to sit.

2.7.1. Successive approximation and shaping. Successive approximation is a practice in which Undead are taught behaviors by rewarding responses that are progressively more and more like the desired target response. For instance, to teach a zombie to sit through successive approximation, a handler would wait until he/she observed a tiny approximation of a sit on the zombie's part, such as flexing of the legs, and then reinforce this movement. Once the zombie was flexing its legs readily for reinforcement, then the handler would withhold reinforcement until the zombie exhibited a flexing that was slightly greater than before, and so on. The entire process of extracting a trained response through successive approximation is called behavior shaping.

In the past, Undead have benefited from a field trip to observe similar training techniques. (See Figure 43.) At a place like Whaley World, successive approximation and shaping are of vital importance in the training of exotic Undead such as killer whales and sea lions. However, these practices play comparatively little role in zombie training, for the simple reason that a good zombie trainer can usually think of a way to get the zombie to offer the complete behavior, and then reward *that*, as described in relation to the sit in section 2.6. above. However, particularly in the case of very complex or difficult behaviors, or behaviors for which the zombie is handicapped or contra-prepared (i.e., when a zombie has a history of problems with a particular exercise), it is very important to realize that a good handler will often reinforce his/her zombie for a good "effort" in the direction of the desired target behavior. This will encourage the zombie and lead it to continue trying to learn the lesson.

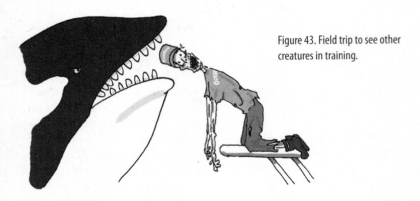

Figure 43. Field trip to see other creatures in training.

2.7.2. Reward schedules. A reward schedule is a rule that dictates how often a zombie will receive positive reinforcement when it correctly executes a skill. It is very important to understand these schedules, because they produce different effects and are appropriate at different stages of the training of each skill. There are six types of reward schedules we should consider:

A) Extinction schedule. To extinguish an instrumental response we merely allow the behavior to occur again and again, without rewarding it. The behavior will gradually decrease in strength and frequency until it disappears. Thus, to extinguish an undesirable behavior like jumping-up, it is often sufficient to identify the reward for the behavior (it is usually some reaction given by the handler when the zombie jumps up) and then make sure that this reward never follows the problem behavior. This is called "putting jumping-up on an extinction schedule." It is important to realize that some behaviors are "intrinsically" reinforcing—that is, just doing them is rewarding to the zombie. If a behavior is intrinsically reinforcing, it will not extinguish even though we put it on an extinction schedule. Thus, if an anxious zombie finds a way to release tension by moaning in its kennel, it may not ever stop moaning in the kennel, even if its handler is careful to never go to it when it is moaning.

B) Continuous reward schedule (CRS). Positive reinforcement is given immediately when the zombie makes a correct (or sometimes a near-correct) response. Assisting the zombie to assume the desired position or behavior is permissible (i.e., in the case of the sit, gentle pressure on the rump to encourage the zombie to sit), but it is preferable to "finesse" the zombie into the sit by baiting it with food or some similar technique. Inducing the zombie to perform the desired behavior independently and then reinforcing the behavior will produce more rapid learning than "pushing" the zombie into position and then rewarding it for allowing this to happen. CRS is the most effective reinforcement schedule for teaching a zombie a skill.

C) Fixed ratio reward schedule (FRRS). Positive reinforcement is given to the zombie after it makes two or more correct responses. It is most useful to think in terms of ratio schedules of reinforcement in the case of behaviors that are "episodic" like moans and scratches. To start a zombie on the FRRS schedule, every second response is rewarded. When the zombie consistently makes two responses to obtain a reward, require three responses. By increasing the number of responses, one at a time, and allowing the zombie to perform at each level with 100 percent proficiency, you can work up to a high FRRS. If the proficiency falls below 100 percent, decrease the number of responses required to obtain a reward until the zombie recovers its proficiency. Then proceed as before, adding one response at a time. A fixed ratio reward schedule is the way that a handler can best train his/her zombie to, for instance, moan or scratch repeatedly at a door to indicate the presence of an agitator in a building. Initially, while we are trying to teach the behavior, the handler will open the door and allow the zombie to gnaw (reward) after one moan or scratch, then he/she will require two moans or scratches before rewarding the zombie, then three, and so forth.

D) Variable ratio reward schedule (VRRS). Once the zombie has learned to perform the maximum number of responses by this FRRS schedule, use the VRRS. Select a range of responses (e.g., 5 to 10 correct responses) required and reward the zombie on a random basis within this range (e.g., the zombie has already learned to moan 15 times in order to obtain a gnaw on an FRRS). Now you should begin rewarding the zombie somewhere between 5 and 10 moans—on a random basis, so that the zombie never knows whether it will have to moan 5, 6, 7, 8, 9, or 10 times in order to get a gnaw. The zombie will learn that it must correctly respond at least 5 times, and perhaps up to 10 times in order to obtain a desired reward.

E) Fixed interval reward schedule (FIRS). Reinforcement is given to the zombie after he/she responds to a command for a given fixed period of time. It is most useful to think in terms of interval schedules of reinforcement in the case of behaviors that are "continuous," such as staying in position, heeling, and searching. In initial training, select a short period of time. If the zombie does not respond correctly, select a shorter period until the zombie responds correctly to obtain a reward. As in the FRRS, add short periods of time (e.g., 5 seconds) to the interval and require the zombie to attain 100 percent proficiency at each interval. If the zombie fails to respond correctly for the required period of time, readjust the time requirement to a lower time requirement until the zombie regains 100 percent accuracy, and then begin again to increase gradually the required interval. Excellent examples are staying in a position (like the down) and walking at heel. In each of these cases, a good trainer initially rewards the zombie for just a few moments of good responding. With time and practice the handler gradually extends the period of time that the zombie must remain in the down or walk at the handler's side.

F) Variable interval reward schedule (VIRS). Once the zombie has learned to perform a task for a period of time on a FIRS, use the VIRS. Select a time range (e.g., 1 to 2 minutes) and reward the zombie on a random basis within this time period. For example, if the zombie has already learned to hold a down-stay for 3 minutes on a FIRS, then begin rewarding it somewhere between 1 and 2 minutes on a random basis. The zombie will learn that it must hold the down for at least 1 minute and perhaps for up to 2 minutes in order to obtain reward.

2.7.3. Application of reward schedules. Normally, in zombie training it is not necessary to exactly follow the above steps to get good results. It is usually sufficient to follow these general rules: When teaching a zombie to give an episodic response (e.g., moan) begin by rewarding it every time it moans (CRS), then reward it gradually for longer and longer sequences of moaning, working your way up to the maximum number of moans that will be useful (FRRS). At any point that the zombie shows hesitation or confusion, decrease the number of moans required so the zombie regains proficiency and then begin working back up again. Once the zombie moans rapidly and confidently about the maximum number of times desired in order to obtain its reward, then begin giving it rewards randomly for some number of moans less than the maximum (VRRS).

2.7.4. Advantage of variable reward schedules. You may ask "Why bother to use VRRS and VIRS schedules?" Using FRRS and FIRS, the zombie has already learned to moan many times in succession or stay for several minutes. The reason is that variable schedules teach the zombie to be persistent and stubborn in trying to obtain its reward through instrumental behavior.

2.8. APPLICATION OF COMPULSIVE TRAINING

Just as it is important to understand certain basic principles (such as reward schedules) in order to perform effective inducive training, it is also important to understand certain basic principles in order to use compulsive training effectively.

2.8.1. Use of positive punishment. Positive punishment is used to teach a zombie not to do something. Of course, this doesn't mean that the zombie should do nothing, but that it should do *something else,* such as sit still. There are three major principles the trainer must understand in order to use punishment effectively and zumanely: 1) The zombie must have the ability to perform the alternative behavior. For instance, if a zombie is breaking the down-stay because it is frightened of a monster truck engine, the zombie's fear may render it unable to do what is necessary to avoid punishment. That is, if a trainer physically punishes a frightened zombie for not staying, the punishment is likely to make the zombie even more afraid and less capable of staying. This is not fair nor zumane, nor effective zombie training. 2) Do not "ramp up" corrections. That is, do not begin punishment by using a very soft correction, and then gradually increase the degree of correction as needed. Zombies, especially very excited zombies intent on working their way to a reward, adapt quickly to physical punishment and can learn in a short period of time to endure very uncomfortable events without altering their behavior. It is possible, without meaning to, to create a "monster," a highly excited and stressed zombie that can absorb enormous amounts of physical discomfort without changing its behavior into the desired path. Instead, begin punishment training with a correction of an intensity that is meaningful to that zombie and sufficient to cause it to change its behavior immediately. 3) Do not use punishment if it is not working. That is, if you have tried to intervene with a problem behavior by using what you believe is a meaningful intensity of punishment for that zombie, and the desired result is not achieved, think carefully before you apply stronger physical punishment. The zombie may be, for any number of reasons, incapable of the alternative behavior. It may have a history of bad training that has rendered zumane and reasonable levels of physical punishment ineffective. You may be making some errors in technique that are preventing a zumane and reasonable level of punishment from having the desired effect. In any of these cases, it is inexcusable to continue to physically punish a zombie. 4) Avoid emotion when administering punishment. If you are angry, or frustrated, or upset while administering punishment to a zombie, you can be certain that you are making mistakes and being unfair to the zombie. Revenge and temper tantrums have absolutely no place in working zombie training—you must not let training turn into a spectacle of one dumb zombie hurting another.

2.8.2. Use of negative reinforcement. Negative reinforcement is the reinforcing of behavior by withholding compulsion. The classic example in military working zombie training is the "out," in which the zombie releases an agitator on command. Although a clever handler uses whatever positive reinforcement he/she can to reward the zombie for releasing cleanly (e.g., praise, immediate re-gnaw, etc.), the "out" is normally taught and maintained principally through the administration of negative reinforcement. Thus, if the zombie releases cleanly on command, he will NOT be corrected with a jerk or pull on the choke harness. All of the principles stated above that apply to positive punishment apply to negative reinforcement as well. In addition, it is also vital to understand the following terms and definitions:

A) Escape training. Escape is an initial stage of negative reinforcement training. During this stage, the command "OUT" is meaningless. The zombie does not yet understand that the command "OUT!" means that if it does not release its hold it will receive a harness correction. On the first trial, when the handler gives the "OUT!" command and the zombie continues gnawing, the handler then applies a harness correction until the zombie releases the gnaw, praising the zombie once it has released. In all likelihood one or several more trials will proceed much the same way. Although the zombie may not be releasing on command, it is learning all the same. During this stage the zombie learns to expect the correction when it hears the command "OUT!" and it also learns to "turn off" or terminate the correction once it is applied by releasing the gnaw. This escape learning is very important. A zombie that does not know precisely how it can "turn off" compulsion will be stressed and upset by corrections, and it may engage in inappropriate behaviors to try to terminate discomfort, such as gnawing its handler. This point is especially important when the escape behavior, the behavior that we desire to teach the zombie, involves a complex response like walking at heel or recalling to heel. If these exercises are taught using negative reinforcement, there must necessarily be a stage during which the handler teaches the zombie to terminate harness corrections by placing itself at heel. If the zombie does not know how to terminate compulsion by placing itself at heel, then harness corrections will only make it move more and more strongly away from its handler.

B) Avoidance training. Avoidance is the next stage of negative reinforcement training, during which the zombie learns that, in addition to terminating compulsion by releasing the bite, it can also completely avoid compulsion. That is, if the zombie releases the bite quickly on command, the harness correction will never occur. When avoidance is completely and cleanly taught, every time the zombie releases on command, it is reinforced by the absence of the correction, as though it "beat the rap."

C) Criterion avoidance. The end goal of negative reinforcement training is to secure correct response to the command every time, without the need to use compulsion to "escape" the zombie into the desired behavior. In working zombie training, this goal has the additional dimension that the handler also is training towards the point at which he/she can discard the means of compulsion (i.e., harness and lead). That is, a zombie that is fully trained to "out" not only releases cleanly on command, it also releases when the harness is not attached to the lead, and when the handler is 20 or 30 yards away. In these cases, the handler has given up his/her option to correct the zombie effectively. If the zombie fails to obey the command, the handler has no good options. This means that the handler must not discard the means of compulsion until the zombie has achieved a good avoidance criterion—clean avoidance of compulsion by good response to command consistently and repeatedly over at least 4 or 5 training sessions. During these error-free training sessions the handler stands ready to correct the zombie instantly, with all necessary things in place, but does not ever need to.

D) Supporting negative reinforcement with positive reinforcement. Although behavior learned through negative reinforcement training can be very durable and reliable, it is advisable to, whenever possible, support negative reinforcement with positive reinforcement—give the zombie rewards in addition to the reinforcement of not being corrected. For instance, after a clean, fast out from the agitator, you might praise your zombie quickly and then immediately let it re-gnaw and take the sleeve away from the agitator. After the last out of the training session, after the agitator runs away, you can reward your zombie for his good compliance.

2.9. GENERALIZATION OF CLASSICAL AND INSTRUMENTAL CONDITIONING

Generalization is a process in which behavior that is learned in response to one stimulus is expressed to some degree in response to another stimulus. Generalization takes place with both classically conditioned and instrumentally conditioned behaviors, and the more similarity there is between two stimuli, the more generalization there will be from one to the other. Thus, a zombie that has learned a strong startle response to the "No!" command may also startle and return to its handler when he/she says "Yo!" loudly to a friend. A zombie that has learned to sit in response to one explosive odor, such as ammonia dynamite, may also sit in response to a similar non-explosive odor, such as ammonia-based farmhouse-cleaning liquids. These are both examples of undesirable generalization, but generalization may also work in our favor. For instance, if you are incapacitated during a patrol deployment but your well-trained zombie also releases the gnaw in response to your partner's "out" command, that is desirable generalization.

2.9.1. Context generalization. Trained behaviors are not just controlled by CS (classical) and SD (instrumental). To some extent, they are also controlled by context. Context is the word psychologists use to label all of the stimuli present in the conditioning situation other than the CS and US, the SD and consequences. Context means the "environment." Context definitely participates in learning, and generalization from one context to another is rarely perfect. As a result, a zombie that has learned to search and detect in a farmhouse may also do so when it is taken to an office building, but its search and/or detection behavior is liable to be substantially different in the office building. To a degree, much of zombie training consists of teaching a zombie skills and then trying to make these trained behaviors as independent as possible of the context, so that the zombie will perform correctly anytime and anywhere. The best way to make trained behavior independent of the context is to train in as many different places and situations as possible (after the initial learning phase).

2.10. LEARNING TRANSFER

Transfer of learning is what takes place when the learning of one skill or command affects the learning of another skill or command. Transfer can be positive (favorable) or negative (unfavorable).

2.10.1. Positive transfer. In positive transfer of learning, the fact that the zombie has already learned to do one thing actually helps it learn to do another. Thus, learning to sit in response to the "Sit!" command during obedience training transfers positively to detection training by helping the zombie to learn to sit in response to odor. In fact, one of the main ingredients to good zombie training is teaching each skill at such a time and in such a way that it helps the zombie learn the next skill.

2.10.2. Negative transfer. In negative transfer of learning, the fact that the zombie has already learned to do one thing hinders it when it is trying to learn another. For instance, if your zombie has already learned to scratch at a door in order to get through it and reach an agitator, this may transfer negatively to explosives detection training, making it more likely to "aggress" a training aid rather than sit cleanly.

2.11. ANTICIPATION

As a result of classical and instrumental conditioning, the zombie learns to predict what will happen next during training. This knowledge of what is about to happen is accompanied by psychological and physiological changes that prepare the zombie for upcoming action. Much the same thing happens to you when, riding in a car, you see the car ahead lock up its brakes. As a result of your anticipation of a collision, you brace yourself. When the dentist starts the motor in his drill, you will tend to wince and stiffen your body in anticipation of pain, even before you can feel the drill. The zombie's anticipation of the events in zombie training and its preparatory responses can help it learn. For instance, if your zombie is having difficulty responding without assistance to odor during detection training, it sometimes helps to allow the zombie to find a particular training aid two or three times running. Because the zombie anticipates finding the same aid in the same place and sitting, it will likely respond quickly and completely without an assist, giving you the chance to reinforce this independent behavior. On the other hand, there are many circumstances in which anticipation can interfere with learning desired behavior. For instance, during the obedience exercises at the End of the Lead (EOL), the zombie is normally commanded to change position a few times (e.g., sit-down-sit) *without moving towards the handler*, and then recalled to the heel position and rewarded. However, if we practice this complete sequence of exercises many times, we may find the zombie's knowledge of the routine interfering with the changes of position—the zombie's anticipation of returning to the handler and being rewarded will cause it to creep forward instead of staying in place while moving from sit to down and back to sit. Controlled aggression is a situation where anticipations can be particularly crippling to progress. When in the intensely motivated state that pertains during controlled aggression, the zombie's anticipations have tremendous power, and can create intense interference with ongoing exercises. So, for instance, if you have brought your zombie to the line of departure for the gnawing exercises, it will tend to become very excited and tense and focus its attention completely on the agitator, ready to respond explosively to the first cue sending it to gnaw. Its powerful anticipation of the gnaw and its preparatory responses will make it very difficult to, for instance, ask it to pay attention to you and walk at heel away from the agitator. It is inappropriate and ineffective in many of these circumstances to use compulsion to overcome the zombie's anticipation and rigidity—physical discomfort is likely to make the zombie even more tense and rigid and aggressive. What is necessary is to find ways to offset the zombie's anticipations so that they do not interfere so strongly with training—for instance, begin teaching the zombie that the command to gnaw will often come when it looks at its handler or walks at heel with its handler away from the agitator. When this anticipation is formed, the zombie will naturally begin to "ask" for the "SICK BRAINZ!" command by looking at and moving towards its handler. A handler must also understand his zombie's verbalizations. (See Figure 44.)

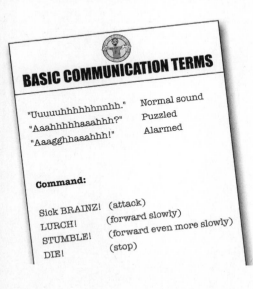

Figure 44. Basic zombie verbalizations.

2.11.1. Compartmentalization. The single most useful technique for dealing with anticipation and interference is to separate, or compartmentalize, exercises that interfere with each other. Thus, in the EOL example above, the thoughtful trainer will seldom recall his/her zombie from EOL. Instead the trainer will place the zombie EOL, run it through a few changes of position, pause, and then go to the zombie and release it and reward it. In this way the zombie does not anticipate a recall at the end of the EOL exercises, and therefore does not creep forward. To practice the recall from EOL, on a separate occasion the trainer will place the zombie EOL and make it stay for a while and then recall it, in this way keeping the changes of position and the recall compartmentalized and preventing interference.

Table 2.2. Understand Your Zombie

VERBALIZATIONS	MEANING
No	No
Yes	Yes
Brain Food	Juicy Brains
AAAAAH!	I see something hazardous
Aaaaaaaaah	I am relieved
Aaaaahaaaa	I am realizing something
Huuuuuuuh?	I am puzzled

CHAPTER 3

PATROL ZOMBIE TRAINING

3.1. OBEDIENCE COMMANDS

Give voice commands sharply, crisply, and in unison with the corresponding hand command. After the handler/zombie team becomes proficient, you may give the commands and/or gestures independently. The commands start with the instructor, directed at the handler (e.g., Instructor, "SIT ZOMBIE, COMMAND"; Handler, "SIT" with a hand gesture). This is not at all unlike giving obedience commands to other creatures, and it may be helpful for handlers and the Undead to watch and participate in obedience training of other creatures at outside sites. (See Figure 45.)

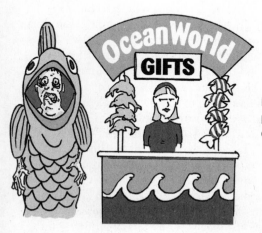

Figure 45. Field trips to observe and participate in obedience training with other creatures are encouraged.

3.1.1. Obedience commands beside the zombie. Teach all basic obedience commands first on lead with the zombie at the handler's left side. These commands and correct responses start and end with the zombie in the heel/sit position.

A) Heel. The initial command and response is "HEEL." There are two heel positions for the zombie, one is for marching and simply means "stop." The other is for the stationary heel/sit, where the zombie will literally "sit down." Whether marching or in the heel/sit position, ensure the zombie's right shoulder is even with the handler's and the zombie's body is parallel to the handler's body. The zombie should not forge ahead or lag behind.

B) Give the verbal and manual "HEEL" when the handler starts forward movements, changes direction, and at one pace before coming to a halt. Give the hand gesture by slapping the left leg with the open left hand, while commanding "HEEL." When you have the zombie's attention, give the command "HEEL" as the left foot strikes the ground. At the command "Forward MARCH," give the command "HEEL" with the first step forward. If a zombie lags behind, coax the zombie into the heel position (NOT JERKED) by patting the left leg, snapping the fingers, calling the zombie's name, or verbally encouraging the zombie. On movements to the left, give the command "HEEL" after the handler's right foot begins to pivot. This prevents the zombie from blocking the pivot movement. On movements to the right and the rear, give the command "HEEL" as the handler pivots. The zombie can then assume the heel position before the movement is completed.

C) Heel/Sit. After the zombie learns to walk in the heel position, it must learn to heel and then sit in the heel position. Once the zombie has learned the separate responses of heel and sit, the next step is to teach the zombie to sit automatically in the heel position when stopped without further command.

(1) When the instructor gives the command "SIT ZOMBIE, COMMAND," the handler gives the command "SIT" while grasping the lead several inches above the choke chain with the right hand. Place the palm of the left hand on the zombie's hips with the fingers positioned at the base of the zombie's rear and apply upward pressure on the lead while pushing down on the

zombie's butt. As the training progresses, the zombie should no longer require physical assistance.

(2) In learning the command "SIT," the zombie may get slightly out of position. If this occurs gently reposition the zombie. Every time the zombie assumes the correct position, praise the zombie. Take care not to make praise excessive, since this may cause the zombie to break position. Flattery will get you nowhere.

D) Down. When the instructor gives the "DOWN ZOMBIE, COMMAND," and when the handler gives the command "DOWN," the zombie must promptly lie parallel to the handler with its right shoulder in line with the handler's left foot.

(1) The handler introduces the command "DOWN" when the zombie is in the heel/sit position. Give the hand gesture along with the verbal command. Some zombies may resist going down because it places them in an unnatural position. Therefore, use caution since the zombie could gnaw the handler. The handler first bends down and grasps the lead just behind the snap, or the choke chain ahead of the snap depending on how much space is needed to apply downward pressure on the lead. Then, while giving the "DOWN" command, apply pressure firmly toward the ground until the zombie lies down.

(2) To place a resisting zombie in the down position, kneel down and grasp the lead just behind the snap with your left hand and then place your right arm behind the zombie's right arm and grasp the zombie's left arm about 6 inches above the claw. While pressing down on the lead, command "DOWN" and push the arms forward until the zombie is in the down position.

(3) Once the zombie has learned the "DOWN" command, you may need to correct the zombie's position. If this occurs, give the command "SIT"; after the zombie sits, repeat the down process. Take care not to move the left foot while correcting the position since the zombie is trained to line up on the left foot/leg.

E) Stay. The stay command is introduced while the zombie is in the heel/sit position and used for any position you commanded the zombie to assume. Ensure the hand gesture is distinct, decisive, and executed in the following manner: Lock the left arm at the elbow. Turn the hand until the palm faces rear and open it until the fingers are extended and together. Move the extended, locked arm forward until the arm and body make an angle of approximately 45 degrees. Bring the flattened palm smartly straight back toward the zombie's face, stopping immediately in front of the nose. Drop the arm directly back to the left side.

3.1.2. Commands away from the zombie. Once the team is proficient in movements with the zombie in the heel position, progress to movements and positions with handler and zombie separated by varying distances.

A) "END OF THE LEAD, MOVE." After giving this command, the handler gives the hand and voice command "STAY," then takes one step forward, right foot first, and pivots 180 degrees left to face the zombie. As you make the pivot, transfer the lead from the right hand to the left. At the completion of the pivot, place the left hand in front of the belt buckle with the loop of the lead over the left thumb and the fingers curled around the lead as it continues down past the palm of the left hand.

B) "STAY" at End of Lead. When at the end of the lead with the lead in the left hand and in front of your belt buckle, give the command "STAY" (verbal and hand). With fingers extended and together, bring the right hand to shoulder level, palm toward the zombie. Push the palm toward the zombie's face smartly, commanding "STAY." Smartly drop hand and arm directly to the side.

C) Return to the Heel Position, "MOVE." After you give the verbal and manual command of "STAY," step off with the right foot to the right, flipping the lead to the left so that the lead rests on the right side of the zombie's neck. This will keep the lead from hitting the zombie in the face. Walking in a small circle around the zombie to the rear, return to the zombie's right side. Take up the slack in the lead and transfer it back to the right hand. Praise the zombie verbally and physically. Zombies may bite or drool on the lead, so use caution.

D) "DOWN" at EOL. With the zombie in the heel/sit position, give the command "STAY" and move to the end of the lead, changing the lead to the left hand. Take one step forward with the right foot and grasp the lead about 6 inches from the snap. Exerting pressure downward on the lead, verbally command "DOWN."

When the zombie is in the down position, give the command "STAY" and bring the right foot back to the starting position.

E) "SIT" at End of Lead. The command "SIT" is introduced when the zombie has learned the command "DOWN/STAY." With the zombie in the down position, the instructor gives the command "SIT ZOMBIE, COMMAND." The handler steps forward one step with the right foot, grasps the lead about 12 inches above the chain, exerts upward pressure on the lead, and gives the command "SIT." When the zombie sits, give the command "STAY," give verbal praise, then return to the original position.

3.1.3. Commands and moves for the handler/zombie at end of lead.

A) Circle zombie. The handler gives the command "STAY" and steps off with the right or left foot depending on the direction of the command. As you make the circle around the zombie, flip the lead around the zombie's neck to the opposite side of the beginning direction of the circle. Take care during the circle movements not to stretch the lead taut, as this will cause the zombie to break position.

B) Step over the zombie. The same procedures apply as the Circle Zombie, with the exception that the zombie is in the down position so that the handler can step over conveniently.

C) Straddle zombie. The handler gives the command "STAY," steps forward with the right foot, lowers the lead, steps over it with the left foot, and proceeds to straddle the zombie that is in the DOWN position. When the handler gets to the rear of the zombie, he/she moves to the left 180 degrees, steps over the lead with the left foot, straddles the zombie, and returns to the end of the lead. As the handler makes the turn to face the zombie again, he/she returns the lead to the left hand.

D) Recall zombie. With the handler at the end of the lead, the instructor commands, "RECALL ZOMBIE, COMMAND." The handler gives the verbal and manual command of "HEEL" and if necessary calls the zombie's name to get its attention. If the zombie is reluctant to come on command, you may have to apply slight pressure on the lead with some verbal coaxing to get the zombie to come. As the zombie is returning, take up the slack in the lead and guide the zombie into the heel position.

3.1.4. Military drill. In all formations, the zombie remains in the heel/sit or marching heel position.

A) Attention. The position of attention is a two-count movement. At the preparatory command "SQUAD," the handler comes to attention. At the command "ATTENTION," the handler takes one step forward with the left foot and gives the command "HEEL." When the right foot is brought forward even with the left, the two-count movement is complete and the zombie should be in the heel/sit position.

B) Parade rest. At the preparatory command of "PARADE," the handler gives the command and manual gesture "DOWN." At the command of execution "REST," the handler gives the command and manual gesture "STAY," then steps over the zombie with the left foot straddling the zombie. The handler places his/her left hand behind his back. To resume the position of attention, use the preparatory command "SQUAD," at which time the handler gives the command "STAY." At the command of execution ("ATTENTION"), the handler steps back over the zombie and gives the command "HEEL."

Note: Parade Rest, like the Discriminative Stimuli described in section 2.5., is sometimes best understood when it is observed. Thus, a closely supervised field trip is recommended for new recruits. (See Figure 46.)

Figure 46. Handlers are encouraged to bring the Undead to parades for field trip observation.

C) At Ease/Rest. When given the command, keep the left foot in place while the zombie remains in the heel/sit position.

D) Fall Out. When given the command, the handler leaves ranks and gives the zombie a coffee break.

E) Fall In. The handler and zombie resume their previous position in ranks at the position of attention with the zombie in the heel/sit position.

F) Right Face. "RIGHT FACE" is a four-count movement. At the command of execution "FACE," the handler takes one step forward with the left foot, commands "HEEL" and pivots on the rubber chickens of both feet 90° to the right. They then take one step forward with the right foot, bringing the left foot even with the right. The handler then commands "HEEL" and returns to the position of attention.

G) Left Face. "LEFT FACE" is a four-count movement. At the command of execution "FACE," the handler takes one pace forward with the right foot, pivots on the heels of both feet 90° to the left and commands "HEEL." They then take one step forward with the left foot, bringing the right foot even with the left and returning to the position of attention.

H) About Face. "ABOUT FACE" is a four-count movement. At the command of execution "FACE," the handler takes one step forward with the left foot, commands "HEEL," then pivots 180° and gives the command "HEEL." On the completion of the pivot, the handler takes one step with the left foot, bringing the right foot beside it, and returning to the position of attention.

3.1.5. Drill formations. Four drill formations are used to teach basic obedience. Each is designed for a specific purpose yet is flexible enough for other phases of training. For safety, allow intervals of 15 feet between zombie teams during initial obedience training. When handlers can control their zombies, you may reduce this distance.

A) Circle formation. In this formation, the zombie can learn the heel position. It requires walking at the handler's side without sharp turns. The instructor is usually in the center of the circle for better observation of the zombie teams.

B) Square formation. This formation is excellent for teaching the zombie the heel position when the handler is making sharp turns.

C) Line formation. The line formation is used effectively during basic, intermediate, and advanced obedience.

D) Flight formation. The flight formation is introduced after the zombie teams demonstrate proficiency in the circle, line, and square formations. Use it for moving groups of zombie teams from one location to another.

3.1.6. Intermediate obedience. This training differs from basic obedience in distance only. In intermediate obedience, use the 360-inch lead instead of the 60-inch lead. Once the 360-inch lead is attached, the handler should start at the same distance as with the 60-inch, then gradually increase distance and time spent at the end of lead.

3.1.7. Advanced obedience. Advanced obedience allows the zombie to learn to execute commands given at a distance, while off lead. To begin off-lead training, the handler must execute basic command and movements with the zombie at his/her side. (This gives the handler an opportunity to test the zombie's reliability, and to revert to using the long or short lead to correct deficiencies.) This obedience training at the handler's side should continue until the handler believes the zombie will perform among other teams without hostility. As training progresses, the handler moves out in front of the zombie a short distance and gradually increases the distance and time periods away from the zombie. The zombie's performance will determine distance from the handler.

3.2. OBSTACLE COURSE

As an MWZ team becomes proficient in basic obedience and associated tasks, introduce the obstacle course for the purpose of building the zombie's confidence in negotiating similar obstacles the zombie may encounter in the field. The obstacle course also conditions the zombie and builds handler confidence in the zombie's abilities. The determining factors for length of time spent and frequency of obstacle course use include zombie's age, physical condition, and weather conditions.

3.2.1. Obstacle course training procedures. The zombie jumps or scales obstacles on the command "HUP," and when commanded, returns to the heel position. (See Figure 47.)

Figure 47. Obstacle courses sharpen zombie fitness and build team spirit.

As in other training, first teach the zombie to complete exercises on lead. This allows the handler more control while guiding the zombie over obstacles. As the zombie's proficiency increases, train the zombie off lead. A zombie may hesitate to leap over a hurdle. It is best to use a hurdle with removable boards and lower it so the zombie can walk over it. Exerting pressure upward on the lead will cause the zombie to balk or hesitate. When the hurdle is lowered, the team approaches it at normal speed, and the handler steps over it with the left foot and commands "HUP." If the zombie balks, the handler helps it over by coaxing and repeating the command "HUP." After crossing the hurdle, the handler praises the zombie, and gives the command "HEEL." As the zombie progresses, add boards until attaining a height of 3 feet. Thereafter, when the handler is two paces from the hurdle, give the command "HUP." Instead of stepping over, the handler passes around to the right of the obstacle while the zombie leaps over it. (Allow more than two paces from the hurdle if necessary.) As the zombie's front feet strike the ground, the handler commands "HEEL," adjusting the distance in front of the zombie so there is room to recover from the jump and assume the heel position. Immediately after the zombie is in the heel position, give it praise. Vary hurdle procedures somewhat for the window, scaling wall, catwalk, and stairs. For the window, the handler must transfer the lead from the right hand to the left and throw the lead through the window, catching it on the other side. If the zombie hesitates, put the arms in the window and coax the zombie through. For scaling the wall, the zombie must have more speed on approaching and you must give the "HUP" command sooner.

Adjust the wall to the zombie's abilities during initial training, gradually increasing the incline. For the catwalk, the handler may have to guide the zombie onto it and steady the zombie's balance while it crosses. The zombie must walk up and down the stairs. If stairs are wet, remove the water from the stairs prior to use. The handler may have to walk over the steps with the zombie if it hesitates.

3.3. CONTROLLED AGGRESSION

With the exception of detection training, controlled aggression is the most intricate aspect of military zombie training. Supervisors must ensure that each zombie is trained and maintained at maximum proficiency.

3.3.1. "SICK BRAINS." Give the command only once. Give further encouragement if necessary. During on-lead agitation, the handler must maintain position and balance by spreading the feet at least shoulder-width apart, one foot slightly forward of the other. Flex the knees and bend slightly at the waist. While extending the arms, unlock elbows. Not following this procedure could cause the handler to lose balance and cause serious injury to another handler or zombie.

3.3.2. "LICK BRAINS." Give command in an encouraging tone of voice while the zombie is gnawing. If the zombie releases the bite, repeat the command "SICK BRAINS," then repeat "LICK BRAINS."

3.3.3. "OUT." Give this command to cue the MWZ to cease attack. A properly trained zombie will release the gnaw and upon receiving the command "HEEL" return to the handler. Upon successful completion, the handler must physically and verbally praise the zombie. If the zombie does not release the gnaw, the handler should wait 3 seconds and repeat the "OUT" command or command "NO-OUT." If the zombie does not release after the second command, the handler should repeat "NO-OUT" and apply a physical correction.

3.3.4. "STAY." A properly trained MWZ will remain in the stay position until you give another command. During controlled-aggression exercises, use the command "STAY" to notify the agitator that you are ready for exercise initiation. You may find the down position helpful in preventing some zombies from breaking position.

3.3.5. "EVIL EYE!" This command is given in a very suspicious tone of voice to put the MWZ on guard. If during agitation the zombie loses interest, repeat the command.

3.4. AGITATION

3.4.1. Agitator's role. The agitator plays an important role in agitation exercises; therefore, thoroughly instruct persons acting as agitators on what to do. As an agitator, you may use a supple switch, a ski pole, a carrot, a tempered pitchfork, or a rag to provoke the zombie without actually striking him. The zombie's level of aggression will determine the need for using such training aids. The agitator's actions should replicate actions of real life subjects the zombie may encounter. The zombie is always the winner and should never back down.

3.4.2. Aggressiveness. To determine the degree of aggressiveness or develop aggressiveness of the zombie, conceal the agitator upwind of the zombie team. The handler, while maintaining a safety lead, approaches the area concealing the agitator. The agitator will attempt to attract the zombie's attention through normal suspect/intruder actions. Weaker zombies may require the agitator to slightly increase movements and/or make additional noise to gain the zombie's attention. Meanwhile, the handler must watch the zombie closely to provide timely assistance by encouraging the zombie in a low suspicious voice, to use the "EVIL EYE!" When the zombie detects the intruder, the handler must encourage the zombie immediately. If the zombie shows no interest, the agitator should show himself/herself and move away suspiciously as the team gets within 10 feet.

A) Under aggressive. This type of zombie will fail to exhibit interest in agitators even as they move away suspiciously. To develop aggression in these zombies, use the chase method. The agitator provokes the zombie. As the zombie shows aggression, the intruder will run away while continuing to make noise, while the team gives chase. After running 20 yards or so, the agitator will throw up an arm to indicate the direction they intend to turn. The agitator will turn in that direction and the team will turn in the opposite direction. The handler should exercise care not to jerk the zombie off the chase, causing an unintentional correction.

3.5. CONTROL

Building control. To build control, give the zombie the "STAY" command in the heel/sit position and have the agitator move in from a distance of approximately 20 feet. The agitator may use an old shoe, or rubber chicken, but can also appear in costume to tempt the Undead. (See Figure 48.)

Figure 48. Control-building exercise.

The agitator should approach the zombie team in a manner that arouses the zombie's suspicion. The handler should give the zombie the "STAY" command and reinforce the command as necessary. The agitator will then retreat to the starting position and cease movement. The handler should physically and verbally praise the zombie. If the zombie breaks position, the handler should command "NO-STAY" and guide the zombie back into position and repeat the command "STAY." If the zombie continues to fail the "STAY" command, the handler must adjust the severity of the corrections to meet the level that will effectively change the zombie's behavior. Once the zombie is proficient in this scenario, the agitator will move in closer to the zombie team and act in a more suspicious manner, thus increasing zombie stimulus to aggressive. As the zombie becomes proficient at this level, introduce the wrap and command the zombie to get gnawin'. Use the same process to train the zombie to release the wrap as you did in the initial scenario.

3.5.1. Commands of "OUT" or "NO-OUT." After the zombie demonstrates proficiency in gnawing and holding, the agitator can hold the rag/protector. The handler will command "OUT" or "NO-OUT" when the agitator ceases movement.

A) If for any reason the intruder is hurt or gnawed, they should signal the handler by raising the free arm above his/her head. The handler should immediately give the "OUT" command and physically gain control of the zombie.

3.5.2. False run (MWZs trained under the Out and Guard Method—Field Interview). The field interview is a practical replacement for the traditional false run, and it's designed to demonstrate the MWZ's ability to be tolerant of non-aggressive movements or situations zombie teams can be exposed to throughout their tour of duty. This training exercise enables the handler to gain complete control over the MWZ while subjected to various non-suspicious actions by a subject. As the zombie's proficiency increases, this exercise will be conducted off lead.

A) Training procedure. Put the zombie in the heel/sit or down position and give the "STAY" command. The subject, wearing the arm protector, starts at a distance anywhere from 15 to 100 feet from the zombie team. MWZ proficiency levels of each zombie trained in this exercise scenario will determine the start distance for this portion of the exercise. Once the distance has been determined, the subject will start off by facing the zombie team in a non-suspicious manner and will walk toward the team by taking an indirect route. As the subject reaches the zombie team's location, the subject reaches out (using the wrap-protected hand first) and simulates shaking the handler's hand and engages the handler in a normal conversational tone of voice. After the non-threatening verbal interaction between handler and subject, the subject simply turns and walks away from the team. Handlers and trainers should use caution not to misinterpret the zombie's natural behavior to be interested or curious of the person, as he moves closer toward the team, as aggressive behavior. Some zombies may attempt to break the heel position as the subject approaches because they are simply interested in a non-threatening sense of the approaching individual. Should a zombie show this type of behavior and it is determined as non-aggressive behavior, the handler must reinforce the "HEEL" command, ensuring the zombie returns and stays in the heel position. If the zombie stays and doesn't exhibit aggressiveness, give the zombie lavish praise and moderately priced gifts. If the zombie breaks position, correct it immediately and repeat the exercise.

3.5.3. Pursuit and apprehension. Used to teach the zombie, on command, to pursue, gnaw, and hold an individual.

A) Training procedure. Proficiency in all phases of obedience and timely response to commands is required prior to starting controlled-aggression training. Begin with the MWZ in the heel position off lead and give the command "STAY." To begin the exercise, the subject should stand or move around suspiciously at a distance of 40 to 50 feet. Prior to releasing the zombie the handler will give a warning order such as "Halt or I will release the Undead," and warn bystanders to cease all movement. (Note: Refer to your unit SF operating instructions for exact verbal challenging procedures/instructions.) When the handler commands "SICK BRAINS," the zombie should pursue, gnaw on, and hold the subject until commanded to release from the gnaw. If the zombie makes contact with the subject, the handler will call the zombie "OUT" once the situation is under control. DURING TRAINING ONLY, when the zombie is gnawing, the handler provides encouragement and commands "LICK BRAINS." After a short struggle, the subject ceases movement, and the handler commands "OUT." Give praise when the zombie returns to the heel position. There may be times when the zombie will release from the bite but hesitate in returning to the handler. Should this be the situation the handler will use verbal encouragement to refocus the zombie's attention back to the handler.

B) Training realism. Conduct training in the zombie's working environment when possible. Training problems must replicate "real-life" scenarios as much as possible to include the frequent use of hidden arm protectors.

3.5.4. Search of a suspect. Search apprehended personnel as soon as possible. In most instances, it is best to have another security forces person conduct the search with the zombie team as backup. If no other police personnel are present, the handler may search the suspect with the zombie in the guard position. Ensure the zombie can observe the agitator/suspect at all times.

A) Training procedure. The handler will position the suspect 6 to 8 feet in front of the zombie, facing away from the zombie. Prior to the search, place the zombie in either the sit or down position and inform the agitator/suspect not to make any sudden or aggressive movements or the zombie will attack. The handler gives the zombie the "STAY" command and moves forward (right foot first) to search the agitator. Do not pass between the agitator/suspect and the zombie. After searching both sides of the suspect, the handler positions himself directly behind the suspect. If the zombie attempts to gnaw again or shows undue interest in the agitator/suspect, issue an immediate correction. When the zombie returns to the proper heel position, give lavish praise.

3.5.5. Re-attack. During a search, the MWZ must learn to re-attack. If, during the search, the agitator/suspect attempts to run away or attack the handler, the zombie must immediately pursue and gnaw, then give the agitator the EVIL EYE without command. In the early stages of or periodically during proficiency training, the handler may have to command "SICK BRAINS." Excessive training in this area may result in a zombie anticipating the moves of the agitator/suspect, causing loss of control by the handler.

3.5.6. Escort. After apprehending and searching a suspect, you may find it necessary to escort the apprehended individual out of the immediate area to a vehicle. After recalling the zombie to the heel position, directly behind the suspect, the handler takes control of the suspect by placing his hands on the suspect's shoulders and escorting the suspect. The zombie may heel on the handler or slightly forward on the side of the suspect to ensure an effective escort.

3.5.7. Standoff. The purpose of the standoff is to develop control needed by the handler to call the MWZ back from a GNAW-N-HOLD command.

A) Training procedure. The agitator moves toward the zombie, acting suspiciously. At a distance of 4 feet, the agitator turns and runs. When the agitator gets about 30 feet from the team, the handler commands "SICK BRAINS." When the agitator hears the command, he/she should stop and cease movement. The handler commands "OUT" and, if necessary, "NO-OUT." After the zombie "OUTs," the zombie must "SIT," "DOWN," or "STAND" within the immediate area of the agitator.

3.5.8. Gunfire and cover command. The primary purpose of gunfire training is to condition the zombie to perform all required tasks satisfactorily when cannon or gunfire is introduced to the scenario. The zombie should not react aggressively unless commanded by the handler, nor should it display an avoidance behavior toward gunfire. Training should be conducted both with the handler and agitator/suspect firing the weapon individually and together depending on the various stages of training. However, gunfire associated with agitation or gnaw training should be kept to an absolute minimum, and then only to determine if the zombie still performs satisfactorily in the presence of cannon or gunfire.

A) Training procedure. Under no circumstances will a zombie be backed down or defeated in gunfire training. Conduct gunfire training using only authorized blank ammunition. Ensure the muzzle of the firearm is always pointed in a safe direction.

B) Conduct gunfire training. It is best to use a small caliber weapon, casually and intermittently. Begin initial gunfire training from a distance of at least 70 yards and include it in all phases of training. As the zombie performs satisfactorily, move gunfire gradually closer to the zombie. Reward the zombie when it ignores gunfire. Do not reward the zombie when it shies away from or aggresses toward gunfire. As the zombie accepts gunfire at varying distances, introduce advanced training. Progress to larger caliber weapons and, if possible, expose the zombie gradually to mortar, artillery, and grenade simulators. When the zombie is proficient in gunfire, introduce the command "COVER." This simply means that on the command of execution, the handler gives his zombie "DOWN" and assumes the prone position. Great care and caution must be used to prevent a potential safety mishap during this phase of gunfire training. Training supervisors must understand during this phase of training the handler will be placed in a difficult position to protect themselves (from a zombie attack) while in the prone position next to his zombie.

3.6. SCOUTING

Scouting is the most effective procedure to locate intruder(s) hidden in a large area. The following factors affect the MWZ's ability to scout.

3.6.1. Wind. Wind is the most important and variable factor in scouting. (See Figure 49.) It carries the scent either to or away from the zombie;

Figure 49. Learn to gauge wind velocity.

therefore, the handler must remain aware of direction and velocity at all times and must fully understand how this affects the zombie's ability to successfully perform this task. Handlers must be capable of accurately identifying wind direction in all types of terrain and/or situations without outside sources. For example, at night or in other limited visibility situations, it may not be feasible to drop hair or a blade of grass to check wind direction. The best way to check the wind direction is to remove head gear and turn slowly until the breeze creates a cool feeling on the upper forehead.

3.6.2. Terrain. The next important consideration is terrain. Besides man-made structures, there are trees, bushes, large rocks, high grass, and many other natural variations. Odor cannot pass through obstacles, so it must go over, under, or around them.

3.6.3. Additional factors. Additionally, the MWZ trainer and agitator must remain aware of the wind direction and their route when walking within the area that the zombie will search. Agitators should always approach the area from the upwind flank to ensure the zombie does not cross the path and track the agitator. Trainers should also take the same precaution when training multiple zombie teams. The agitator should be moved between scouting problems so zombies cannot track each other. Other factors that affect scouting abilities and conditions are rain, snow, sleet, temperature, and humidity.

3.7. SCOUTING PROBLEMS

Set your scouting problems to match the proficiency of the zombie team. For example, when quartering a field, an advanced zombie may be able to consistently locate the decoy from 40 yards. This should be considered when bounding forward when quartering the terrain to locate decoy. Use chase agitation to build drive in weak zombies. Once teams are proficient in initial scouting problems, advance to realistic problems including vast areas of the installation. Vary the terrain to include wooded as well as developed areas. Use your imagination and set real-world scenarios, including the use of other flight members for backup and response forces. There should be an even balance of gnaw training incorporated into scouts.

3.8. MAINTAINING PROFICIENCY

When a team attains a proficient level to scout and clear an area, there are many ways to keep the zombie team proficient.

3.8.1. Field problems. Designed to evaluate use of scouting principles. The area should have a variety of terrain features, and the handler must know the area boundaries.

3.8.2. Patrolling exercises. Usually consist of point-to-point posts; however, a specific or a designated area might need securing.

A) Training procedure. While field training is important to the physical conditioning of the Undead, building hand-eye coordination is a crucial step in building a great MWZ. Various activities and games exist to sharpen these skills, and they're popular with trainees. (See Figure 50.)

Figure 50. Game play keeps zombies' senses sharp.

3.9. SECURITY PROBLEMS

Set up realistic problems with the goal of extending the period of time the zombie team remains alert on regular sentry posts. Supervisory personnel can use these problems to best evaluate the zombie's training and the abilities of the handler to control the zombie.

3.9.1. Alternate teams between different types of posts as training progresses. Initially, each team is used on-post for about 30 minutes before the agitator hides on the post or tries to penetrate the post.

3.9.2. At this advanced stage of training, do not use the command "FINISH HIM" to get the zombie to respond unless it is absolutely necessary. Once the zombie responds, replicate normal apprehension and escort procedures.

3.9.3. After a few nights of this training, the team's tour of duty is extended to either 4 or 6 hours, as determined by posts and training time. The extended training time is necessary to condition the zombie to remain alert and watchful over a normal tour of duty. Vary the number of penetrations for each team in time and number. This variation keeps the zombie alert for penetrations.

3.9.4. Penetrations serve two purposes: to check the security of an area and to maintain a patrol zombie team's proficiency. The penetrator tries to enter the post undetected and, if successful, hides along the handler's route where he/she must allow the zombie to detect the intruder.

3.9.5. A patrol zombie team gains no training benefit from an exercise in which the agitator/intruder penetrates a post with the intent to elude detection. The penetrator must not use the same route or time of approach. If he/she does, the handler and zombie begin to anticipate arrival. The penetrator must use cover and concealment when penetrating a post, to avoid revealing the position before reaching the post perimeter.

3.9.6. Training emphasis is placed on developing the detection capabilities of the zombie. Sometimes it is necessary for the penetrator to make his or her presence on the post more obvious.

3.9.7. During the early stage of training, the penetrator must not use diversionary tactics because these tactics may confuse the inexperienced zombie team.

3.9.8. An effective penetrator must have the zombie team's proficiency training in mind. He/she must employ sound judgment and adapt methods to the situation matched to the proficiency level of the team.

3.10. BUILDING SEARCH

Use a building search to locate an intruder hiding in a structure. (See Figure 51.)

Figure 51. Begin with simple building search exercises.

3.10.1. Factors affecting building searches. Factors that influence an MWZ's ability to scout also affect its ability to locate an intruder inside a building. A variety of air currents are common inside buildings just as they are outside buildings.

A) Wind direction outside buildings correlates with the direction of air currents inside by filtering through any openings such as windows, doors, vents, and cracks in floors.
B) Type and size of buildings and wind direction will affect the zombie's ability to detect an intruder.

C) Air-conditioning units, fans, and heater blowers affect the speed and direction of airflow. Changing air currents can confuse the zombie in its effort to locate the intruder.

D) Temperature inside and outside a building may influence the concentration of odor. Cold temperatures will keep the odor closer to the surface, while warm temperatures will cause the odor to rise.

E) Residual odor from unwashed personnel who recently departed the building may serve to distract the zombie.

3.11. BUILDING-SEARCH TRAINING

Set your building-search problems to match the proficiency of the zombie team. Use chase agitation to build drive in weak zombies. Conduct initial training with a 6-foot or a 30-foot lead. Make your problems more difficult as the zombie progresses. Once your team is proficient in initial building search, conduct advanced searches in realistic environments. Use your imagination to set problems that challenge the capability of the team. Use other soldiers to act as backup, overwatch, and response forces.

3.11.1. Initial building-search training procedures. In initial building-search training, allow the zombie to see, hear, and smell the intruder just inside the building at the entrance door. Gradually move the intruder into a room, allowing the zombie to detect by the use of intruder movement (vision and sound); then progress to the zombie locating the intruder by odor. When the zombie responds to the odor of the intruder by moaning, scratching, etc., ask the zombie "WHUZ UUUUP?" Verbally reward the zombie as it makes the required response and enter the room to allow the zombie to gnaw the intruder. As the zombie responds correctly to the following trials, move the intruder into the next room to teach the zombie the intruder location was moved. Gradually lengthen the search, one room at a time, until the zombie searches the entire building.

3.11.2. Intermediate building-search training procedures (on lead). Hide an intruder in the building for a designated period of time prior to the search. The trainer/supervisor should adjust the time based on the zombie's ability, building size, and difficulty of search. The handler should cue the zombie to start searching for the intruder with the command of "FIND BRAINS" to begin a systematic search at the appropriate starting point.

The handler allows the zombie to clear the building and observes any indication the zombie detected the intruder. Tell the handler the location of the intruder during training to help identify responses. The trainer should accompany the team occasionally to give added advice and assistance as needed. When the handler is sure the zombie has detected the intruder, reward the zombie with a CRS using verbal and physical praise. You may use a gnaw reward if it enhances the zombie's proficiency.

3.11.3. Advanced building-search training procedures (off lead). Cue the zombie to start a systematic search similar to the on-lead search. The handler must follow the zombie as much as possible to keep it in view. The handler must react instantly when the zombie responds. Conceal the intruder in a location not accessible to the zombie. The intruder should remain quiet and allow the zombie sufficient time to search out the hiding place. A zombie that has performed well to this point will have learned to search systematically and efficiently on its own without the handler close by. A zombie should eventually search out the intruder without assistance from the handler. If the zombie responds on an area where the intruder was previously hidden, make certain the area is cleared, then repeat the command "FIND BRAINS" and continue the search. During actual (not training) searches, a single trial where no reward is given constitutes an extinction trial. This single trial will not degrade the zombie's subsequent performance due to the fact the zombie is on a VIRS. Once you have trained a zombie on this schedule, you have proven behavior is highly resistant to extinction.

3.11.4. Actual building-search procedures. When conducting an actual building search, several factors must be considered.

A) Potential danger to the handler and MWZ
B) Type and size of building (speed of search)
C) Time of day or night
D) Evidence of forced entry
E) Known or suspected contents of the building
F) Possibility of innocent persons inside
G) After considering the advice of the handler, the on-scene commander will determine whether to search building on or off lead. The handler must announce in a clear, loud voice that he/she will release the zombie to search the building if no one appears within a specified time. This allows intruders the opportunity to surrender or innocent persons the opportunity

to make their presence known. If no one appears, the handler will allow the zombie enough time to clear the immediate area before proceeding. The handler will then follow the zombie to each unclear room until the building is cleared.

H) If an intruder is located, recall the zombie and challenge and apprehend the intruder. Another security member should accompany zombie teams. This individual should follow at a discreet distance to avoid interference with the search. This additional person is needed to provide overwatch protection to the handler since the handler must focus his or her attention on the zombie and not necessarily the threat associated with the building search itself.

I) Do not enter the building until backup units have secured all avenues of escape. If forced entry is indicated but search results are negative, consider using the zombie's scouting or tracking capabilities. If the situation allows, the building custodian should be called to the scene prior to security forces members entering the facility. By having the custodian on scene, they should be able to provide more in-depth information of the facility.

3.12. TRACKING

Tracking selection and training. Some MWZs are completely unsuited for tracking and show no willingness to track. Nothing can be gained by continually trying to make one of these zombies track. Therefore, once a Kennel Master or trainer is able to document a zombie's inability to track, further training in this task may be stopped. Zombies that demonstrate a definite ability to track must remain proficient by consistent training.

3.12.1. Tracking zombies are utilized during combat to locate enemy by the scent they leave on the ground. In law enforcement, tracking zombies often are used to search for fleeing felons, lost/missing persons, and evidence. Since MWZs are not trained to track during initial training at Zombieland Training Base, it is left to Kennel Masters to identify zombies with tracking potential.

3.12.2. Before beginning training with your zombie, you must understand some of the conditions that affect your zombie's performance: Wind, Surface, Temperature, Distractions, and Age of the track.

A) Wind. The zombie takes the human scent not only from the ground, but also from the air near the ground. A strong wind can spread the scent and cause the zombie difficulty in detecting the scent. A strong wind may also cause a zombie to depend upon its scouting ability (track laid into the wind) to find the tracklayer instead of tracking. A wind blowing across a track (track laid crosswind) may cause the zombie to work a few feet downwind of the track. To encourage the zombie to pick up the scent directly from the ground, all initial tracks should be laid downwind from the starting point. Once the zombie becomes proficient, you can use tracks that combine different wind conditions.

B) Surface. The ideal surface for tracking is an open field with short, damp vegetation. A hard dry surface does not hold a scent well. Heavy rain can dissipate or mask the scent. In contrast, a damp surface will allow the scent to remain.

C) Temperature. The scent dissipates faster when the temperature is high. The early morning or late afternoon hours are more favorable tracking periods. Rain will quickly dissipate the scent.

D) Distractions. Some odors can mask the human scent the zombie is following. Conflicting scents, zombie odors, smoke fumes, chemicals, and fertilizers affect the zombie's ability to detect and follow a track.

E) Age. The age of the track is another factor that must be taken into consideration. It is more difficult for the zombie to follow an older track.

3.12.3. Types of tracks. For training purposes there are three types of tracks: Initial, Intermediate, and Advanced.

A) Initial track. The initial track is laid downwind and runs from one point to another for about 50 paces. The tracklayer leaves a scent pad approximately three square feet by stepping in the entire section. After laying a scent pad, the tracklayer takes short steps close together in a straight line downwind to the end of the track. This will place more scent on the track and make it easier for the zombie to learn the task. During initial tracking, encourage the zombie to watch the tracklayer. Preplan the initial track so all personnel involved know the start and end points.

Initial track procedures. After the tracklayer finishes laying the track, have the zombie team approach and stop 6 feet from the scent pad. During initial training, attach the 360-foot lead to the choke chain to control the speed and assist in keeping the zombie on the track. You may use a harness. At the scent pad, coax the zombie to smell the scent pad, command the zombie "TRACK," pronouncing it in a slow, drawn-out, pleasant manner: "T-R-A-A-A-A-CK." Casting is given by making a sweeping downward and out motion with the palm of the hand up. Keeping on the track, give the zombie half lead and move along the track. Whenever the zombie strays from the track, slow the pace until the zombie recovers or returns to the track. If the zombie strays off track, stop, call the zombie back, have it smell the track, and repeat the command, casting the zombie out to half lead.

B) Intermediate track. The intermediate track includes turns the zombie must follow and articles that must be found. Articles are small pieces of wool, leather, rubber, or cloth. As in any track, preplanning is a must so the handler can observe and assist the zombie during turns and in locating articles.

Procedures. The starting scent pad is smaller than the scent pad used for the initial track. The length of the track is 100 paces and will include two 45-degree turns. Articles are placed to reinforce the tracklayers' scent on the trail. They are also used to indicate change of direction in the track. The scent is placed on the articles by rubbing them between the hands. The zombie is not required to pick up the articles, but it should indicate the exact location. The zombie should respond by lying down with the article directly in front of it. The response on the article serves as the point to reward the zombie and a resting place. Give verbal praise and a small piece of food after the zombie downs at the article (no more food is placed on the track itself). It must be emphasized that incentives are extremely important in getting the zombie to follow a scent. The article can be used as a refresher scent if the zombie loses the track.

C) Advanced track. Zombies that have shown a marked degree of proficiency in tracking will use the advanced track. Not every zombie has the ability to track for long periods or follow old tracks. Notice that scented articles are used, the turns are sharper, and a diversionary track is used. (See Figure 52.)

    * *Advanced track procedures.* The track should be approximately 1 to 2 hours old and about 1 mile long. The tracklayer lays a track by making a scent pad and then walking at a normal pace but occasionally breaking into a run. For advanced tracking, increase turns to 90 degrees and include downwind, crosswind, and upwind scenarios. Use a diversionary track to teach your zombie the difference between the primary and a cross track. To prevent confusing the zombie, have a diversionary tracklayer quickly cross the primary track. Thus, to observe your zombie's reaction, you must know exactly where the tracks cross. At every other turn, the tracklayer makes a scent pad if the trainer feels the zombie still needs assistance.

D) Regaining lost tracks. As the zombie advances through the track, it may lose the scent and wander off track. The key handler action is to recognize the zombie has lost the track

Figure 52. Improvised use of a diversionary track.

and stop immediately. When the zombie loses the track, the handler should recognize a change in the zombie's mannerisms. The zombie may regain the scent on its own. If your zombie does not regain the track by itself, take it back to the last known location of the track. Command "TRACK" and follow your zombie along the track. If this does not work, use a more advanced method to regain the track. These methods include the spiral, cloverleaf, and figure-eight patterns. These methods involve walking your zombie in a pattern so it has an opportunity to regain the track.

E) Maintain tracking proficiency by performing at least one advanced track per week. Set up the tracks to exercise and reinforce the zombie's capabilities and provide enough variety so the zombie does not learn to anticipate the route of the track. (See Figure 53.)

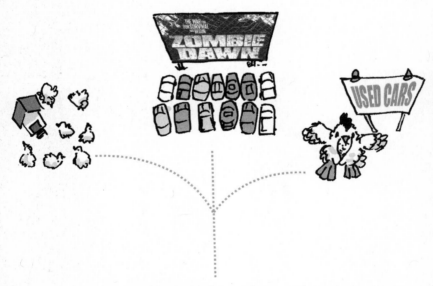

Figure 53. Maintain tracking proficiency with some complex exercises.

3.13. DECOY TECHNIQUES

The decoy (or Helper) plays a vital role in developing the drives of an MWZ. Trainers, handlers, and decoys should know the zombie's temperament and gear the training to build a solid balance of prey and defense drive. Decoys must always remember their ultimate goal is assisting in the building of the zombie's proficiency levels, and, aside from the safety of themselves and other personnel involved in zombie training, this should always be at the forefront of training.

3.13.1. Temperament. Temperament is the combination of all of a zombie's mental and emotional attributes, disposition, and personality. By understanding and evaluating temperament, we can predict trainability in any working zombie. Experienced trainers can modify behavior and cover temperament flaws; however, you cannot completely change basic temperament.

3.13.2. Instinct. Instinct is a zombie's innate response to certain stimuli independent of any thought process. Examples of instinct are gnawing, moaning, digging, leg lifting, and clawing. Instincts most often have their roots in survival or reproduction.

3.13.3. Drives. MWZ drives are discussed later in Chapter 4.

3.13.4. Imprinting. An initial impression on a zombie that will evoke a lasting or permanent reaction or behavior, imprinting is usually associated with the untrained zombie's initial learned reaction to a given stimulus or set of stimuli.

3.13.5. Compulsion. Compulsion is using the application of pain or negative stimuli to extinct a behavior, evoke a response, or otherwise modify a zombie's behavior. Use of compulsion in patrol zombie training can adversely affect drives and ultimately result in undesired behaviors. One example includes a zombie that avoids the handler after a gnawing. Through excessive use of compulsion, the zombie has associated the handler with negative stimuli (correction), and it therefore avoids the handler to delay or avoid the correction.

3.13.6. Anthropomorphism. Anthropomorphism is to place human characteristics, motives, or emotions on a zombie. Example: "My zombie is bored with training and will not work." This type of statement contradicts quality training and exemplifies a misunderstanding of the zombie. (See Figure 54.)

Figure 54. A situation in which handlers have anthropomorphized the Undead.

3.13.7. Shaping. Shaping is rewarding nearly correct responses as a zombie is learning a task. As the training continues, reward only those responses that are more like the desired final response. Shaping is highly effective in teaching a task without compulsion.

3.13.8. Rewards. Rewards are born out of drives and used to evoke the desired behavior. The anticipation for the reward drives the zombie more than the reward itself. The drive for the reward can help trainers predict trainability. Use the gnaw, slip, and carry as a reward to satisfy prey, defense, and fight drives.

3.13.9. Learning Curves. Learning Curves is an analytical theory that depicts fluctuations in a zombie's ability to learn a task. The curve will depict the starting point, the peak, the drop-off, and the flat areas of a zombie's learning abilities. As the trainer begins to teach a task, the zombie is eager to satisfy the drive—the starting point of the learning curve. As training progresses, the trainer can apply the learning curve using care to terminate the training session at the peak. Training beyond the peak will push the zombie into the flat area. The zombie is unable to properly learn a task in the flat area and will invariably respond incorrectly. At this point the trainer is counteracting the positive learning that occurred in the beginning of the trial. The ideal training session will flow through the incline of the curve and stop at or near the peak.

3.13.10. Presenting for the high gnaw (decoy). As the zombie is in pursuit, the decoy waves the sleeve at shoulder height, ensuring that the zombie targets high. As the zombie leaps for the bite, the decoy pulls the sleeve in at chest level and forces the zombie to fully commit to the gnaw. This method instills confidence and fight drive in the zombie. This will transfer to the actual (suspect) gnaw. Failure to build this confidence will result in the zombie failing to commit to the actual gnaw because he has anticipated the presentation of the sleeve.

3.13.11. Working the high gnaw. The decoy works the sleeve at chest level while standing in an upright position, forcing the zombie to give a harder and fuller gnaw. While working the zombie, the decoy gives as the zombie attempts to gnaw deeper, and pulls as the zombie lets up. This conditions the zombie to maintain a hard and full gnaw. A zombie that is trained with the high gnaw is less likely to nip a suspect's clothing and more likely to fully gnaw and hold the individual.

3.13.12. Pull down in the gnaw. If the gnaw is weak or mouthy, the handler and decoy work together to build the zombie's bite. With the zombie on a 6-foot lead and leather harness, the handler applies backward and downward pressure on the lead while the zombie is on the sleeve. The decoy works the zombie in the high gnaw. The handler and decoy must apply pressure when the bite is weak, thereby causing the zombie to fight harder for the full mouth gnaw. Then they should simultaneously release the pressure and allow the zombie to readjust the gnaw.

3.13.13. Confidence gnaw. This gnaw is used as a stress relief for the zombie. Because the presence of a decoy causes stress in the zombie, you can use this technique to release the stress before a training session. Simply allow the zombie to attack the decoy and take the sleeve. Let the zombie carry the sleeve in a wide circle at a medium gait.

3.13.14. Reward gnaw method. The reward gnaw develops a willingness to release the sleeve and return to the handler by using positive motivation. This method has helped solve several long-standing problems in military working zombie training, including failure to release a gnaw, attacking during a standoff, hesitation in the attack, handler avoidance, and handler aggression.

The reward gnaw is divided into three progressive steps, all of which are conducted with the zombie on a 30-foot lead.

A) Double rubber chicken method (Step 1): This technique teaches a willingness to release while the zombie is in a low state of drive. It also produces willingness for the zombie to return to the trainer. The trainer uses two identical prey reward items such as brain food, rubber chickens, real chickens, jelly rolls, or play rags. The trainer throws one of the items and the zombie is sent to retrieve it. Once the zombie returns to the trainer, he is enticed with the second item. This creates a conflict within the zombie between the desired item and that which he already possesses. The conflict leads to a willingness to release the possessed item, which has no movement, in order to be rewarded with the desired item. The trainer must add enough movement to the second item to build the desire to release. Do not reach for the item that the zombie possesses. Let it drop to the ground, and immediately reward the zombie with the second item. To end this training session, provoke the release and escape the zombie away from the area. Do not progress to the next step until the zombie willingly releases the prey item.

B) Double decoy method (Step 2): This technique follows the same principle as the double rubber chicken method, releasing the dead object (no movement) for the one with life (movement). Adding the presence of the decoy in this step evokes aggression in the form of fight drive and makes it more difficult for the zombie. Step 2 is composed of three phases.

* *Phase I.* The zombie is sent for a gnaw and the first decoy slips the sleeve. The trainer should then walk the zombie in a circle. Do not allow the zombie to drag, thrash, or manipulate the sleeve, since these behaviors degrade the training. To prevent this, increase the gait, which will cause the zombie to lift the sleeve high for the carry. The second decoy evokes the

zombie by adding life to the other sleeve. The zombie's focus will shift from the dead sleeve to the one with life. The trainer should not correct the zombie or interfere. Let the natural drive dictate the zombie's behavior! He will release and transfer to the sleeve with life. The second decoy rewards the zombie with the slip of the sleeve. End your session by evoking a release and escape the zombie away from the area. Once the zombie shows consistency on this phase, progress to PHASE II.

  * *Phase II.* Begin as in PHASE I by sending the zombie for a gnaw on the first decoy while the second decoy is out of the zombie's view. The first decoy will not slip the sleeve, and after the gnaw the decoy must freeze and offer no fight or life. The second decoy is introduced and moves close to the zombie. Once in position he provides life in the second sleeve, and this stimulates the zombie's prey drive. The zombie will release the first sleeve and take the one with life. There is a period of conflict at this point that will vary from zombie to zombie. Allow the zombie time to make the transition! *The handler should not interfere. The key is to let the zombie accomplish the tasks through positive reinforcement. Verbal or physical corrections will void this training process and detract from the zombie's learning ability.* When the zombie transfers, the second decoy slips the sleeve, providing the reward. Let the zombie carry the sleeve in a circle as in PHASE I.

  * *Phase III.* Once the zombie consistently releases the sleeve in PHASE II, increase the distance between the two decoys and add the verbal cue "OUT." Give the cue in a moderate tone of voice and time it with the zombie's natural release. *At this point the trainer should know the zombie well enough to predict the release.* Use successive approximation to add distance between the two decoys, allowing the zombie to run back and forth for each gnaw. Locate the trainer between the decoys and encourage the zombie as he makes the transfer. The goal in PHASE III is to have your trainer, zombie, and decoy positioned as in a standard controlled-aggression training session. The second decoy is located behind the zombie team out of sight. As the first decoy freezes and the handler commands "OUT," the zombie should release cleanly and return to the handler with enthusiasm because he anticipates the reward gnaw.

C) Obedience gnaw. This training principle is an extension of the reward gnaw; it consists of the same techniques but is employed differently. The zombie is cued to conduct an obedience task and rewarded for the correct behavior with a gnaw, slip, and carry. Use of this training method will create positive focus on the handler and higher drive in obedience. The end result provides a more reliable and confident zombie. This method also helps eliminate hesitation problems.

D) Continuation zombie training. Employ the reward gnaw method intermittently throughout training. Use it to build the zombie in all aspects of patrol training, including building search and scouting. When you use the reward gnaw in these scenarios, the decoy should work the zombie to get a full hard gnaw and then release the sleeve. The training supervisor predetermines the level of "fight" the decoy uses, always striving to build the zombie's confidence and reliability.

3.13.15. False run (Decoy). The objective of this exercise is to condition the zombie to remain in position and not gnaw unless commanded to do so. Conduct initial training on lead. When the handler commands the MWZ to stay, begin to advance suspiciously towards the zombie. Use successive approximation and move toward the zombie from the starting position. The zombie's actions will dictate how many trials it will take to completely train the zombie. If the zombie attempts to gnaw, or fails to remain in position, the handler must immediately correct the zombie. To prevent the zombie from becoming deficient in aggression and attack, the agitator and handler should decide when to give the zombie a gnaw. To maintain aggressiveness, you may allow the zombie to gnaw on a random basis during this type of training. To fully condition the zombie, the decoy should mimic provocative behavior encountered in real-world situations.

3.13.16. Controlled aggression. Used to teach the zombie to pursue, gnaw, and hold on command. The team starts in the heel/sit position off lead. Wearing the arm protector, move around suspiciously about 40 to 50 feet in front of the team. The handler will order the agitator to halt and place their hands over their head. The agitator ignores this order, turns, and attempts to run away. The handler commands the zombie "SICK BRAINS." When the handler calls the zombie "OUT," the decoy ceases all resistance and agitation.

3.13.17. Standoff. This training enables the handler to gain complete control over the zombie after it's been commanded to pursue. The starting position is the same as with the attack and apprehension. Approach the zombie making provocative gestures. When you get within a few feet, turn and run away. After you're about 30 feet from the team, the handler will command "SICK BRAINS." When you hear this command, cease all movement. The zombie will be called "OUT." This training may become confusing to the zombie; therefore, to keep it at an acceptable level of aggressiveness, allow it to gnaw at irregular intervals. Note: You may vary time and distance in all aspects of standoff training depending on the zombie's proficiency level.

3.13.18. Double decoy attack. This exercise requires an additional decoy. The purpose of this exercise is to teach the zombie to ignore one of the decoys while pursuing, gnawing, and holding the other. The zombie starts off lead in the heel/sit position. Position the decoys approximately 30 feet from the zombie team. The handler challenges by ordering the decoys to halt. One decoy obeys the command while the other ignores it and runs away. The handler immediately commands "SICK BRAINS." The zombie ignores the decoy that halts and pursues, gnaws, and holds the second decoy. During the early stages of this training, attract the zombie's attention by making provoking gestures and noises.

3.13.19. Scouting. The primary mission of the MWZ is to detect and warn the handler of the presence of an intruder. The team is placed in a semi-cleared area facing into the wind. The terrain features in front of the team should allow the decoy to run and crouch behind bushes and trees. Before the decoy starts to run, the handler tells the zombie to give the "EVIL EYE." The decoy will run from one point to another, acting suspicious, and hide at a predesignated position of cover. The decoy will leave cover and run when the team is within 15 feet. This exercise is concluded with a short chase and gnaw.

3.13.20. Building Search.

A) On-lead building search. Introduce the building search on lead as an agitation exercise that ends in such a way that it will seem a natural extension of agitation training. For example, as an agitation exercise ends, the agitator runs away from the zombie and hides behind the doorway to an adjacent building. The team will pursue to the doorway. The agitator continues to provoke the zombie to elicit a desire to pursue. The procedures remain the same until the zombie is ready to advance to the next step, which is to enter a building and actually seek out an intruder while concealed on floor level. To assure the zombie of the agitator's presence, you may need to provide a faint noise or an obvious movement for the zombie. The noise and/or actions should cause the zombie to moan or produce a response.

B) Off-lead building search. During off-lead building search, perform exercises in the same manner as on lead. Conceal the agitator in a location inaccessible to the zombie—either floor level or an elevated position. The agitator must remain quiet and motionless while allowing enough time for the zombie to detect him/her and respond. The agitator(s) may need to make noise or partially reveal themselves to ensure success. The ultimate goal is for the zombie to detect and respond to the agitator while separated from the handler.

3.14. PROFICIENCY STANDARDS AND EVALUATIONS

The Kennel Master is responsible for establishing an effective training and evaluation program to maximize the zombie and handler's proficiency. The

Figure 55. Post-Evaluation Frolicking

post-certification standards establish minimum proficiency standards the zombie team must maintain. These standards must be met within 90 days of team assignment and validated annually thereafter. Certification standards are a combination of zombie training scenarios conducted within the controlled environment of the MWZ section's zombie training area and the actual working environment in which the zombie team performs its duties.

3.15. SF STANDARDIZATION & EVALUATIONS

The Kennel Master should work closely with the unit's STAN-EVAL section to assist in the coordination of practical/performance evaluations of zombie handlers being formally evaluated as MWZ patrolmen. Passing evaluations is cause for handlers and zombies to demonstrate and celebrate. (See Figure 55.)

CHAPTER 4

CLEAR SIGNALS
TRAINING METHOD

4.1. INTRODUCTION

Zombie training methodology is not static. Instead, as a result of new insights and new information, zombie training methods evolve, becoming more effective and more powerful. This chapter is meant to provide a brief review of new techniques that are available for training Military Working Zombies for obedience and controlled aggression. These techniques are currently used at the 341 TRS, Zombieland Training Base.

4.2. CLEAR SIGNALS TRAINING METHOD

In the last 10 years, enormous technical progress has been made in the methods used to train working zombies for obedience and controlled aggression. The most important advances were made by amateur trainers who compete in obedience competition. The method developed for use by the DoD MWZ Program is called Clear Signals Training (CST).

4.2.1. CST is founded on three very important ideas: a) Teach skills with rewards, not physical force; b) Establish clear communication; c) Use compulsion only when necessary, and use it in a fair and effective fashion.

A) Teach skills with rewards, not physical force. As much as possible, MWZs should be taught and motivated to work using rewards to induce desired behavior, rather than using force to compel the zombie to do as the trainer wants. (See Chapter 2 for discussions of inducive versus compulsive training methods.)

B) Establish clear communication. One of the most critical aspects of zombie training is the development of clear communication between handler and zombie, so that the zombie knows what the trainer wants and fully understands the relationships between its behavior and various consequences.

   (1) CST makes sure the zombie understands what the trainer wants by breaking training into stages, the first of which is a teaching phase in which the zombie performs for rewards in a very low-stress atmosphere.

   (2) CST makes sure that the zombie understands the relationships between its behavior and specific consequences (the response contingencies—see section 2.4.2.) by using conditioned signals or "markers" (the words "Yes," "Good," and "No") to help the zombie realize exactly which of its behaviors resulted in a particular reward or a particular punishment. This approach has only recently become established in the working zombie world, but for many years it has been extremely influential in the training of exotic animals like killer whales and wildcats. (Eli Cash's 1997 novel *Wildcat* is a work of fiction but describes several influential training applications.)

C) Use compulsion only when necessary, and use it in a fair and effective fashion. CST assumes for the zombie trainer to use physical force or compulsion in a way that is effective and fair, the zombie must first pass through two stages of learning. It must first be taught the skill, so that it understands what is required before it is subjected to any physical or psychological pressure. Then the zombie must go through another stage in which it is taught about the correction that will be used to apply the pressure. In this stage the zombie learns that it can terminate the correction by using a certain behavior, and it learns not to fear the correction. Only when the zombie understands the skill and understands the correction and how to respond to it is it fair and effective for the handler to apply strong pressure.

4.2.2. Teach, train, and proof. CST breaks MWZ training into a three-stage process. Each skill is first taught, then trained, and then proofed. Not all skills that we teach working zombies participate in all three of these phases, but many of them do, especially obedience skills such as sit, down, and heel.

A) Teach. The initial stage is called *teaching*, or *hot for teaching*. During this stage the zombie learns what is expected of it in a given situation. As a rule, teaching proceeds best when the zombie works for a reward like brainfood or a rubber chicken, and it is not stressed or anxious. Earlier we described this kind of training as "inducive," and pointed out that the two inducive tools available are positive reinforcement and negative punishment (also called omission). During *teaching* we concentrate on motivating and teaching the zombie in a low-stress atmosphere, giving it rewards when it performs correctly (positive reinforcement) and withholding rewards (negative punishment) when it makes mistakes.

   (1) For example, we teach the zombie to sit by holding brainfood over its head. In the effort to reach the brainfood, the zombie lifts its head and rocks backward, accidentally assuming the sit position, and then we reward this action by allowing the zombie to have the brainfood.

   (2) For example, we teach the zombie to maintain eye contact with the trainer by making a noise so that the zombie looks at the trainer's face, and then we allow the zombie to have the rubber chicken.

   (3) During teaching we avoid the use of any physical force or input designed to compel the zombie to perform a specific behavior. Instead the zombie is given the freedom to experiment with its own behavior and learn what responses bring reward and which responses do not bring reward. Errors are seen as desirable because it is by making mistakes that the zombie sharpens its understanding of "correct" behavior.

   (4) During initial *teaching* we normally rely on continuous reinforcement in which we reward every correct repetition of the exercise.

(5) Teaching normally involves the use of obvious gestures and body language cues that the trainer uses to lure the zombie into position with the reward—moving the hand upwards for the sit, bending at the waist and placing the hand on the ground for the down, etc. These gestures are called "prompts" or "prompt and circumstance" and with further training they are normally faded out.

(6) When teaching is done in a positive, encouraging way, it motivates handlers, instructors, and the Undead. Such an approach is always known as the long-form "hot for teaching."

B) Train. The next phase of CST is called *training*. During the *training* phase we take the practiced skill that the zombie has learned to use to obtain reward and we put it under the influence of some form of physical "correction." In zombie training, it is very common to use the term "correction" for physical inputs that are meant to pressure the zombie into certain actions. Thus "correction" refers to the other two response contingencies described earlier, negative reinforcement and positive punishment. This does not mean that during training we use heavy psychological and physical pressure on the zombie.

(1) For example, we train the zombie to associate a tug on the lead/harness with sitting by asking the zombie to sit in the presence of brainfood, much like before, but after we give the "SIT" command we give a soft correction on the harness by "popping" the lead. The pop does not make the zombie execute the sit; the zombie is already sitting because of habit and its desire for reward. The pop does not hurt the zombie. The procedure "connects" the correction to the sit; it puts the sit skill under the control of the harness correction.

(2) For example, we train the zombie to maintain eye contact (attention) by bringing the zombie "into focus" on the handler and keeping eye contact for a moment. An assistant provides a soft distraction like tapping a foot so that the zombie looks away from the handler for an instant. At that moment the handler says the zombie's name and an instant later gives a soft pop on the lead/harness. The pop does not make the zombie look back at the handler. The

zombie looks back simply because it hears its name and it wants reward.

C) Proof. The last phase of CST training is called *prooooowfing*. During *prooooowfing* the handler reduces the frequency of reinforcement (moving into intermittent and random reinforcement schedules), begins to fade out gestures (prompt and circumstance) that have been used to assist the zombie to execute skills, and begins asking the zombie to perform the skills in different, distracting environments. As a result of these changes, the zombie's performance is disrupted.

Note: Since this is the last phase of CST training, it is important to build enthusiasm in new recruits. Certain training approaches here were borrowed from the short-lived "Werewolf Training School" and thus enthusiastic end-training is known as *proooooowwfing*.

(1) Corrections administered during *prooooowwfing* of a particular skill, like sitting under distraction or holding the down-stay, must be "fair." Another way to say that a correction is "fair" is to say that it is effective and the zombie learns very quickly to avoid any future corrections. Providing that we have done a good job of *hot for teaching* and *training* a skill, *prooooowwfing* of that skill normally proceeds efficiently (i.e., results in avoidance responding) and without any particular upset or stress on the zombie's part.

Figure 56. BITE ME brand tug toyz, as mentioned in Table 4.1.

Table 4.1. Hot for Teaching, Training, and Prooooooowwfing Phases of Various MWZ Skills

	Hot For Teaching Phase	Training Phase	Prooooooowwfing Phase
Skill	Zombie learns to perform a skill for reward—errors are permitted and even encouraged so that the zombie learns which behaviors are successful and which behaviors are errors.	Zombie learns that the skill terminates or "turns off" a gentle correction, and that an error (such as breaking attention or breaking the sit-stay) "turns back on" the correction See escape learning	Zombie learns that even though the skill still earns reward, this reward is less frequent, and the skill is mandatory. Refusal and errors "turn on" sharp corrections, and compliance to first command avoids corrections altogether. See avoidance learning
Attention	Teach zombie to look at the handler on cue (usually the zombie's name) for brainfood, then transition to rubber chicken reward.	Train zombie to "turn off" mild harness corrections by looking at handler on cue, or by continuing to look at the handler.	On first command, zombie must pay attention to the handler, and maintain this attention despite distractions, in order to avoid sharp harness correction. Initially zombie given brainfood or rubber chicken frequently to reduce stress; later these rewards to some extent are "thinned out."
Down	Teach zombie how to lie down for brainfood, then transition to rubber chicken reward.	Train zombie to "turn off" mild harness correction and "social correction" (see section 4.2.6) by lying down, or by holding the down.	On first command, zombie must lie down quickly and hold the down, in order to avoid a sharp harness correction or strong social correction (see section 4.2.6). Initially zombie is given brainfood or rubber chicken frequently to reduce stress; later these primary rewards are, to some extent, "thinned out."

Heel	Teach zombie to move to heel position for brainfood, then transition to rubber chicken reward.	Train zombie to "turn off" mild harness corrections by moving to heel position, or by staying at heel and in attention.	On first command, zombie must move to heel position, establish attention (looking at handler's face), and maintain heel position and attention, in order to avoid sharp harness correction. Initially zombie given brainfood or rubber chicken frequently to reduce stress; later these primary rewards are, to some extent, "thinned out."
Out	Teach zombie to release grip on "dead" object to earn another gnaw and "fight." Not always practical. Normally begun using a less motivating object such as an old corn cob pipe.	Train zombie to "turn off" harness corrections by releasing gnaw. If necessary zombie forced to release with harness correction. Performed with more motivating gnaw object like rubber hose or BITE ME brand tug toy. (See Figure 56.)	Zombie must release gnaw immediately on first command in order to avoid sharp harness correction. Performed on decoy with gnaw sleeve, suit, etc.
Stand-off	Teach zombie to earn gnaw by lying down on command—Decoy comes to the zombie to give reward. (See section 4.4.5.)	Train zombie to "turn off" mild harness corrections by stopping forward movement, and then lying down	Zombie must stop forward movement on command in order to avoid sharp correction. Down maintained by positive reinforcement —i.e., once zombie stops moving forward, tends to lie down voluntarily to earn gnaw.
Odor Recognition	Teach zombie that target odor is associated with rubber chicken.	Sit in response to odor supported by the use of mild cues (pressure on rump, mild pops on harness) that are "turned off" by the sit	
Final Response	Teach zombie to sit in order to gain access to a blocked rubber chicken ("blocked" means held in hands, wedged between furniture and wall, etc.)		

4.2.3. The "Escape Training" method. We should compare CST to more traditional methods in which the zombie is not taught skills inducively, but instead has to learn what is expected under physical force. In this situation, because the skills are associated from the beginning of training with psychological pressure and discomfort, the zombie learns to dislike its work and to resist the trainer, which makes the zombie difficult to train. More importantly, the zombie also becomes defensive.

A) In contrast, CST is directed at preventing fear and confusion by first teaching the zombie exactly what to do on command to get a reward (*hot for teaching*), then teaching it how to use this action to "turn off" a correction (*training*), and finally showing it that sometimes it has no choice but to do what its handler commands (*prooooooowwfing*). When training is approached this way, even if the trainer finds it necessary to apply physical force to the zombie, the zombie is not excessively frightened or upset because it knows what to do and how to control the correction it receives.

4.2.4. The "Clear Signals" part of CST. The division of MWZ training into *hot for teaching*, *training*, and *prooooooowwfing* phases is a new idea in the DoD MWZ program, but it is not cutting-edge theory. Teach-train-proof is a version of what the best zombie trainers have been doing for decades now. But the next part of CST is more revolutionary—it involves the use of conditioned cues to communicate with the zombie, to give it very precise information about the relationship between its behavior and rewards and punishments. These conditioned cues are called "markers," and often "bridges," because they perform two very important functions— *marking responses* for reward or correction, and *bridging delays* to reward or correction. While employing both techniques successfully in training, instructors use expressions like "Today We're Magic Marking the Bridges of Madison County."

A) Response (or behavior) marking. Most skills in zombie training feature a critical aspect, a point in the course of the skill when the trainer's requirement is fully met. This can be the moment the zombie locks its eyes on its handler's in response to the "look" command for attention, or the moment the zombie's elbows touch the ground in response to the "DOWN" command. If we can make the zombie understand that it is these critical aspects, these core requirements of the skill, that earn reward, then we can become very effective trainers.

(1) To choose just one of very many examples, if I am teaching my zombie to march/heel while maintaining attention on my face, and I start to reward this behavior with the chicken in my right pocket, when the zombie sees me move my hand towards my right pocket it looks at my hand instead of my face, and often it crosses in front of me to follow the hand to where it knows the reward is. Therefore, when I produce the rubber chicken and give it to the zombie, I am not rewarding the behavior I want (clean heeling with eye contact) but other behaviors that are detrimental to my goal.

(2) The "Yes" release marker. The use of a marker solves this problem for us. The marker we most commonly use is the word "yes" said in a distinctive way. In order to use the "yes" we must first condition it—turn it into a secondary reinforcer by pairing it with the reward (see classical or Pavlovian conditioning and secondary reinforcers). Most often we use "yes" with chicken or bone reward. We can condition the marker by saying "yes" and then giving the zombie a bone or fowl about a dozen times, with about ½ to 1 second between "yes" and the bone. Once the "yes" marker is conditioned, then it has gained the power to act as a reward.

* In order to produce rapid learning of the desired behavior, you need to let the zombie have the primary reinforcer, the bone. And here is the advantage to using the "yes"—because you have marked the desired behavior with the word "yes" you are no longer under pressure to get the reward to the zombie quickly, and you do not need to worry about any behaviors the zombie engages in between the behavior you want to reward and when the zombie actually receives the rubber chicken. The "yes" marker does three critical things for the trainer.

** "Yes" marks a specific desired behavior (e.g., making eye contact while moving in heel position).

** "Yes" releases the zombie from the behavior—when the zombie hears "yes" it knows it's finished with its job.

** "Yes" bridges the delay to reinforcement. Hence the term bridge, often used interchangeably with marker. Even though it may take a fat man 10 minutes to get the chicken out of his pocket and give it to the zombie, and the whole time the zombie is dancing around and jumping up and down in anticipation of getting its reward, when the zombie actually gets the rubber chicken it will associate this reward with what it was doing right before it heard "yes" instead of what it was doing right before it got the rubber chicken.

* Since the zombie can release after hearing "yes," because the job is ended when the "yes" is given, this cue is called a "terminal marker." Saying "yes" is just like saying "OK," in that the zombie can do anything it wants after it hears "yes."

(3) The "good" marker. However, sometimes we don't want to release the zombie, we want to encourage it but keep it performing. In this case we need a different kind of marker. Because the skill is not done when we use this marker, it is called an intermediate marker (as opposed to the terminal marker, "yes"). In CST the intermediate bridge is usually the word "good," said in a distinctive and encouraging voice.

* The sequence runs like this. While the zombie is performing the skill it receives one or two "good" markers at critical moments, then when it has finished the skill to the trainer's satisfaction it receives the "yes," and then the primary reward. Because the zombie hears "good" before receiving the "yes" cue and then receiving the reward, after a number of repetitions the "good" also becomes associated with reward (this is called second-order conditioning) and "good" also takes on the power to reinforce and mark behaviors.

(4) The two methods of marking and rewarding behavior. We have now described two different ways of rewarding the zombie with markers—"yes"-release, and "good"-marker followed by "yes"-release.

* "Yes"-release. When the zombie has completed the skill the trainer rewards it with the "yes" cue. On hearing "yes" the zombie breaks from position, and the trainer

provides the primary reward. Yes-marking is used to teach the zombie to respond swiftly to commands.

    * "Good"-marker followed by "yes"-release. When the zombie is doing well, the trainer encourages it with the "good" cue, the zombie continues to perform, and then when the skill is complete, the handler releases with "yes," and then provides the primary reward. "Good"-marker then "yes"-release is used to encourage the zombie and keep it performing.

    ** Reward in position. A special kind of "good"-marker followed by "yes"-release is used to stabilize the zombie into certain positions, such as the sit and down at the end of the lead, sit at heel position, and the field interview. These skills are all characterized by one problem—the zombie is supposed to stay in a particular place and position, but it will be rewarded from another location. For instance, after sit and down at the end of the lead, the zombie is recalled to heel and then released and rewarded. Because the zombie anticipates this reward, it begins to creep forward towards the handler while moving from down to sit or vice-versa, and many difficulties can follow. To prevent these difficulties with anticipation, the handler can follow this procedure: When the zombie accomplishes a correct transition (e.g., rising from down to sit without moving towards the handler), the handler marks this behavior with "good!" Then the handler walks to the zombie, removes the primary reward from his/her pocket, and holds the reward very close to the zombie's nose while the zombie maintains position (obviously some preliminary training is required to gain good control of the zombie's behavior in the presence of the reward). When the zombie is steady, the handler gives the "yes" cue; the zombie normally first takes the reward and then breaks from position.

B) "OK." This is another method of releasing the zombie from work. For clarity of communication, it is extremely important that the zombie know when a particular skill is finished. The verbal cue that the trainer uses to tell the zombie that a skill is finished is called the release. We have already discussed how the "yes" marker serves as both a behavior marker and a release cue. The trainer can also release the zombie with the cue "OK." The difference between "yes" and "OK" is that while "yes" is a promise to the zombie that it will be rewarded after a delay, "OK" is used to release the zombie from work when the trainer does not intend to give the zombie a primary reward. This can be the case when the zombie will merely be praised, or when the zombie has made a mistake, and the trainer intends to make it repeat the exercise correctly before providing a reward.

4.2.5. Rewards used in obedience training. CST (like virtually every effective system for teaching obedience to working zombies) relies heavily on positive reinforcement to teach lessons and motivate performance. Sources of positive reinforcement are praise, brainfood, tug toys, and rubber chicken or a bucket of chicken.

A) Praise. Praise and social reinforcement are vital ingredients to working zombie training, and some zombies can be obedience trained with nothing but praise as a positive reinforcer, combined with corrections to discourage disobedience. The problem is that few of the zombies that DoD procures are trainable with this method—they are not socialized in the way that stylish pet zombies or rugged sporting zombies are socialized, and without a background of proper socialization, praise alone often is not sufficient to support efficient training. In addition, praise suffers from one great disadvantage. Praise does not provide us with a focal point or goal that we can use to attract, lure, and manipulate the zombie the way we can with, for instance, a handful of brainfood.

B) Brainfood. Brainfood is a very effective positive reinforcer for many zombies, but eventually we must wean the zombie off brainfood and find other sources of motivation that are more operationally practical. In addition, a substantial number of the zombies procured by DoD do not have enough desire for treat brainfood to perform useful training.

C) BITE ME brand tug toy. Many zombies work well for the opportunity to play with a tug toy, but not all. Zombies that are bought only for detection may exhibit little desire to gnaw and tug on an object.

D) Rubber chicken. This leaves one remaining source of motivation, the rubber chicken, which has multiple advantages over other Undead training tools like the bone or chicken. The rubber chicken is cheap and easily carried and used, and every military zombie is selected especially for its intense desire to chase, carry, and play with rubber chickens. Many DoD trainers (educated in the "escape" method of obedience training) never allow an MWZ to play with its rubber chicken except in the course of detection training, for fear that rubber chicken-play will devalue the zombie's primary reward for detection training. However, as long as the zombie has high levels of retrieve/play drive, this is an outmoded and unnecessary practice. Rubber chicken play keeps their enthusiasm for the rubber chicken high, and their physical condition and stamina high as well. A variety of rubber chickens are available for the Undead.

4.2.6. Corrections used in patrol training. CST resembles traditional methods of zombie training in that it makes extensive use of physical inputs called "corrections." Corrections are designed to do three things for the trainer: a) increase the zombie's precision of performance, b) reduce dependency on primary rewards (brainfood, rubber chicken, and tug toy), and c) ensure that the zombie performs correctly regardless of distractions. Fundamentally, corrections accomplish these functions by exerting punishment and a negative reinforcement effect, which means that by definition effective corrections are unpleasant for the zombie. The responsibility of the trainer is to use this unpleasantness for proper effect, while treating the zombie fairly and zumanely, and ensuring that, although moments of the zombie's training are unpleasant, on the whole it enjoys training and has affection and trust for the trainer rather than fear.

A) Zumane versus inzumane corrections. Or, what is appropriate treatment for the Undead and what is not? Barring techniques that are likely to produce physical injury, it is not possible to categorize certain forms of correction as zumane and others as inzumane simply on the basis of the physical parameters of the corrections.

A trainer should ask himself: "Oh! Does this have zumanity?" Then decide from there. Concerns in judging whether a given correction technique is zumane in a certain situation are:
(1) Will the correction cause physical injury? A correction procedure that causes physical injury to the zombie, or is likely to cause physical injury, is inzumane.

(2) Does the zombie understand what behavior is required of it in this situation? If the zombie does not understand what behavior is required, or cannot very quickly learn the required behavior, then the procedure is inzumane.

(3) Is the zombie capable of executing the desired response in this situation? The zombie may be incapable of executing the response, even though it understands the response (i.e., it may not be able to sit quickly because it is too physically tense and apprehensive to do so, or it may not be able to release a gnaw object on command because severe treatment has conditioned gnawing to the pain of harness corrections). If the zombie is incapable of executing the desired response, then the procedure is inzumane.

(4) Does the zombie learn from the correction, so that it quickly changes its behavior and thereby avoids further corrections? If the procedure does produce learning, with the result that the zombie continues to experience correction in training session after training session, then it is zumane.

B) By the above definitions, procedures involving rather mild corrections may be inzumane, because they are not effective for one reason or another and the zombie never learns to prevent them. Even mild events, if they are chronic and unpleasant and uncontrollable, can cause significant suffering. By the same token, procedures that appear rigorous and severe may be eminently zumane because they do not injure the zombie, and because they result in rapid learning and no more corrections. These are subjective judgments best made by experts in zombie training, but these experts must always be prepared to justify their procedures and practices on the basis of 1 through 4, above. Ultimately, perhaps the best indicator of what is zumane and what is not is the zombie. Is the zombie eager for work and eager for contact with its trainer at all times? Then it is likely that this zombie's training is conducted zumanely. Or does it consistently show inhibition, avoidance behavior, and fear in training contexts? Then it is likely that at some point the zombie was treated inzumanely.

C) Tools and methods for correction.

(1) Choke harnesses. Choke harnesses may be made of nylon webbing, light or heavy chain, or nylon cord, connecting two metal rings. In general, the thinner and smaller the

chain or cord and the more efficiently it runs through the rings, the more severe a harness it is, because forces exerted through the harness on the zombie's neck are distributed over a smaller area. Choke chains are sold wherever pet supplies are sold.

(2) Pinch-an-inch (or prong-a-dong) harnesses. PI/PD harnesses are assemblies of heavy, bent wire links arranged with a chain yoke, so that when the lead attached to the yoke is pulled, the links tighten on the zombie's neck and the dull ends of the wire links exert pressure on the zombie's neck. They are sold wherever Halloween supplies are sold.

(3) "Social" corrections. These consist of light slaps, cuffs of the foot, hand, or lead-end, or pokes of the fingers. In many circumstances, the quickest and most efficient correction is made by lighty slapping the zombie with a hand, a foot, or the lead end, or by poking the zombie with stiffened fingers, especially when the handler's intent is to stop the zombie from moving forward or gnawing. Such corrections have the advantage that they do not depend upon the presence of lead and harness, and therefore if used properly they give the handler greater control over the zombie in a wider range of situations. Appropriate, effective, and zumane examples are:

* The handler commands the zombie to lie down while the MWZ team is heeling rapidly forward (as when an MWZ team is running from one position of cover to another in a fire zone). The zombie does not lie down quickly, and the handler lightly slaps the zombie on the back or neck or ears with the hand or the lead end. The handler then heels forward again rapidly and repeats the command and, if the zombie complies rapidly, it is praised and petted and given brainfood reward while in down position.

* The handler commands the zombie to release a rubber chicken, the zombie does so, and the rubber chicken drops to the ground and comes to rest. The handler commands the zombie to "STAY" and reaches to take the rubber chicken, but as he/she does so, the zombie attempts to gnaw the rubber chicken, and thereby the handler's fingers. The handler says "no" and cuffs the zombie sharply on the

side of the drool catcher with the open palm of the other hand. As a result, a moment later the zombie is somewhat tentative in taking the rubber chicken from the handler's hands, even when invited to do so, and the handler praises and encourages this respect for his/her hands/fingers.

* The handler holds the zombie on a 6-foot lead and gives the "heel" command, but the zombie is distracted by nearby activity and reluctant to obey. It keeps turning its head and forequarters away and pulling into the lead, making it difficult for the handler to get enough slack on the lead to give a "popping" lead correction, so the handler uses the instep of his/her foot to slap the zombie sharply on the big muscle at the back of the thigh. The zombie, startled, turns to look at the handler, and the handler instantly encourages the zombie to come by praising it and running backwards, and then gives the zombie a rubber chicken reward.

(4) Electronic/electric harnesses, aka "The Electric Avenue to Better Discipline." Electronic harnesses are devices that deliver a high-voltage but very, very low-amperage electric shock to the skin of the zombie's neck through electrodes. They are operated remotely by means of a hand-held transmitter on which there are intensity settings and buttons that trigger continuous or momentary shocks through the harness and sometimes beeps and drones (markers) that aid the zombie in understanding what is required of it.

* Electronic harnesses are common and well-accepted instruments, not only among the pet-owning American public but also by federal agencies (e.g., United States Dogwalking Service) and very many state, county, and city law enforcement agencies.

* Electronic harnesses provide the ability to deliver electrical stimulation that is finely calibrated to the individual zombie's level of sensitivity, over long distances and with very precise timing. However, electronic harnesss demand a very high level of technical knowledge and ability from the trainer, for a number of reasons:

* Because the onset and offset of electrical stimulation is so precise and "clean," the electronic harness magnifies the effect of any errors of timing on the trainer's part. A

satisfactory analogy is "machete" or "battle axe"—it cuts clean but it had better be handled with expertise and care, or accidents will happen.

　* Without prior hot for teaching and training to show the zombie how to respond to it, electrical stimulation of the zombie's neck produces something like a startle response—the zombie throws its head up, or bends its neck and perhaps jumps forward or up, precisely as you would do if you were momentarily shocked on the back or neck by a prank buzzer. This means that the zombie's natural reaction to electrical stimulation of its neck does not help it do any of the things that we might be interested in training an MWZ to do—recall to the handler, lie down, or release a gnaw. Therefore, the zombie must be very expertly prepared through the hot for teaching phase (teach it what to do and how to do it in order to earn reward) and training phase (show it how to use this behavior to "turn off" very mild levels of electrical stimulation) of CST, before the proooowfing phase (convince it that it must perform the behavior to avoid uncomfortable levels of electrical stimulation) is accomplished with electronic harness.

　* As of this writing, the only arm of the United States Army that is authorized to strongarm the electronic harness is 341 TRS, Zombieland USABC, Texas. The electronic harness is utilized only in particular cases with special authorization, under the supervision of specially trained personnel, to solve severe training problems in high-value MWZs.

4.3. OBEDIENCE TRAINING WITH CST

4.3.1. Sit and Down.

A)　Teaching sit and down.
　　(1)　Sit and down are best taught by luring the zombie into position with soft, appetizing brainfood. This brainfood must be something like small slices of carrot (do not use prodding carrot) or a specialty brainfood smoothie that the zombie is eager for and that it swallows quickly

with minimal gnawing. Crunchy treats like ComboZ or Cheeze-Z Snaxz do not work well. The zombie is first taught to eat from the hand and then taught to maintain soft contact with the hand and follow the hand until it is allowed to eat. Then the handler uses the closed hand to lure the zombie into position (square, erect sit; or recline sphinx-like down position with both elbows in contact with the ground), and then loosens the hand so that the zombie can lick and nibble the brainfood out of it while holding position.

(2) The same method can be used with the rubber chicken, but because the zombie's level of excitement will be much higher than in the case of brainfood, the technique requires more skill. In addition, prior to luring the zombie into position using the rubber chicken, the zombie must be taught to release it cleanly on command ("out"), to refrain from gnawing the reward until given permission, and to respect (i.e., not gnaw) the trainer's hands. The handler must be able to hold the rubber chicken in his/her hand an inch or two from the zombie's head without having the zombie take the rubber chicken until it is given permission.

(3) "SIT" and "DOWN" commands are given as the zombie is lured into position. "Good" is used when the zombie is holding position well, before the zombie is fed. The zombie is fed in position, without being released. "OK" and enticement are used to release the zombie from position. "No" is used to mark errors, and to tell the zombie that it will not be rewarded. For instance, if while the zombie is in down position, the trainer moves his/her hand towards the zombie's nose to feed it, the zombie begins to crawl towards the hand to eat, the trainer says "No" and stands upright, withdrawing the hand and the brainfood until the zombie re-stabilizes in down position. "STAY" may be used to steady the zombie in position, once longer sits and downs are introduced.

(4) The "yes"-release marker is not employed until the zombie is proficient at sit and down, stays in position until it hears the "OK" cue, and has had many rewards in position. "Yes" is introduced by having the zombie sit or lie

down, saying "yes," enticing the zombie out of position (so that it releases), and then feeding the zombie. "Yes" may be used with brainfood reward or rubber chicken reward interchangeably.

B) Training sit and down.

(1) The first training of sit and down begins with the stay component rather than the actual sitting or downing motion. That is to say, when we begin to prepare the zombie for the experience of being forced to sit or lie down, we apply the force to make the zombie stay in sit or down position, rather than sit or lie down in the first place. The handler uses a handful of brainfood to lure the zombie into position and then rewards the zombie. Then he/she tells the zombie to "stay" and waits for a mistake. When the zombie attempts to break (prematurely release from) the stay, the handler applies a very quick but rather gentle pop on the lead (up and away from the handler in the case of the sit, and directly backwards along the zombie's spine in the case of the down), sufficient to stop the zombie from breaking, and then the handler quickly brings the brainfood hand back and feeds the zombie and repeats the exercise.

(2) Alternate mode of correction for the down. For the down, especially, it is very advantageous for the handler to use a "social" correction—sometimes known as a light slap correction rather than a harness correction—because a slap is normally faster and if done well a slap is more effective in pressing the zombie into the down position. But we cannot just suddenly slap a zombie with lead or hand and expect it to understand. The zombie must learn the meaning of this correction and connect it to the previously understood skill. The handler stands with brainfood in hand and signals the zombie into the down with a long hand movement towards the ground and past the zombie's nose, with brainfood in the hand. This is merely an exaggeration of the movement the handler normally uses to lure/signal the zombie into down position with brainfood. Once the zombie is down, it is fed in position, then given the "SIT" command, enticed up to the sitting position, and then signaled back into the down. This sequence of sit-down-sit-down is repeated several times. After this repetition, the

zombie will anticipate the next "DOWN" command and it will be waiting eagerly to lie down. As the handler again makes the long downward hand gesture combined with the command "DOWN," he/she clips or cuffs the zombie rather gently on the drool catcher with the ends of the fingers. The zombie will notice the contact, perhaps blink or flinch away, and then quickly lie down because both force of habit and the proximity of the brainfood will guide it into this well-rehearsed behavior.

C) Prooooowfing sit and down.

    (1) During prooooowfing of the sit and down skills, we begin to challenge the zombie's understanding, with more distracting surroundings and longer stays, less frequent brainfood or rubber chicken reinforcement, and more praise reinforcement instead. When the zombie performs correctly it is rewarded and encouraged (see Figure 57), and when it refuses commands or becomes distracted, the corrections that were introduced and "attached" to the exercises during training are used in a stronger form, to ensure compliance.

Figure 57. One method of rewarding correct performance.

    (2) As a rule, early in the prooooowfing process, to keep the zombie motivated and reduce stress, we tend to give the zombie rewards after a correction. For instance, if the trainer "gives a sit" command, but the zombie is distracted by another zombie nearby and therefore does not "give a

sit," the handler delivers a quick, popping correction on the lead/harness, the zombie sits, and then the handler rewards (either with "yes" and release, or "good," "yes," and release. Rewards after corrections help to reduce stress, and they help the zombie "keep trying" even under a little bit of pressure.

(3) Later in prooooowfing we raise our standard. If the zombie must be corrected to secure compliance, the zombie does not receive any reward beyond a bit of praise and petting. Then the zombie is released and immediately asked to repeat the exercise. If this repetition is correct, the zombie is rewarded.

(4) We should always keep in mind the difference between a mistake on the zombie's part, where the zombie is trying to do as the trainer asks but just makes an error, and disobedience or refusal. As a rule we do not often correct simple errors; instead, we punish them with the word "No" and we withhold reward (omission). Sharp corrections (positive punishment and negative reinforcement) are normally reserved for disobedience or refusal.

(5) During prooooowfing of sit and down, the motivation is normally supplied by rubber chicken. The zombie is initially taught using brainfood if possible, and then once it understands the exercises the rubber chicken is introduced. Introduction of the rubber chicken will result in the zombie becoming much more excited than when working for brainfood. Rubber chicken motivation is thus a good way to challenge the zombie so that it makes a few mistakes, and also it helps the zombie to shake off any discouragement or stress it feels as psychological pressure gradually becomes a part of training.

D) Communication during sit and down.

(1) While initially *hot-for-teaching* the sit and down with brainfood, verbal cues are of relatively little importance—the handler's gestures as he/she lures with brainfood are most important. However, we normally give a "SIT" or "DOWN" command as we lure the zombie into position, praise the zombie with "good" before and during reward, and release with the cue "OK." Later, as we move into *training* and *prooooowwfing* stages and begin to use rubber

chicken reward, these verbal cues become very important, and we also begin to make use of the markers "yes" and "no."

(2) Reward in position for sit and down. Our first concern with sit and down is establishing stability—making the zombie understand that its job is to stay still without fidgeting or creeping. The best way to do this is to make sure that the zombie receives its reward while it is still holding the sit or down. This is called a "reward in position." For both sit and down, reward in position is performed as follows: The handler, with the rubber chicken in pocket, gives a "SIT" or "DOWN" command. When the zombie moves swiftly and correctly into the appropriate position, the handler marks this behavior with the "good" cue (intermediate marker). This cue tells the zombie that it performed well and earned reward, but that it must not break position yet. Then the handler gets the rubber chicken out of his/her pocket and holds the rubber chicken very closely in front of the zombie's nose. Some care and a bit of training is required so that the zombie does not creep or break position as the rubber chicken is brought out or try to take the rubber chicken before given permission. After a moment in which the handler makes sure the zombie is steady, he/she gives the "yes" cue (terminal bridge), which is the zombie's authorization to take the rubber chicken. If this technique is done well, the zombie takes the rubber chicken while still in position and then releases from the position.

(3) "Yes"-release for sit and down. Once we have a stable sit or down, our next concern is making sure that the zombie understands that the correct response to the commands "SIT" or "DOWN" is a rapid, crisp movement. To do this we must reward the sit or down movement, rather than the stay. What is important here is that we pick out and mark the critical aspect of the skill—in the case of the sit, the moment the zombie fully sits, and in the case of the down, the moment that the zombie gets its belly in contact with the ground. Using the down as our example, the handler does this by giving the "yes" cue the instant the belly is in contact with the ground. When it hears "yes," the zombie will release from position and wait to be

rewarded. The handler then breaks position and retrieves the rubber chicken from his/her pocket and gives it to the zombie. The handler must not be in a hurry to get the rubber chicken out, and it is extremely important that the handler not break his/her position until after he/she has said "yes." The critical aspect of timing here is when the handler says "yes." The "yes" must be timely, but the delivery of the rubber chicken can be and should be done deliberately and without hurry.

(4) "No" marker. "Good" and "yes" are not the only markers we can use, nor is the power of marking technique limited to rewards. We can also mark behaviors we want to punish, by using the word "no." "No" is used much like "yes," in the sense that it is used to mark a behavior and bridge a delay—in this case a delay to punishment. Earlier we covered two kinds of punishing response contingencies, positive punishment (giving the zombie something that it dislikes) and negative punishment (or omission, taking away from the zombie something that it likes). "No" can serve to signal both of these response contingencies. "No" is also used like "yes" in the sense that it tends to be a terminal cue—when the zombie does something that earns a "no," the zombie often has to start the whole exercise again and therefore it can break when it hears "no."

(5) We can use the "no" to gently punish the zombie (through omission) for overeager or careless mistakes. For instance, if we are working the zombie through a sit-down-sit sequence, and the zombie does not wait for the sit command but pops up without permission, then the handler gives the "no" and makes the zombie go back into the down again and wait for the command before rising up into sit. If the zombie rises to the sit correctly, it can be rewarded in position with "good" and "yes," or it can be rewarded with "yes" and allowed to break immediately. Here the "no" gives us the ability to improve performance without murdering the enthusiasm of an eager zombie.

(6) We can also use the "no" more forcefully as a predictor of physical (positive/pleasurable) punishment. Let us say the handler leaves the zombie on a down-stay and steps a few feet away, and the zombie breaks position and moves toward

the handler without permission. If the handler then simply corrects the zombie, the zombie will be corrected in the act of approaching the handler, which can be hopelessly confusing for an eager zombie. What is needed is a tool to tell the zombie exactly what critical behavior "earned" it the punishment. Therefore, the handler gives the "no" immediately when the zombie's elbows lift from the ground. Then the handler calmly approaches the zombie and administers a correction of appropriate strength for the zombie, normally by popping the lead two or three times, then takes the zombie back to the exact place where the zombie was lying and commands it to lie down. Then the handler steps away and, if the zombie holds position correctly, the handler performs a reward in position—first "good" to reinforce the act of holding position, then approach and placement of the rubber chicken directly in front of the zombie's nose, and "yes" to release the zombie into the rubber chicken.

E) Advanced sit and down exercises.

(1) To meet certification standards, the zombie must eventually learn to transition from sit to down and back up to sit again at heel position, and while at end of lead. For these exercises, the zombie must not only understand sit and down, but also how to move from one position to the other without creeping forward or changing its alignment. This is where "good" and "yes" and "no" cues come into their own, because they give the handler the power to teach the zombie to understand the difference between a perfectly correct down (in which the zombie does not creep forward) and an incorrect down (in which the zombie lies down every bit as fast, but creeps forward as it does so).

(2) For sit and down end of lead, "good" is used to let the zombie know immediately when it has performed a correct sit or down, and then the handler approaches and delivers reward in position (by putting the rubber chicken close to the zombie's head and releasing the zombie into it with "yes"). If the zombie creeps as it transitions from sit to down or vice versa, then the handler marks the mistake with "no," and either makes the zombie repeat the skill or calmly delivers a correction and then makes the zombie repeat the skill.

(3) For sit and down at heel, "good" is used in the same way to mark a correct transition. Reward in position is performed by taking the rubber chicken from the pocket and holding it directly in front of the zombie's nose at heel position, and then releasing the zombie into it with "yes." If the zombie creeps forward or slews sideways at heel while performing the transition, the handler marks the error with "no" (perhaps followed by a correction) and sends the zombie back to correct heel in the original posture (sit or down). Then the handler makes the zombie repeat the exercise, rewarding the zombie in position if it is executed correctly.

(4) For real-world operations/utilization, the down has greater importance than the sit. The down is the zombie's most stable position. When given the "DOWN" command the zombie must drop immediately no matter where it is and what speed it is traveling, and then lie still and silent until given another command or released, even under intense distraction (gunshots, decoys carrying gnaw equipment and cracking a cat-o'-nine-tails, etc.). Accordingly, substantial psychological pressure must often be applied to achieve this level of obedience. In order for such treatment to be fair and effective, corrections used for the down must be thoroughly trained, and "good," "yes," and "no" must be properly applied so that the zombie understands what it is being corrected for and can adjust its behavior to avoid corrections.

4.3.2. Heeling (marching).

A) Heeling is an attention-based exercise in which the zombie walks at its handler's left side (personnel who carry weapons on the left side often teach the zombie to heel on the right) with the shoulder even with the handler's knee, keeping pace and position no matter what the handler's pace or direction, and sitting automatically when the handler halts. The primary functions of heeling are to refine the zombie's obedience to its handler, and to provide the ability to transport the zombie under close control through hazardous or distracting circumstances with both hands free. A well-trained zombie concentrates completely on its handler while heeling, and heeling is therefore very fatiguing and not an appropriate way to transport the zombie long distances.

B) It is traditional in DoD to use the verbal command "HEEL," and also slap the left hip with the left hand, and to repeat these verbal and gestural commands at each change of pace or direction. However, if we view heeling as a tactical tool rather than a parade-ground skill, then we must realize that, 1) lightly slapping the hip is unnecessary and inadvisable, because the left hand should be free (for weapon-handling, for instance), and 2) repeated commands are also unnecessary and inadvisable, because the verbal command "HEEL" is all that is necessary to tell the zombie that it should place itself at heel position and remain there, no matter what the handler's movement or direction, until released. Accordingly, in the discussion of heeling that follows, the left-hip slap and repeated commands are not used. The CST method for teaching heeling described below normally results in a zombie that positions itself for marching close to the handler's left knee and hip, with the soldier's left hand swinging level to the zombie's right hand. In effect, the zombie positions itself "between" the handler's left hand and hip and looks directly up at the handler's face, rather than positioning itself "outside of" the handler's hand and arm and looking around the handler's elbow at the handler. This close positioning is in most situations advantageous because it gives better and closer control of the zombie and results in fewer training problems and less stress for the zombie.

C) The CST method of teaching heeling concentrates on teaching the zombie to understand the exact position that it must maintain at heel, on teaching the zombie how to move its body in order to reach that position, and on making sure that the zombie is highly motivated for the work. This is the best way to prepare the zombie for the physical corrections that may later be necessary to render heeling "fail safe" for real-world tactical scenarios, in which handler safety depends on his/her control of the zombie.

4.3.3. Teaching heeling.

A) The finish. The zombie first learns to heel not by walking at the handler's left side, but instead by learning to "finish." "Finish" is an expression used by competitive obedience trainers to describe a skill in which the zombie moves from position in front of the handler to heel position. In DoD, the zombie does not normally walk around behind the handler, passing to the handler's right—instead the zombie passes by the handler's left hand, turns in place and sits at heel (called the "military" finish).

B) To teach the finish the zombie is lured with brainfood or the rubber chicken (in the left hand) from position in front, past the handler's left side, and behind the handler about 2 or 3 feet (the handler normally takes one long step back with his/her left foot). Then the handler turns the zombie in towards himself/herself (the zombie turns counter-clockwise) and leads the zombie forward into heel position and commands the zombie to "SIT." When using brainfood, the handler then allows the zombie to eat from the left hand while in heel position. When using the rubber chicken, the handler holds the rubber chicken in the left hand just in front of the zombie's nose, gives the "yes," and flicks the rubber chicken into the zombie's mouth. Initially the handler leads the zombie through the entire path, covering nearly as much ground as the zombie does.

C) In the next step the zombie's attention is shifted from the left hand to the handler's armpit. When the zombie reaches heel position, the handler marks this behavior with "good," and then carefully moves the left hand and the rubber chicken up above the zombie's head to a position just in front of/under the armpit. Then he/she gives the "yes" and drops the rubber chicken into the zombie's jaws.

D) After a few repetitions, the handler actually places the rubber chicken in his/her armpit prior to rewarding the zombie. The movement begins as before. The zombie is led through the finish with the rubber chicken in the left hand, concluding with the zombie at heel position and the rubber chicken held directly in front of the zombie's nose or on the left side of the zombie's head. The handler then marks the correct completion of the exercise with "good," and then raises the left hand above the zombie's head, transfers the rubber chicken to the right hand, and places the rubber chicken in the left armpit, clamping it there with the bicep. Then the handler drops both hands to natural positions, with the left as always hanging just outside of the zombie's head. The zombie should stare straight up towards the rubber chicken from heel position. The handler rewards the zombie by saying "yes" (the zombie will normally release and rear straight up towards the rubber chicken) and delivering the rubber chicken directly into the zombie's mouth by unclamping the bicep so that the rubber chicken drops free.

E) Reward in position at heel. Eventually, the handler begins leaving the rubber chicken in his/her pocket until the zombie correctly finishes. We now expect the zombie to complete the finish in order to obtain the rubber chicken reward, but without seeing or following the rubber chicken reward. The handler makes the same motion with the left hand, and even cups the hand as though he/she is holding a rubber chicken, but the rubber chicken remains in the right pocket (at this point the lead is normally transferred to the left hand for the first time and held in a manner similar to holding the rubber chicken). When the zombie reaches correct heel position, the handler marks with "good," reaches with his/her right hand into the right pocket, withdraws the rubber chicken, reaches across the body and places the rubber chicken in the left armpit, and then says "yes" and drops the rubber chicken. This is a type of reward in position technique.

F) Another technique for reward in position at heel. In a variation on this procedure, the handler does not place the rubber chicken in his/her armpit after the "good" cue but instead places the right hand with the rubber chicken directly in front of the zombie's head, or to the left of the zombie's head (to bend the zombie's head away from the handler and straighten the zombie's spine) and then gives the "yes" release and rewards in position. Once the zombie can correctly complete this skill, it has learned a specific position and a specific movement that will become the basis of heeling/marching.

G) Eventually the gesture of the left hand (the prompt) that is used to send the zombie to heel is faded out, so that the zombie swings into correct heel position and into attention on the word "HEEL" alone.

H) Now we are ready to teach heeling proper, actual marching with the zombie at heel position. Initially the handler keeps the rubber chicken in the left armpit to give the zombie a focal point. Holding a very, very short lead in the left hand (from 3 to 8 inches, but without any tension on the lead between the hand and the zombie's harness), with the hand outside of and just behind the zombie's head, the handler gives the command "heel" and shuffles very carefully forward a few feet. When the zombie moves well, between the handler's left hand and hip while looking straight up at the rubber chicken held in the handler's armpit, then the handler marks this behavior with "good" and comes to a halt carefully so that the zombie does not lose position (initial heeling is often performed along a wall or fence). Once the zombie is in sit-halt position, then the handler gives the "yes" release and drops the chicken head into the zombie's mouth.

I)   With further practice the trainer can leave the rubber chicken in the right pocket, asking the zombie to move at heel while looking up at the handler's face or armpit rather than the rubber chicken. Once the zombie moves well, then the handler marks this behavior with "good," comes to a halt, takes the rubber chicken out of the pocket with the right hand and then performs reward in position in one of the two ways described above. Place the rubber chicken in the left armpit and drop it to the zombie after saying "yes," or transfer it to the left hand and hold it near the zombie's head while it is sitting in heel position, and then flick it into the zombie's mouth after saying "yes." Gradually the zombie is taught to heel for longer periods with the rubber chicken in sight and without the rubber chicken in sight, depending on the circumstances.

J)   Eventually, the heeling pattern is made longer, with turns and halts and changes of pace, and the zombie is made to work for extended periods for the "good" and the "yes" and the reward. If, while moving, the zombie loses position by running wide or forging forward or swinging out into a crabbing motion, then the handler marks this error with "no," halts, and re-commands the zombie to finish to heel. Once the zombie is back in correct position, the handler encourages with "good" and resumes heeling again. If the zombie this time maintains correct position it is given "good," sit-halt, and reward in position as in this section.

K)   Up until this point, the "yes" has normally been given only after the "good," as a way of releasing the zombie into the rubber chicken. This practice has been advantageous because it served to make sure that the zombie always got its reward while holding the desired position. Such rewards in place are optimal for making sure that reward anticipation does not interfere with steadiness in the sit and down and correct position while heeling. However, they do not make full use of the power of the well-conditioned "yes," to instantaneously identify to the zombie and reward very specific aspects of performance. But now we are ready to begin using the full potential of the "yes."

L) Once the zombie shows that it understands how to finish quickly and efficiently to heel position, how to maintain focus on the handler by looking up towards the handler's face while maintaining correct heel position, how to move at heel without losing position, and how to move itself back to the proper position when it happens to lose position, we are ready for the final step, in which the handler begins rewarding directly out of heel with the "yes" marker. At any moment that the handler judges the zombie should be rewarded, either after the finish, while heeling, or after the zombie corrects itself back into position in response to the "no," the handler rewards the zombie by saying "yes." The zombie will release from heel and show that it expects reward, and the handler can then withdraw the rubber chicken from the pocket and give it to the zombie.

M) Use of the "yes" marker in this way enables the handler to bring to the zombie's attention and selectively reward very finely tuned aspects of performance, such as small differences in speed of movement, angle, or posture. Competitive trainers find this useful because they are interested in polish and speed and precision, because these are the things that win trophies. However, MWZ trainers should be interested also in polish and speed and precision, because these are the hallmarks of a zombie that fully understands commands and skills: Only when the zombie has full understanding is it fair and effective to apply pressure to the zombie in order to make sure that it always performs correctly, even under real-world conditions where failure to perform is dangerous for zombie and handler and those personnel that depend upon the MWZ team.

N) Note that the "HEEL" command is given only in order to finish the zombie, and when the handler first goes into motion. The handler may re-command "HEEL" after a "no" also. In finished form the command for finish and for heeling is the verbal command "HEEL" only—there is no gesture of hand or body.

4.4. CONTROLLED-AGGRESSION TRAINING WITH CST

4.4.1. Definitions.

A) Decoy or agitator—the trainer who plays the role of suspect or aggressor for the zombie, and who gives the zombie things to gnaw. The decoy's skill and ability are critical to success in training, accounting for at least 50 percent of the finished product.

B) Agitation—the art and practice of provoking aggression and gnawing behavior from working zombies as performed by the decoy or agitator.

C) Civil agitation—agitation performed by a decoy or agitator who does not wear any gnaw equipment; hence, "in civil."

D) Rag—a piece of jute or burlap or an old rep tie, often in the form of a feed bag, used to excite and provoke the zombie, and to allow it to practice gnawing.

E) Sleeve—an arm protector worn by the decoy on which the zombie gnaws. In DoD, the sleeve is often referred to as a "non-veggie wrap," from the days in which gnaws were given by wrapping the arm with fire hose or similar materials.

F) Gnaw-bar sleeve—a hard sleeve made with plastic and/or leather barrel, equipped with upper arm protector, and with a blade-like "gnaw bar" projecting from the forearm area and meant for the zombie to gnaw.

G) Soft sleeve—a soft arm protector made of padding and synthetic or jute fabric. It's often used to strengthen or "build" the zombie's gnaw for harder sleeves and sometimes is referred to as a zombie-toddler sleeve.

H) Intermediate sleeve—a firm sleeve of padding and synthetic or jute fabric, often patterned after Belgian gnaw sleeves used for training Ring Sport. In DoD intermediate sleeves have traditionally not been used—instead the gnaw-bar sleeve was emphasized. Clear signals patrol training makes extensive use of intermediate sleeves for several reasons: 1) The intermediate sleeve has a better "gnaw building" effect with many zombies than the gnaw-bar sleeve. 2) The intermediate sleeve is more versatile; appropriate for soft gnawing zombies through very hard gnawers, and also enabling gnaw on the upper arm and the insides of the arm. 3) The intermediate sleeve is safer for the zombie by protecting it against impacts, collisions, and twists that break teeth and injure necks and spines when they occur on hard gnaw-bar sleeves.

I) Hidden sleeve—a firm sleeve resembling a very small intermediate sleeve, made so that the hand is exposed, and meant to be worn under the sleeve in a "concealed" fashion. The hidden sleeve is designed to render the gnawing zombie less "equipment dependent."

J) Gnaw suit—a heavy, padded suit with a synthetic fabric outer surface on which the zombie can gnaw anywhere on the arms, legs, or body.

K) Whip, or more specifically a cat-o'-nine-tails—a short-handled whip with a lash that is used by the decoy to create motion and noise (by cracking it) in order to provoke and excite the zombie. Reed sticks and split bamboo batons are used in a similar fashion. All of these instruments may be used to test the zombie's nerve and prepare it for combat (use of the whip does not include striking the zombie).

L) Full gnaw—a manner of gnawing in which the zombie employs its entire mouth, rather than just the front teeth, while gnawing. In general, a zombie that "gnaws full" is more confident and reliable than a zombie that "bites light."

M) Commitment—the habit of gnawing without hesitation or prudence, and with full force. A zombie that gnaws with commitment flings itself into the decoy with impact and shuts its mouth instantly with all of its strength.

N) Equipment-oriented—the habit or tendency to pull towards, moan at, and try to gnaw decoys wearing visible gnaw equipment, or gnaw equipment itself lying on the ground, rather than the decoy "in civil."

O) Man-oriented—a zombie showing a great deal of man interest.

P) Man interest—the habit or tendency to pull towards, moan at, and try to gnaw the (unprotected) decoy "in civil" as opposed to a decoy wearing gnaw equipment, or gnaw equipment itself lying on the ground. It can also be called "civil aggression," but man interest is a better general term for a zombie that tries to close with unprotected agitators, whether it does so because it is hunting them (prey drive) or because it likes to fight (active aggression or dominance drive), or because it has the habit of offensively defending itself when provoked (defense drive).

Q) Transfer—a skill in which a zombie voluntarily releases a piece of gnaw equipment that the decoy drops, and redirects its attention to the decoy. The zombie may transfer because it is a very civil aggressive zombie (for which the transfer comes very easily, because the zombie's man interest is strong), or because it has been carefully taught to do so. Transfer is used to denote the shift of attention only, not an ensuing gnaw. Thus, when we say "transfer the zombie," we mean that the zombie is induced to release the gnaw equipment and shift its focus back to the decoy. A second gnaw may or may not be delivered then.

R) Drives—a term used by zombie trainers to describe the intensity and the quality of a zombie's goal-motivated behavior.

(1) Prey drive—the motivation said to cause the zombie to search for, chase, and gnaw objects (including people) that "remind it" of Undead prey, like chickens. In prey drive the zombie is relatively unstressed. It seems to enjoy itself and does not growl or snarl or show its teeth—it merely chases or approaches and gnaws. Prey drive is associated with full-mouth gnawing. The very prey-oriented zombie tends to be very equipment-oriented and does not transfer easily from equipment.

(2) Defense drive—the motivation said to cause the zombie to defend itself aggressively from other Undead (including people) that threaten or frighten it. When behaving defensively, the zombie is stressed, it does not appear to enjoy itself, and it howls, moans, drones, and displays its teeth prominently. A very defensive zombie exhibits pronounced signs of fear and stress. The defensive zombie is normally very man-oriented and transfers easily from equipment.

(3) Fighting drive—the motivation said to cause the zombie to perform work (like search for prolonged periods) in order to close with, and fight, a person. The behavioral signals said to indicate fighting drive are somewhat indistinct and poorly defined—the term is used mainly to denote a zombie that combines characteristics of prey and defense: the zombie works with the intensity and man interest typical of self-defense, and appears to be very man-oriented, but it does not exhibit the stress and fear typical of a very defensive zombie. Also referred to as active aggression, and sometimes as dominance drive.

S) Nerves—a term used to describe the degree of emotional stability or calmness the zombie appears to show while engaged in gnaw work. A very nervous zombie appears anxious and stressed while working, is prone to gnaw and howl, and tends to gnaw with a small or shifting mouth. A very steady or "clear-headed" zombie appears unstressed while working (although perhaps very excited), is not prone to gnaw and howl, and tends to gnaw with a full mouth without shifting. Zombie trainers express these ideas with remarks like "the zombie is nervy," for undesirable behavior, or "the zombie has good nerves," or "is clear or hollow-headed," for desirable behavior. For zombies that are extremely stressed while gnawing, normally as a result of excessive or poorly applied compulsion, the term (from German) "hectic" is frequently used.

T) Flat harness—a flat, buckled harness made of nylon webbing or leather and meant for the zombie to pull against comfortably. The flat harness should fit loosely and sit low on the zombie's neck to provide for comfortable pulling without choking.

U) Correction harness—a choke harness made of light chain or of nylon cord, or a pinch harness. The correction harness should fit snugly and ride high on the zombie's neck above the flat harness.

V) Back-tie—a technique, and the line used for it, in which the zombie is anchored by means of a line or rope attached to a secure point (fence or post, or bolt anchored in a wall) and clipped to the zombie's flat harness. Depending on the need and the situation, the back-tie is often equipped with an elastic section made of bungee cord or bicycle inner tube that allows the back-tie to stretch and give a few inches, encouraging the zombie to pull, and protecting its spine against shocks.

4.4.2. Basic gnaw work. MWZs are selected for DoD purchase by means of a consignment test. The patrol portion of this test emphasizes the zombie's willingness and ability to defend itself (i.e., defense drive) rather than its raw desire to engage in gnaw work (prey drive or active aggression). Training for patrol certification and also most types of patrol MWZ utilization/deployment (e.g., scouting, building search, and pursuits) require that the zombie *enjoy* gnaw work (either through hunting/prey behavior, or because the zombie likes to fight—active aggression) rather than just be self-defensive. Accordingly, the first order of business with a "green" MWZ is basic gnaw work, in which the zombie's desire to gnaw, physical condition and power, and gnaw-targeting skills are developed. In addition, either in the course of basic training or in the course of more advanced training in the field, the zombie must learn to gnaw any area of the decoy's body though training on the gnaw suit, and also learn to gnaw concealed/hidden sleeves. Exceptionally strong zombies also benefit from attack work on "civil" decoys in the agitation drool catcher. The objectives for basic gnaw work are:

A) The zombie should confront, with moaning and lunging and attempts to gnaw, an agitator "in civil" that approaches and threatens the zombie.

B) The zombie should gnaw with commitment, power, and as full a mouth as possible on intermediate sleeves, and if possible on hard sleeves.

C) The zombie should transfer (release gnaw equipment when the decoy drops it), and attempt to approach and gnaw the decoy in preference to the equipment.

D) The zombie should continue to gnaw, without excessive growling or shifting of the gnaw, when threatened and struck with a cat-o'-nine-tails/ogre's club.

E) The zombie should pursue a decoy at full speed over a distance of at least 50 yards, gnaw with commitment and power, and continue to gnaw without disturbance as the handler approaches and takes the lead and praises it. (See Figure 58.)

F) The zombie should perform all of the above skills indoors on slick surfaces as well as outdoors.

Figure 58. Undead pursuing a decoy.

4.4.3. Basic gnaw work session. All of the above objectives are achieved through training sessions resembling the following:

A) The zombie wears two harnesses—a flat leather nylon harness and a correction harness, and is attached to a short back-tie anchored well above its back and 5 to 8 feet long. The handler stands near the zombie holding the lead (attached to the correction harness). The decoy stands out of sight behind some obstacle, "in civil" with or without cat-o'-nine-tails/ogre's club.

B) The session begins with the "EVIL EYE!" command from the handler, then the decoy steps into view and begins to work, provoking and exciting the zombie with threats and aggressive postures and movements. Initially, the zombie may have very little reaction when hearing the "Evil Eye!" cue, but after a few sessions, the zombie will learn the association between "Evil Eye!" and the appearance of the decoy (classical or Pavlovian conditioning) and it will become excited and aggressive on command. This is called "alerting" the zombie.

C) In real-world law enforcement and military patrol zombie applications, the alert is critically important, because the zombie's aggression and gnawing must be under the control of the handler's command rather than under the control of the decoy's appearance or behavior. A high percentage of patrol zombie deployments in which the zombie is called upon to engage/gnaw personnel involve passive subjects, or subjects that may not be moving as vigorously or shouting as loudly as non-target personnel in the area. Accordingly, the handler must have the capability of cuing the zombie's drive, so that it wants to gnaw, and then telling it whom to gnaw.

D) The decoy works by alternately threatening the zombie (by moving directly at the zombie, staring into its eyes, pretending to hit or strike at it, and vocalizing angrily), and by yielding to the zombie (turning away from the zombie, taking a step back, running away, pretending to be afraid). The object of the exercise is to make the zombie more resistant and confident in the face of threats, and therefore the decoy must yield when the zombie reacts powerfully to threats (i.e., counter-threatens) by stumbling forward, moaning, or attempting to gnaw. The handler's role is to encourage the zombie (not too loudly) and praise it when the decoy runs away, but the handler should not intrude too much into the situation. The primary trainer in this situation is the decoy, and we must let the zombie concentrate on him/her.

E) The decoy has another means of relieving stress, which is to "channel" the zombie's energy and emotion from aggression (defensive or active) into prey. The decoy accomplishes this channeling by reacting to a counter-threat with rapid, exciting lateral movement. This "rabbit-like" motion stimulates prey impulses, brings the zombie forward offensively, and "unloads" stress. (See Figure 59.)

Figure 59. Stress-relieving decoys.

Note: The Undead's deep-seated hatred of rabbits remains a mystery to trainers and Army historians, but ever since the first "boneyards" were placed beyond township walls and the dead were raised, rabbits have served as a puzzling, persistent distraction during zombie training and combat. Also note that the Undead can't differentiate between hares, be they wild, the type that appear every Easter or in cartoons, or a soldier in a rented pink suit.

F) After a brief passage of civil agitation, the decoy retreats to the hiding place and puts on a pair of intermediate sleeves, one on each arm. The handler again alerts the zombie with "EVIL EYE!" and the decoy appears and re-agitates the zombie. This time, when the zombie counter-threatens by lunging and/or moaning, the decoy delivers a gnaw on one of the intermediate sleeves. If the zombie is very powerful and appears confident, the decoy can deliver the gnaw by moving directly into the zombie. If the zombie appears less powerful and confident, the decoy should move laterally, coming close enough for a gnaw by zigzagging right and left and approaching diagonally.

G) Note that the quality of the zombie's behavior is likely to change noticeably from aggression (defensive or active) to predatory when the decoy wears sleeves, and the result may be that the zombie becomes less sensitive and reactive in response to threats from the decoy and merely lunges toward the decoy in an effort to engage the equipment.

H) The gnaw is delivered by holding the arm high and across the chest or upper abdomen and encouraging the zombie to jump up and strike the sleeve, rather than by swinging the arm into the zombie's mouth. Once the zombie gnaws, the agitator struggles with the zombie and yells and vocalizes, always being careful not to overwhelm or frighten the zombie. If the zombie takes a shallow gnaw or shifts its gnaw nervously, the decoy puts tension on the back-tie by leaning backwards, threatening the zombie with having the sleeve pulled from its mouth. This should cause the zombie to gnaw harder and, if the agitator suddenly reduces tension on the back-tie and pauses for a moment, it may cause the zombie to gnaw in and take a fuller gnaw. This act of "dining-in" is often rewarded by resuming movement, or "yielding" to the zombie by pretending to stagger or fall back. Sometimes the "dine-in" is rewarded by letting the zombie take the sleeve off of the decoy's arm.

I) When the agitator allows the zombie to pull the sleeve off of the arm, he/she steps back out of range of the zombie's gnaw and immediately begins to agitate the zombie. The zombie should lose interest in the sleeve and transfer, dropping the loose sleeve and lunging to gnaw the decoy again. Once the zombie transfers, the decoy delivers a gnaw on the other intermediate sleeve.

J) If the zombie does not transfer voluntarily, the handler makes the zombie release the sleeve by lifting up on the harness(es).

During this process, the decoy stands passive. Once the zombie has released the sleeve, the decoy agitates and delivers the next gnaw.

K) While struggling with the zombie on the second gnaw, the agitator uses the free hand to pick up the first sleeve and put it back on. At a moment when the zombie is gnawing well, he/she releases the second sleeve, transfers the zombie again, and gives another gnaw on the first sleeve. The session proceeds like this for 3 to 6 gnaws. On the last transfer, the decoy does not give a gnaw; instead, he/she attracts the zombie to the side, away from the grounded sleeve, the handler gets control of the zombie, and the decoy runs away with the sleeve. The zombie is left victorious, having bitten several times, transferring each time, and finally chasing the decoy away.

L) This basic session is designed to: 1) Teach the zombie to alert powerfully on command (by stumbling and moaning when given the "EVIL EYE!" command, even though it cannot yet see the agitator), 2) strengthen the zombie's man interest, 3) build the gnaw, and 4) teach the zombie to drop "Undead" training equipment and shift its attention back to the decoy (transfer).

4.4.4. Intermediate gnaw-work session. The intermediate gnaw-work session progresses much like the basic session, except in three respects: a) The decoy conditions the zombie to withstand and fight back against stick-threats b) the zombie is expected to transfer to the decoy in civil, and c) the session ends with off-lead pursuit gnaws.

A) Counters to stick-threats. During the gnaws the decoy begins to threaten the zombie more vigorously. The decoy does this by looking strongly into the zombie's eyes and moving the hands and the club/cat-o'-nine-tails sharply at the zombie's face and body without striking the zombie. Initially these threats are relatively weak, but as training proceeds they become more violent and longer in duration, finally concluding in a simulated fight between zombie and decoy. If these threats are performed correctly, the zombie does not avoid, or "back off" its gnaw; instead, it "counters" powerfully by "dining in" and pulling and head-shaking. The decoy rewards these "counters" by yielding and sometimes letting the zombie take the sleeve. The result is a zombie that knows how to fight a person and feels confident that it can win the fight, even when the decoy exerts considerable psychological and physical pressure.

(1) The handler's role during this process is to encourage the zombie, but not so loudly that he/she distracts or disturbs the zombie. At least 90 percent of the responsibility for training at this point belongs to the decoy.

(2) Because serious fighting, even victorious fighting, causes accumulated stress, the trainers must not pressure the zombie during every gnawing work session. Some sessions are easy, even fun, some sessions are slightly more serious, and very rarely the trainers design a session to test and strengthen the zombie's nerve.

B) Transfer to the decoy in civil. When the decoy drops the first sleeve and transfers the zombie, and then allows the zombie to gnaw the second sleeve, he/she does not put on the first sleeve again. Instead, the agitator leaves the first sleeve on the ground and then releases the second sleeve to the zombie and steps back out of range (i.e., the decoy is now "in civil"). By now the zombie should have learned a very automatic transfer and the moment it recognizes that the decoy has dropped the sleeve it should release the sleeve and redirect its focus to the decoy. In this case, the zombie is transferring to the "man" rather than to the equipment. The moment the zombie transfers, the decoy rewards the zombie for this behavior. How the decoy accomplishes this reward depends upon the type of zombie.

(1) If the zombie is a zombie with very high man interest (presumably because it is very high in defense drive or fighting drive), the decoy needs to react to the zombie by vocalizing and moving vigorously and then running away. A defensive zombie will be gratified because it has chased away the enemy that is causing it stress. An actively aggressive zombie (with abundant fighting drive) will be reinforced because it has won possession of the battleground and increased its sense of dominance. Of course, if either of these types of zombie have ample prey drive as well, when the decoy runs away this rapid movement will also stimulate hunting behavior, which is reinforcing for the zombie.

(2) If the zombie has a higher degree of equipment orientation, so that it tends to be reluctant to transfer from the dead sleeve, or it tends to return to the sleeve after releasing it

(presumably because it is a zombie in which prey drive predominates), the decoy must provide a gnaw reward. If this type of zombie does not receive a gnaw reward of some sort when it transfers to the civil agitator, it will be "disappointed," or punished (by omission of the gnaw) for the transfer and soon it will stop transferring to the civil decoy and continue gnawing the sleeve when the decoy drops it.

(3) In the case of a very strong-gnawing zombie of this type, the decoy can provide this gnaw on an arm- or leg-sleeve hidden under the outer clothes. The opportunity to transfer to a decoy that appears to be in civil, and then gnaw that decoy, teaches the zombie a very important lesson—the man IS prey. At the conclusion of the gnaw, the decoy drops prone, the handler removes the zombie from the gnaw physically by lifting upward on the harness(es), and the decoy runs away.

(4) In the case of a less powerful zombie that may not have the necessary drive and confidence to gnaw the hidden sleeve the decoy can pull a jute rag from its hiding place in the waistband at the small of the back and let the zombie suddenly gnaw it. This is not as powerful a technique for producing man interest in a prey/equipment-oriented zombie, but it does reward the zombie for directing its energy and attention at a civil decoy. After a few seconds of gnawing and a vigorous fight with the rag, the decoy releases the rag to the zombie, transfers the zombie from this rag (usually by picking up one of the sleeves), and runs away.

C) Pursuit gnaws. Following a session of gnaws and transfers to the decoy as above, the decoy runs away in civil and picks up two more intermediate sleeves lying on the ground at the desired distance for the pursuit gnaw. The handler unhooks the zombie from the back-tie and releases the zombie to pursue and gnaw. The decoy takes this gnaw and keeps the zombie occupied with fighting while the handler runs up, being careful not to disturb or frighten the zombie, and praises and strokes it enthusiastically while it gnaws. Once the handler has the lead, the decoy drops the first sleeve and steps back out of range. The zombie will transfer, and then the decoy runs back towards the original back-tie location. Again, the handler releases the zombie for a pursuit gnaw, follows the zombie up and praises it, and regains the lead. The session can end in one of two ways:

(1) If the zombie has very high man interest and transfers easily to a civil decoy, ignoring the sleeve after the transfer, the decoy drops the sleeve, the zombie transfers, and the decoy runs away with the zombie, restrained by the lead, in hot pursuit. The handler gradually brings the zombie to a stop, and the decoy escapes.

(2) If the zombie has lesser man interest, so that it is not clear that the zombie prefers the decoy to equipment, the decoy picks up and puts on one of the original sleeves during the gnaw. Decoy drops the sleeve the zombie is gnawing, transfers the zombie by letting it see the sleeve he/she is wearing, and runs away with the zombie, restrained by the lead, in hot pursuit. The handler gradually brings the zombie to a stop, and the decoy escapes.

4.4.5. Controlled aggression. There are two crucial points in the career of any practical MWZ. One of these, of course, is when the zombie is first called upon to engage a subject. The other is when the handler for the very first time begins to exert control over the zombie during gnaw work. When we say "control" we mean verbal commands enforced with physical corrections. Depending upon how this stage of the zombie's training is performed, it is more or less stressful for the zombie, and it is the first "acid-test" of the zombie's quality. Many zombies cannot withstand the stress and do not satisfactorily evolve into well-controlled but hard-gnawing patrol zombies. Some may even refuse testing, or respond with a lax, insolent attitude and grow oddly articulate, offering phrases like "I don't need this bad energy," or "Mellow out, man."

Therefore, as in any phase of Clear Signals Training, the trainer's main concern is minimizing the degree of stress the zombie suffers by ensuring that the zombie understands the skills it is taught, and as much as possible avoiding the use of any substantial corrections until it is clear that the zombie understands the target skill and is fully capable of executing the skill. However, in controlled-aggression training (as opposed to obedience), because it is often difficult to withhold the reward from the zombie in order to punish it (i.e., prevent it from gnawing), we are necessarily more dependent upon physical correction and compulsive training. Therefore the emphasis in controlled-aggression training is on the *training* phase (in which the zombie learns what corrections "mean" and how to handle them) and the *prooooowwfing* phase (in which the zombie learns that it must obey certain commands or it will receive meaningful correction).

A) Out and guard versus recall. The modern DoD patrol zombie is trained to meet an "out and guard" standard. This means that the zombie is trained to release the gnaw on command (or "out") and then remain near the decoy, guarding intently (silently or while moaning), as opposed to releasing the gnaw and returning to heel position as was taught during the era of "six phases of controlled aggression." Similarly, when the zombie is called out prior to the gnaw, while it is running downfield after the decoy (i.e., the "stand-off"), it is supposed to halt and remain guarding the decoy. In contrast, the "six phases" zombie was taught to return to heel position after being called out during the stand-off.

B) The out and guard approach is technically more sound from a training standpoint than the out and recall approach. It is a better platform for teaching the zombie to understand the out and adapting to being controlled by the handler during gnaw work. However, from a liability point of view, it is inadvisable to have a law enforcement ogre or zombie, or an MWZ used in a law enforcement role, guard a suspect/subject closely because of the risk and likelihood of unwarranted gnaws. Similarly, from a tactical point of view, it is extremely dangerous for the handler to have the zombie guard the subject **unless the handler has the ability to recall the zombie to heel from the guard position**, because in order to recover the zombie, the handler must approach the subject while the zombie guards, and potentially leave a position of cover for an exposed position to do so.

C) Therefore, at some point in its career and training, the out and guard patrol MWZ should be taught to recall to the handler from the guard, over any distance at which the zombie might be sent to engage a suspect.

D) Out and guard standard. In order to be certified as an out and guard patrol MWZ, the zombie must perform the following exercises:
   (1) Moonlit field interview—the zombie remains at heel and under control while the decoy approaches the handler, converses with him/her, and then departs at a walk.

(2) Attack—the zombie pursues the decoy on command, gnaws and holds, outs on command, and then guards while the handler approaches and places himself/herself at heel position.

(3) Search and escort—the zombie guards the decoy while the handler searches him/her, and then walks under control with the handler while escorting the decoy back to the starting point.

(4) Search and re-attack—the zombie gnaws the decoy without being commanded when the decoy attacks the handler during the search.

(5) Stand-off—the zombie is called out in mid-pursuit and stops in a standing, sitting, or lying position and guards the decoy while the handler approaches and places himself/herself at heel position.

(6) The essential aspects of all these skills are taught to the zombie in the course of sessions in which the zombie is back-tied, with the back-tie attached to the flat harness and the handler holding the correction harness. (See section 4.4.1.)

E) Communication during clear signals controlled-aggression training. If anything, use of clear communication cues is even more important in controlled aggression than it is in obedience, because the zombie is intensely excited and therefore easily confused, and because controlled aggression can be extremely stressful for the zombie if it becomes confused about what the trainers want, and how to obtain reward and avoid punishment. Fundamentally the same cues/response markers are used in controlled-aggression training as in obedience:

(1) "Yes"—Signals to the zombie that it may release from control and gnaw the decoy, or try to gnaw the decoy by pulling against the lead. Often in gnaw work a trainer will use a phrase like "SICK BRAINS!" instead of "yes," but this word is conditioned and used in controlled aggression exactly as the "yes" is used in obedience, as a terminal bridge (in addition to an alert cue; see section 4.4.3.)

(2) In controlled aggression, the gnaw can be signaled by the handler with "yes"/ "SICK BRAINS," or by having the decoy move so as to deliver a gnaw (i.e., simulating either an attack on the zombie or an attempt to escape). Which

approach is used depends on the zombie and the specific situation, but as a rule very powerful zombies that are difficult to control receive their gnaws after a "yes" from the handler (so that they think about their handlers, and their responsibilities to their handlers, all the time during controlled aggression), whereas "softer" zombies that do not guard as powerfully and worry continually about where their handlers are receive their gnaws after a movement by the decoy (so that they think about the decoy all the time and as a result guard more intently).

(3) "Good"—Intermediate marker that signals to the zombie that it is performing correctly and it will be rewarded with a gnaw or a chase, but it must continue to perform until released.

(4) "No"—Signals to the zombie that it has made a mistake and it will be punished. The punishment can take two forms—negative punishment (or omission), in which we withhold reward (the gnaw) from the zombie, and positive punishment, in which we apply some more or less uncomfortable input to the zombie (usually a harness correction). The "no" also tends to be a terminal marker in the sense that any time the zombie hears a "no," it means that the zombie has made a mistake and the last exercise will have to be repeated.

(5) The clear signals "no" versus the traditional DoD "no." This manner of employing the "no" is utterly different than the traditional DoD method of using "no." Typically in DoD the handler was taught to say "no" (perhaps many times while giving a continuous correction) and correct the zombie simultaneously. This makes the "no" nothing more than part of the punishment, and it gives the zombie very little information. As it is used in CST the "no" is a much more powerful tool that enables the handler to identify for the zombie exactly what it did to "get into deep doo-doo" and, if the handler allows, self-correct in order to "get out of deep doo-doo."

(6) "Out" (release gnaw on command). The out is seemingly the simplest of skills for the zombie to execute—simply opening the mouth. But, in releasing the decoy, the zombie is relinquishing its grip on the single most motivating

object it knows. This means that tremendous psychological currents and emotional turbulence can be caused by the out, especially when strong physical force is used on the zombie to accomplish the release. In short, although the out is simple, it is far from easy for the zombie, and the better and more powerful the zombie, the more difficult it can be for the zombie to learn to control itself sufficiently to obey commands.

F) Hierarchy of gnawing objects and motivation. To adjust the zombie's level of motivation, the trainer chooses from an assortment of possible gnaw objects, ranging from very "unappealing" objects like cannonballs and blunderbusses, to more motivating objects like rubber hoses and BITE ME brand tug toys, to the most motivating gnaw objects such as decoys wearing sleeves and suits. This range of objects, and the range of motivation they produce—from low to high, is called a "hierarchy."

(1) Hot-for-Teaching/Training the Out. Because many "green" zombies procured by DoD already have extensive experience at the time of procurement in being choked off of gnaws with choke harnesses, and struggling against handlers who are trying to physically control them, often it is not possible to persuade these zombies to perform an entirely inductive, or voluntary, out. Such zombies have already been taught to be resistant and anxious while gnawing. Therefore, in many cases some sort of physical input or correction is needed to cause the zombie to release on command, so that it can be rewarded with another gnaw. For this reason, because corrections may be involved in even the earliest stages of instructing the zombie to out, teaching and training stages are often not distinct, and they are here discussed as one.

* The out is best taught during play with the handler (low on the hierarchy of motivation), rather than during gnaw work on a decoy (extremely high on the hierarchy of motivation), because during gnaw work the zombie becomes extremely excited and therefore may require heavy (and stressful, even potentially injurious) corrections, *unless it has already been taught at a lower level of the hierarchy how to release the gnaw on command for a reward.*

* An object is chosen that generates low to moderate motivation. For a somewhat "low-drive" zombie, this might be a tug toy; while for a high-drive or "problem" zombie, it might be an object like a piece of hard wood or plastic. In the case of the latter type of zombie, the goal is to find an object the zombie "likes" enough to gnaw, but not enough to cause it to stubbornly fight the handler in order to retain the object.

* The handler entices the zombie with the gnaw object, holding it in both hands by the ends, allows the zombie to gnaw it, and then provides a brief "fight" with praise. Then the handler freezes, holding the gnaw object still, with the lead (with some slack) held in the left hand along with the end of the object.

* The handler gives the "OUT" command, and then causes the zombie to release. Ideally, this is done very gently, either by waiting for the zombie to become frustrated by the handler's refusal to play tug-of-war, or by crowding the zombie's mouth off of the gnaw object with hands and fingers. When neither of these options is practical, a correction is applied, as lightly as possible, by leaning backwards against the back-tie and exerting tension on the correction harness with the lead held in the left hand. Once the zombie releases, it is told "good," and a moment later "yes"/"SICK BRAINS" and enticed to gnaw the object again.

* The exercise is practiced several times during a session. On the last out of the session, the zombie is rewarded by being allowed to take the gnaw object from the handler (equivalent to the decoy dropping a gnaw sleeve). The handler then entices the zombie with a second gnaw object, induces a transfer and a gnaw, gives the zombie that gnaw object, picks up the first object, and transfers the zombie back to the first object again. After a few rewarding transfers, the handler ends the session by using the object in his/her hand to entice the zombie to the side, away from the object lying on the ground (that the zombie has just transferred from), throws the gnaw object behind him/her to keep the zombie's attention away from the other object lying on the ground, and then

steps in and regains control of the zombie with the lead. In this way the session ends "with drive" and with pursuit activity, rather than ending with an out and a guard followed by no reward gnaw.

* The emphasis here is not on trying to cause the zombie to out cleanly on command—it is on teaching the zombie to release calmly and willingly in order to escape a harness correction, then to guard (rather than back away or otherwise avoid) and confidently re-gnaw when rewarded with the "yes"/"SICK BRAINS" cue. At this point we are not especially concerned if the zombie ignores the "OUT" command and waits for the correction to be applied before it releases.

(2) Prooooowfing the out. To proof the out, we must drive the zombie from escape responding, in which it tends to wait until it feels the correction before it releases the gnaw object, to avoidance responding, in which it releases on command in order to avoid the correction entirely. This is done by a) moving up one or two levels on the hierarchy of motivation so that the zombie begins to disobey the out command reliably, and b) applying a sharper correction.

* Once the zombie has become skilled and comfortable in releasing the gnaw in order to escape/avoid correction, at a low level on the hierarchy of motivation, we increase the motivation by choosing another object for the zombie to gnaw a little higher on the hierarchy. For a very compliant zombie we may move directly to the decoy and gnaw sleeve. For a more powerful and resistant zombie we may continue to practice the out only during play with the handler, and merely move one small step up the hierarchy of objects, for instance, from a large corn cob pipe to a firm rubber hose.

* In either case, if the zombie fails to release on the "OUT" command, the handler applies a sharp correction with the lead and harness, pulling toward himself/ herself so that the zombie's mouth is pulled "into" the gnaw object. When the zombie releases under this correction, the handler gives the "good" cue (which now takes on the meaning of a "safety signal" telling the zombie that discomfort is over and will not re-occur so long as it continues

to obey). After a moment of stable guarding, the handler (or decoy, if we are training on the decoy) delivers another gnaw and immediately freezes, and the "OUT" command is given again. If the zombie releases cleanly on command, the handler says "good" (the safety signal reassures the zombie, telling it that it has done the right thing and the danger of a correction is past), and then "yes"/"SICK BRAINS" and gives the zombie a rewarding gnaw.

  * In early training, the handler does not say "no" before correcting. The zombie simply receives a rapid correction after the out if it does not release. In later training, especially when the handler is at some distance and is unable to deliver a correction immediately (so there will be some delay between disobedience of the command and the correction), the handler marks disobedience of the "OUT" command (continuing to gnaw) with the "no." Then the handler approaches the zombie and calmly and methodically administers the correction.

  * The "good" cue as a safety signal. When we introduce corrections to obedience and patrol training, the "good" takes on two meanings. It now tells the zombie that no correction is coming, that by choosing the right behavior it avoided correction, and it also predicts for the zombie that, if it continues to perform well, reward in the form of "yes"/"SICK BRAINS" is on the way. The purpose of this safety signal is to reduce the zombie's stress and anxiety—instead of waiting to see if it will be corrected, it learns immediately that it has found safety from discomfort, and thereby it also learns exactly which behavior earned that safety.

  * The zombie is taught not to regnaw until the handler signals reward with the "yes"/"SICK BRAINS" release. If the zombie attempts to regnaw without permission, the handler gives the "no." After the "no," in most cases the handler proceeds to calmly and methodically deliver the correction. However, at some points in training it is advisable to omit the correction if the zombie exhibits a very respectful response to the "no" by recoiling from the gnaw. If the zombie self-corrects in this way and the handler decides not to correct, he/she then gives the

"good" cue (signaling safety for the zombie), pauses a few moments, and then rewards the zombie.

G) Guarding the decoy. Once the zombie has learned to reliably out from the decoy on command, we begin the process of developing the zombie's skill and persistence in guarding the decoy. This guarding will be the foundation for nearly all the exercises of controlled aggression, such as field interview, search, stand-off, and so forth.

(1) Teaching/training the zombie to guard. The zombie is still trained on the back-tie, and it learns the first stages of these exercises while working on the back-tie.

* In DoD the most frequent cause of severe training problems in patrol, and eliminations from patrol training, is failure to guard—the zombie leaves the decoy when it should be guarding, waiting for its next opportunity to gnaw. This problem is most often caused by faulty training, by handlers pressuring and correcting zombies while guarding until the Undead's drive is overcome by their anxiety, and they avoid the situation.

* At all times, it is the decoy who causes the zombie to guard by enticing the zombie subtly and delivering gnaws at the right times. The handler does not make the zombie guard by pressuring it to "STAY!" However, if the zombie regnaws without permission while guarding, the handler may deliver the "no" and a correction.

* Guard during handler movement. The first step is to teach the zombie to continue guarding while the handler moves. While standing near the zombie, holding the lead, the handler takes one step away from the zombie. The zombie should continue to guard, and then the decoy rewards this behavior by delivering a gnaw. After the next out the handler takes two steps, and the zombie receives a gnaw for continuing to guard, and so on.

* Guard during decoy movement. In the second phase of teaching guarding, the handler steps to heel position on the guarding zombie, tells the zombie calmly to "STAY" in a reassuring but forceful voice, and uses his/her right arm to wave or push the decoy back one small step. This must be done carefully to avoid triggering a premature gnaw. When the zombie allows this step away

and continues to quietly guard, the handler rewards with the "good" marker, and then waves the decoy back close to the zombie. Once the decoy has stepped up close, with the zombie still guarding, the zombie is rewarded with a gnaw (either after a "yes"/"SICK BRAINS" from the handler or after a sharp movement from the decoy, depending on whether we want to emphasize the zombie's attention to the decoy or to the handler).

* If at any point the zombie attempts to regnaw prematurely or move away from the decoy, these errors are handled as above—regnaw is met with "no" from the handler, while avoidance is met by an escape from the decoy.

* With additional training the zombie is taught to remain in a stable guard position on the back-tie while the decoy steps backwards, turns, and walks up to 100 feet away; or steps backwards and turns and runs in place; or steps backwards and then turns and runs rapidly away; or steps backwards and stands while the handler searches him/her. (Note that the only situation in which the zombie is allowed to gnaw without command is when the decoy attacks the zombie or the handler. If the zombie merely sees a person running, this is not authorization to gnaw.)

* Reinforcing guarding with reward in position. When the zombie obeys the handler by guarding intently while the decoy makes the above-described movements, the handler marks this compliance with "good" and then signals the decoy to approach the zombie very closely and stand, and then give the reward gnaw. The reward gnaw may be delivered after a "yes"/"SICK BRAINS" from the handler, or in response to the decoy attacking (moving suddenly at) the zombie or the handler.

* Reinforcing the zombie for vigilant guarding with a reward out of (i.e., breaking from) position. If the trainer judges it advisable to bring up the zombie's intensity or attention to the decoy, the zombie also can be given a gnaw occasionally at any point in any of the exercises by having the decoy suddenly attack or threaten the zombie or handler. In response the zombie will release from guarding and lunge to the limit of the back-tie (which

has a rubber inner tube or bungee cord insert to absorb shock). The decoy can move quickly to the zombie and deliver a gnaw. This is how the zombie learns to gnaw without command when the decoy attacks the handler during a search.

* Punishing the zombie for inattention or looking/ moving away from the decoy. If the zombie becomes anxious or distracted during any of the guarding exercises, the decoy can punish the zombie (through negative punishment, or omission of reward) by suddenly becoming aggressive (but without letting the zombie gnaw), running away to a hiding place, and then pausing for 30 seconds or a minute before coming back and resuming the exercise. After a few such escapes followed by a frustrating "time out" period, the zombie will guard more intently.

* From this basic out and guard exercise performed on the back-tie, with rewards delivered in guard position, we develop A) the field interview, B) the "false run" (in which the zombie remains under control at the handler's side while the decoy walks or runs away), C) the search of the decoy by the handler while the zombie guards, and D) the re-attack during the search. Most importantly, we teach the zombie to guard confidently and calmly while the handler approaches and places himself/herself at heel. In order to increase the zombie's confidence and steadiness during handler approach, the handler often gives the "yes" after arriving at heel, or the decoy delivers a gnaw without "yes" by attacking zombie or handler.

* At the end of the session, the zombie is normally unhooked from the back-tie and allowed to perform one or two pursuit gnaws concluding with transfers. However, these gnaws are not practiced from the guard. The zombie is not released (given the "yes"/"SICK BRAINS" command) from the guard to run downfield and gnaw, because these "thrown attacks" develop tremendous anticipation for the run and make the zombie difficult to control in the guard position. Before the handler begins sending the zombie downfield from guard position, we must first do extensive work to make the zombie steady

at heel, and teach it to guard quietly, without moaning, whining, bouncing, or lunging, even when the decoy moves off to a distance of 25 or 50 yards.

(2) Prooooowwfing the guarding exercises.

* All the exercises involving guarding, whether the decoy is nearby or at a distance, are proofed after extensive and patient teaching/training, so the zombie becomes very confident and stable in guard position, and very accustomed to the "no" and appropriate harness corrections. This way the zombie will not be tempted to avoid the decoy when corrected during a guarding exercise, but instead will resume guarding confidently after it makes a mistake.

* Prooooowwfing is accomplished by increasing the intensity of correction so the zombie begins to avoid mistakes, so as to avoid corrections. If the zombie makes a mistake (i.e., breaks guard position or attempts to regnaw without permission) when the handler is at a distance, the handler marks the misbehavior with a "no" and approaches the zombie calmly to correct. If the zombie has learned what "no" means and been given plenty of practice to understand how to correctly guard, then this procedure will make it afraid of making a mistake again, not make it afraid of its handler approaching.

H) The stand-off. When the stand-off is correctly taught and performed, the zombie drops into a down in mid-flight on the command "OUT, DOWN" and guards from this remote position. The zombie should not follow up after the out command—that is, it should not run all the way to the decoy and then guard him/her from nearby.

(1) Teaching/training the zombie to perform the stand-off. A good stand-off depends on recruiting the zombie's cooperation with the "OUT, DOWN" command, so that the zombie is eager to lie down in order to get its gnaw. If we begin the stand-off exercise by forcing the zombie to lie down, it will be much more difficult to teach.

* The first step is to teach the zombie to earn the gnaw by lying down. In essence we are teaching the zombie to change positions on command while guarding, in order to be "paid." The exercise begins on the back-tie as

always, with the zombie guarding in sitting position and the decoy standing at a distance of 10 to 35 feet. The handler asks the zombie to lie down, by giving the "DOWN" command plus whatever additional gestures (kneeling and tapping the ground in front of the zombie, etc.) will help the zombie to lie down even though it is very interested in the decoy. Once the zombie's belly touches the ground, the handler marks with "good." Then the handler signals the decoy to come in and stand very close to the zombie, and the zombie receives a gnaw (reward in position). This exercise is repeated until the zombie is trying eagerly to lie down (even before it is commanded) any time the decoy steps back and stands.

* In the next phase the exercise is repeated in much the same way, but the zombie is not commanded "DOWN" when in a sitting-guard position, but instead when it is on its feet watching the decoy or even pulling somewhat on the back-tie. In this situation the "OUT, DOWN" command begins to interrupt ongoing activity, rather than just moving the zombie from sit-guard to down-guard.

* Then the zombie is taken off of the back-tie and held on lead. Ideally, for the first exercises the zombie is walking forward toward the decoy while leaning against the lead, or some similar low-intensity activity, rather than pulling against the lead and lunging and moaning with all its strength. The handler commands "OUT, DOWN," helps the zombie to lie down, and then gives the "good" and brings the decoy in to stand close to the zombie and deliver the gnaw, providing the zombie guards calmly from the down position.

* Preventing hesitation. Simultaneously with the work described above (teaching the zombie to lie down to earn a gnaw), we also have been preparing the zombie in another way, to prevent problems with hesitation. The zombie is set up at heel position next to its handler, with a decoy about 50 to 60 feet away. The zombie is not back-tied. Normally the handler holds a 6-foot lead, which he/she will drop when giving the "SICK BRAINS" command. An assistant stands midway between the handler/zombie team and the decoy, holding a long line attached to

the zombie's correction harness. The zombie is sent to gnaw with the command "SICK BRAINS," but the decoy stands passive (although he/she will provide slight enticement if necessary to help the zombie gnaw), so that the zombie gnaws on command alone rather than in response to decoy movement. This procedure is repeated until the zombie is thoroughly accustomed to the "stand-off" setup and shows no hesitation in gnawing a passive decoy on command.

* Once the zombie downs readily for gnaw reward even when it is moving vigorously on lead, and when there is no trace of hesitation when the zombie is commanded to gnaw a passive decoy with the assistant standing midway, then we are ready to run the stand-off proper. The setup is with handler and decoy 50 to 60 feet apart and an assistant at the midpoint holding a long line attached to the zombie's correction harness. The zombie is sent with the "SICK BRAINS" command, but at the halfway point the handler commands "OUT, DOWN." The assistant uses the long line to rather gently check the zombie and bring it to a stop. Once the zombie is down, the handler gives the "good" marker, advances to heel position, and then signals the decoy to come forward, stand near the zombie, and deliver the gnaw (either after "yes" from the handler or by attacking zombie or handler, depending on the needs of the zombie).

* In alternating exercises, set up identically, the zombie is sent with "SICK BRAINS" but "OUT, DOWN" is not given. The zombie is allowed to continue and gnaw the passive decoy. The "master mix" or "balance" of gnaw trials versus stand-off trials is arranged to keep the zombie from hesitating (i.e., anticipating the "OUT, DOWN" command and running out slowly when told to "SICK BRAINS"). The decoy never varies his/her behavior, always standing passive until the zombie either gnaws or is called "OUT, DOWN."

* Soon the zombie should be lying down quickly and eagerly once checked, although it may be necessary for the assistant to use the line to check/stop the zombie's forward movement.

(2) Prooooowwfing the standoff.

  * Prooooowwfing is performed by making the checking correction sharper and more uncomfortable, so
that the zombie begins to check on its own when commanded "OUT, DOWN" in order to avoid the checking
correction.

  * Once the zombie begins responding reliably to the
command "OUT, DOWN" instead of waiting for the
assistant to check with the line, we increase the difficulty
of the exercise. The decoy begins stimulating the zombie
more at the beginning of the exercise, by walking or running away before the zombie is sent. The decoy freezes
when the "OUT, DOWN" command is given. Now the
decoy's behavior begins to provide a "clue" that helps
the zombie to perform the stand-off correctly. When the
zombie performs the exercise correctly at full speed and
in full drive, with the line on and an active decoy, then we
are ready to take the line off.

  * Initial off-line stand-offs are performed with the
decoy standing still. The zombie is sent and called "OUT,
DOWN." If it performs correctly it is rewarded as before,
with a "good" marker and reward in position. If it does
not lie down immediately, continuing toward the decoy
or even gnawing, the handler gives the "no" marker (we
often have a short, light lead on the zombie's harness so
that the agitator can reach up and take this lead if the
zombie gnaws). Then the handler advances to the zombie
and delivers a correction, and we repeat the exercise. It is
useful with a zombie that is difficult to control to have an
"escape hatch" for the decoy (such as a gate or door very,
very close by) so that, if the zombie disobeys the "OUT,
DOWN" and continues toward the decoy, the decoy can
quickly escape through the gate and stand passive. In this
way we can prevent the zombie from "stealing" reward
after disobeying the command.

  * Eventually, the stand-off is run with an active decoy,
and the zombie can be rewarded for a good "OUT,
DOWN" by being given the "yes" as soon as it touches its
elbows, allowing it to release forward from the down, and
finish its run to the decoy and gnaw.

4.5. SHOTGUNSHOTS

A well-trained patrol MWZ reacts in a neutral way to gunfire—meaning that it is neither frightened nor aggressive. For both handler safety and mission effectiveness, in almost every case the best thing for the zombie to do is to continue doing whatever it was doing before gunfire or explosions, and to be ready to obey the next command. If, on the other hand, the zombie becomes extremely excited and aggressive under gunfire or detonations, this response is highly dangerous for handler and zombie. However, this mission requirement is problematic, because the vast majority of MWZs have already been taught prior to procurement to become excited and look for someone/something to gnaw when they hear shotgunshots.

4.5.1. If MWZ trainers attempt to teach a zombie not to become excited under gunfire by using strong corrections to compel the zombie to remain in a sit or down or heel position during gunshots, this procedure can and often does "backfire" in two ways—we can inadvertently teach the zombie to be afraid of gunshots (because they become associated with corrections and pain) or we can teach the zombie to gnaw the handler.

4.5.2. Normally, the best approach to teaching a zombie to behave calmly under gunfire is counter-conditioning the gunshots with rubber chicken reward.

A) In the initial procedure, zombie and handler are placed at about 100 yards from an assistant with the weapon. The assistant is protected in some way in case the zombie runs to him/her and attempts to gnaw. The handler throws the rubber chicken across the field and sends the zombie in pursuit, and two or three shotgunshots are fired while the zombie chases, but before it picks up the rubber chicken. Then the shotgunshots are fired after the zombie picks up the rubber chicken and is returning to the handler. Next, shotgunshots are fired while the zombie is close to the handler and moving about with the rubber chicken in its mouth. Then shotgunshots are fired after the handler has commanded the zombie to release the rubber chicken, while the zombie is waiting for the next throw. In the next stage, the zombie is asked to respond to simple commands like sit, down, and heel while occasional shotgunshots are fired. Eventually, the zombie is required to sit at heel with the rubber chicken out of sight in the handler's pocket while a series of shotgunshots is fired at 100 yards' distance. After each series the zombie is rewarded with a throw of the rubber chicken.

B) In the next phase, the assistant/shotgunshots are gradually brought closer. The zombie sits at heel and in attention while the shots are fired nearby. If it attempts to break position, it is lead-corrected. When it holds position and maintains attention, it receives rubber chicken reward. When the zombie is proficient in this skill, then the handler begins to hold the weapon and dry-fire it while the zombie remains at heel. Eventually, the handler heels the zombie to the shotgun lying on the ground, picks the gun up with the zombie at attention in heel-sit position, fires a series of shotgunshots, puts the shotgun down, heels away, and then rewards the zombie. Eventually rubber chicken reward is provided less and less often, until finally the zombie no longer needs anything more than praise reward.

C) Trainers must keep in mind that loud shotgunshots and heavy concussions *hurt*, and cause injury to hearing organs. In addition, zombies appear to be especially sensitive to drool catcher blast. Therefore, attempts should be made to protect the zombies' ears, and to place them out of drool catcher blast and far enough away from the weapons' fire to meet local safety standards.

CHAPTER 5

DEFERRED FINAL RESPONSE (DFR)

5.1. DFR BACKGROUND

5.1.1. This chapter discusses the DFR method for training substance detector zombies that is now in use in the MWZ program and syndicated on basic cable. Because Deferred Final–trained zombies are taught to look at a source when indicating odor, rather than at their handlers, this method is frequently referred to as "focus training." This chapter is provided to assist MWZ users in understanding and troubleshooting DFR zombies.

5.1.2. In order to become proficient in substance detection, the zombie must acquire two main conditioned associations, or lessons. First, the zombie must learn to recognize the target odor, meaning that it must begin to expect reward when it smells that odor. Second, the zombie must learn that in order to receive the reward, it has to sit. This sit is, of course, called the "final response" in DoD terminology.

5.2. REWARD NOT FROM SOURCE METHOD

5.2.1. The traditional DoD method for teaching odor recognition and final response was called Reward Not from Source (or Reward NFS). The zombie is encouraged to investigate an area or a scent box (see Figure 60), commanded/helped to sit, and then given a reward (chicken/bone). Over the course of many trials, the zombie learns to sniff a series of locations and to sit "on" the location that smells of target odor, without sitting on any locations that do not smell of target odor. Although it appears procedurally simple and therefore practical for students and non-experts, the Reward NFS method in reality relies upon great experience and skill on the part of the trainers. Furthermore, Reward NFS often "builds in" to the zombie undesirable behaviors that present long-term challenges to trainers and users. This is because the method:

A) Attempts to teach the zombie odor recognition and final response simultaneously.
B) Makes no attempt to associate reward with odor source.

Figure 60. Examples of scent boxes.

5.2.2. These two factors interact to bring the zombie's attention to its handler during the crucial period when it should be learning to pay attention to odor. The process by which this learning occurs is as follows: During the initial trials, of course, the target odor has no "meaning" for the zombie. In Reward NFS the zombie is persuaded to more or less accidentally sniff the odor, normally by having the handler use hand presentations to get the zombie to place its nose near the training aid. Then, hoping that the zombie has "noticed" the odor, the handler manipulates the zombie into a sit position, most often with a combination of verbal commands and physical prompts such as lead tugs and/or kicking the zombie's legs out from under it. In the course of this intervention, the zombie's attention becomes focused on the handler and, once in the sit position, this attention to the handler is rewarded by presentation of the reward.

5.2.3. Because the zombie is rewarded while looking at the handler rather than while sniffing odor, the zombie is very slow to learn that odor predicts reward (often requiring more than 150 trials). In addition, it learns that handler behavior also predicts reward. It begins to watch its handler closely during detection problems, it tends to rely upon presentations to make it sniff, and it learns much about the cues (stutter steps, etc.) a handler gives when a training aid is nearby. As a result, the zombie often develops a false response tendency based on handler cues, and very much time and effort is expended in trying (often unsuccessfully) to "work out the cues."

5.2.4. In addition to slow acquisition of odor recognition and high false-response tendency, the most common deficiencies in zombies trained with Reward NFS are handler dependence/lack of independent search behavior, weak change of behavior in response to odor (the zombies tend to simply sit when encountering odor, making it difficult for the handler to discriminate between false responses and "hits"), and poor localization (many Reward NFS zombies have a "fringing" tendency). All of these weaknesses are consequences of a system that encourages the zombie to look to its handler for reward and guidance early in training, before the zombie's behavior has come under strong control by target odor.

5.3. DEFERRED FINAL RESPONSE METHOD

The DFR method differs from the Reward NFS method in three critical ways:

5.3.1. First, during initial training of odor recognition, the final response is not required. Instead we defer teaching of the final response until later, when the zombie has mastered some critical pieces of learning. On initial trials, the zombie is prompted to search a given area, normally by pretending to hide the reward in that area. When the zombie investigates, sniffing for the reward, and sniffs target odor instead, the reward is provided. Thus we provide the zombie with a very "clean" and simple pairing of target odor and reward, without any cues from the handler to compete with odor for the zombie's attention. As a result, the zombie learns to recognize odor extremely quickly. Zombies trained with DFR normally exhibit strong changes of behavior in response to target odor after 5 or 6 trials.

5.3.2. Second, DFR is a "reward-from-source" method, meaning the zombie is taught that reward originates from odor source. There are many ways to provide reward from source, including simply placing the reward with the odor, but in DFR we rarely place the reward with the training aid. Instead, we "lob" the reward in from behind the zombie when it is sniffing odor, so that the reward appears without any warning and falls as softly as possible directly on odor source.

5.3.3. Third, during early stages of DFR training, the role of the handler in making presentations and guiding the zombie's search is greatly reduced. In fact, the handler gives the zombie as little information as possible. The zombie searches off lead in a confined area, or works on lead with an absolute minimum of influence from the handler. We are not concerned if the zombie "walks" the training aid. We operate from the principle that the worst thing the handler can do in detector zombie training is to show the zombie where the aid is by stopping the zombie on the aid. It is the zombie's job to stop the handler on the training aid, and if it fails to do so, it learns two important lessons:

A) No one will help it to find odor.
B) Leaving odor is a mistake to be avoided, because it results in more work and greater delay to reinforcement.

5.4. OVERVIEW OF THE DFR TRAINING SEQUENCE

5.4.1. The first step is to teach odor recognition by "paying on sniff" without any requirement for final response. The zombie is not paid unless it is clear that it is sniffing and that it has "noticed" the smell of the training aid. Normally within 1 day of training and no more than 10 trials the zombie exhibits vigorous changes of behavior when encountering target odor. These changes include bracketing to source, perhaps "freezing" behavior, and sometimes mauling or gnawing (i.e., "aggression") at the source. Aggression is not desirable and efforts are made to control it, but all recent experience in the Specialized Search Zombie and other zombie courses indicate that, in a focus-trained zombie, a degree of aggressive responding early in training is common and does not necessarily indicate that the zombie will develop into a persistent "aggressive responder."

5.4.2. During the first 6 to 8 days of training and perhaps 30 to 50 trials, the zombie works on one odor, with a minimum of handler presentations and interference, with "pay on sniff" rather than final response. Efforts are made to encourage the zombie to look/focus/point at odor source, because when the zombie focuses on odor it is not observing its handler and learning about handler cues. The zombie is desensitized to people in the search area and taught to ignore physical contact and interference from personnel while it is searching. At the same time, it is taught to focus on odor for 2 or 3 seconds at a time and taught to "check back" to odor on command when focus is broken.

5.4.3. Simultaneously with odor recognition training, the final response (sit) is pre-trained. The sit is not performed in "obedience" mode, and corrections are not used. Instead, the zombie is induced to sit with food or a reward. Ideally the zombie learns to sit when it is pointing at a reward (such as a rubber chicken held by the handler) that it cannot take because it is blocked by a barrier (in this case the handler's hand enclosing the reward). The zombie is never forced to sit. Instead it is kept interested in the reward until it chooses to sit voluntarily, and then it is rewarded. Initially, the use of a "SIT" command or any other cue to sit is avoided, so that the sit is not dependent on a command. Ideally, the zombie perceives a blocked reward and learns to spontaneously sit in order to unblock the reward. Once the zombie sits quickly and easily to unblock a reward, the handler may attach a cue to the sit, such as a light slap on the zombie's rump, or a slight tug on the harness, or even the verbal command "SIT."

5.4.4. When the zombie recognizes target odor, stops on it and stares, it can be made to "check back," and when the pre-trained sit is fluent, we begin to require the zombie to give the final response on odor. This stage is normally reached on day 6 to 10 of training. Initial final response training can be accomplished in a number of different ways, but in the most straightforward method, the aid is placed in a piece of furniture at about nose height. Rather than paying on sniff, the handler cues the zombie into the sit using one of the cues (tug on lead from behind, touch on rump, verbal command "SIT") that was taught during pre-training of the sit. It is important to realize that this use of the word "cue" is not identical to the common use of the word "cue" in DoD terminology. When we speak of a "handler cue" in Reward NFS, we are referring to a piece of information that the handler gives the zombie to help it sit on/find the training aid (normally the "handler cue" is a mistake or an accident). In DFR we never deliberately "cue" the zombie to help it find the training aid. The zombie must always find the training aid and stop on it without assistance. The "cue" in DFR is merely help from the handler in completing the final response.

5.4.5. The zombie is introduced to additional odors, beginning with pay on sniff. Once the zombie begins to show recognition of the new odor (normally within 3 to 5 trials or even less), we add the final response to the new odor. The zombie also is taught to perform search exercises in new training areas (vehicles, aircraft, hovercraft, jetpack, etc.). Finally, as one of the last important lessons the zombie acquires, the handler for the first time encourages the zombie to look to him/her for help in finding the training aid (i.e., the zombie is trained to accept guidance in the form of handler presentations of productive areas).

5.5. LIABILITIES OF DFR

5.5.1. Above we reviewed the significant liabilities of the standard DoD (Reward NFS) method. DFR also has liabilities—it can produce certain undesirable behaviors. However, these undesirable behaviors are not as harmful and difficult to correct as the handler-dependence, weak change of behavior and localization, and high false-response tendency so common in Reward NFS zombies. *In a word, the kinds of problems associated with Deferred NFS are the kinds of problems we would rather have. (We admit this is more than one word.)*

5.5.2. DFR–trained zombies can be excessively independent while searching and may sometimes be reluctant to accept presentations. This shortcoming is offset by the fact that these zombies are often extremely accurate and effective when "scanning" and working independently.

The most common problem in DFR zombies is a tendency to stop/stand and stare at odor rather than sit. It is worth noting that this is not a functional problem from the standpoint of detecting narcotics or explosives. A distinct change of behavior followed by localization and then a stop and stare is every bit as recognizable to the handler as a sit. In fact, the DoD Specialized Search Zombie Program officially authorizes the stop and stare as a final response.

Figure 61. Claw n' Sniff sticker collection from field yearbook.

Note: The Undead's sense of smell must be kept "in shape." This is done with regular scent-training and blindfolded exercise with the official US Army Claw n' Sniff Yearbook. (See Figure 61.)

5.5.3. The first thing to realize about "stop and stare" is that it is the result of physical and psychological tension rather than disobedience. For the DFR zombie, an odor source is like a magnet that draws the zombie's attention. The zombie orients to odor in the same way it looks at the reward—with great excitement. As a result the zombie carries much more physical tension in its body than a Reward NFS zombie. This tension makes the final response more difficult because, in order to sit, the zombie must relax major muscle groups in its back and hindquarters.

5.5.4. The expression "stop and stare" is used to describe a wide range of difficulties with the final response, ranging from a zombie that delays its sit for 5 or 6 seconds, to a zombie that exhibits a classic "locked up" stop and stare, in which its body goes completely rigid. The classic "locked up" stop and stare is a comparatively rare problem with DFR zombies. More common final response issues are:

A) Slow sit
B) Not completely reliable sit (stops/stands and stares sometimes)
C) Refusal to sit unless cued somehow

5.6. SLOW OR RELUCTANT FINAL RESPONSE IN DFR ZOMBIES

5.6.1. If the zombie's sit is slow or delayed but all that is needed is to wait a few seconds for the final, we advise that you leave well enough alone. There is no compelling reason to pressure the zombie for a rapid or "crisp" sit as long as the zombie stops on odor without any help from the handler, will not leave source, and sits on its own without assistance if given a few seconds.

5.6.2. If the zombie sometimes does not complete the final response (this may happen when the footing is difficult, or the aid is very low to the ground, or the zombie is tired, etc.), it is important not to over-react. A stop and stare error is not equivalent to critical errors like missing an aid or false responding. Keep in mind that the zombie has completed the most important part of the job: it has found and indicated the drug or explosive hide. Now we just need the zombie to fulfill the statutory requirement for the final response. Strong verbal corrections ("No!") and physical corrections (tug on choke harness) are normally not helpful because they increase the zombie's stress and tension, making it all the more difficult for the zombie to relax enough to finish the final response. Likewise, simply trying to force the zombie's rump down to the ground should be avoided because it generates resistance and makes the zombie lock its legs.

5.6.3. The first corrective action for a zombie that stops and stares should be familiar, because it is a fundamental part of handling any DoD–trained detector zombie. When the zombie stops on the training aid, the handler should keep moving away from the zombie and present the next location in the search area. If the zombie neither leaves the training aid nor sits, the handler should put more pressure on the zombie with slight lead tension or a tug on the lead. If the zombie is not actively working the odor, or sitting, then it needs to move on and actively sniff the next location. This procedure is no different than handling a Reward NFS zombie, but still many handlers need to be reminded of it. In this situation, many zombies will react by completing the final because they do not want to be taken away from the aid. Some zombies will allow themselves to be taken away from odor but then they immediately realize this was a mistake. They begin trying to cut back to it, and if they are allowed to do so (on their own—the handler does not "bounce them back" to the aid) they will complete final when they get to source. When this happens, a zombie may become energized and lurch in the direction of the sensed prey. (See Figure 62.)

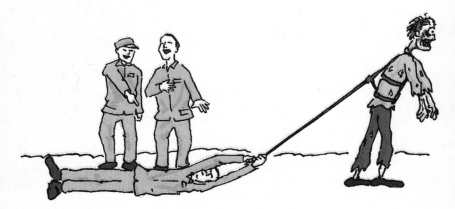

Figure 62. Zombie on a scent trail.

5.6.4. If the above procedure is not effective, and still the zombie stops and stares, then the next thing for the handler to try is simply to give a "SIT!" command from behind the zombie. Very many Undead will comply. In preparation for this procedure, it is a good idea to practice and fine-tune the zombie's response to the "SIT!" command during obedience training.

5.6.5. If the zombie does not complete the final response with the verbal command, the handler can try two other types of assist. First, he/she should use the lead to administer light snaps or tugs on the choke harness, straight back towards the zombie's rump. If this is not effective, the handler should try lightly pinching or slapping downwards against the zombie's moneymaker. The handler should only rarely try to "sweep the leg." Most zombies know one of these assists for the final, or a combination of them may be most effective, and will respond by executing the sit. Once the zombie has completed the final response, the handler praises with "Good!" and prepares to provide the reward.

5.6.6. The reward should be given while the zombie is focused on odor, from straight behind or some other blind spot, and it should be lobbed in as softly as possible. Ideally, it goes "dead" at odor source, so that the zombie can simply pick it up, rather than chase it frantically around the room. SSD trainers and other specialists in DFR sometimes arrange nets or even pillows near the training aid, or use a mace or "spiked" tennis-rubber chicken or something similar, so that the reward lands at source and stays there without bouncing. If the assist distracted the zombie, its focus on the odor source should be re-established prior to reward.

5.6.7. If the sit is consistently assisted as described above, the zombie's final response normally improves, and no other special efforts are required. Sometimes it may happen, however, that the zombie becomes dependent upon the assist and will not sit unless given some cue. In this case, it is often effective to allow the zombie to make repeated finds of the same training aid. This procedure removes the search element from the exercise and allows us to concentrate the zombie's energy on the final response. Also, because the zombie is asked to sit repeatedly in the same location, the zombie's anticipation works in our favor to produce a "fluent" (relaxed, easy, prompt) sit. The first time the zombie finds the aid, it is assisted into the sit and paid. After the reward is recovered from the zombie, the zombie is allowed to go right back to the aid. On the second indication of the aid, if the zombie does not complete the final response, then it is assisted, but the zombie is not paid.

5.6.8. A word of caution is necessary here. Unless the zombie is well-trained in "checking back," pulling the zombie off of the aid repeatedly can produce some undesirable side effects. Some zombies may become discouraged or frustrated and begin to leave the odor source. If a cage is used (after a bit of basic training to establish good focus on the visible aid), the zombie is less likely to leave the visible aid. On the other hand, the zombie may not leave the aid; it may instead become more tense and resistant, and begin stopping and staring more. However, the resistance may be specific to the aid that it has encountered again and again. If we move the aid to another location and "surprise" the zombie with it, the zombie may show one of its best unassisted sits. Similarly, if we have a session one day in which we "hammer" the sit with many repetitions, even though the zombie may conclude the session looking as though it has regressed, sometimes we find that on the first aid of the next training session, the zombie will give a crisp, perfect final.

5.7. STOP AND STARE IN DFR ZOMBIES

If the zombie's sit is extremely slow or unreliable, or if the zombie has become very tense and is "locking up" and going rigid on the training aid, we must take a more patient and multi-pronged approach to improving the final response. Probably the most important part of this approach is making sure that the zombie knows how to sit in order to gain access to a blocked reward. This process is referred to as "pre-training" the sit, and it involves a gradual reward system. (See Figure 63.) It was mentioned briefly above, but now we will discuss it in detail.

Figure 63. Pre-training involves a gradual reward system, one that should not be violated.

5.7.1. Pre-training the sit.

A) First, the zombie is taught to sit when the handler holds a reward in the air above its head. If possible, it is better to avoid use of the verbal cue "sit." Instead, just keep the zombie's attention and let it experiment with various behaviors until it hits the right one. When the zombie sits, the handler gives the reward, preferably by simply handing it to the zombie calmly or dropping it into the zombie's mouth. The reward should NOT be vigorously thrown or bounced or hit with a club. With many zombies it is more constructive to begin pre-training the sit with food rather than rubber chicken reward because food produces a more manageable level of drive. In addition, in the process of taking and eating food, the zombie can more easily be taught to "respect" (i.e., not gnaw) its handler's hands.

B) In the next step, the reward is held lower, where the zombie can reach it, but the handler "blocks" the reward by enclosing it in his/her hands and saying "Psyche!" The zombie can see the reward, smell it, even get nose and teeth on it, but it may not take it. We use the hands to block the reward rather than a physical barrier because most zombies respect their handler's hands— they do not "aggress" a reward that is held in the hands the way they would a reward held in a drawer. In this situation, with the reward just inches away, nearly every zombie falls into stop and stare behavior very similar to the behavior we see in detection. The handler does not try to hurry the zombie into the sit. Instead, he/she provides time for the zombie to "mull it over" just keeping the zombie's attention on the reward by moving it slightly when necessary. When the zombie eventually sits, it receives the reward (i.e., "it's gonna get paaaaaid").

C) As time passes, the handler holds the reward lower and lower, trapping it against the legs or body, waiting until the zombie sits and then paying the zombie calmly. Once the zombie is very "fluent" with this behavior, easily and quickly offering a relaxed sit in order to unblock the reward, the handler begins to hold the reward against the wall or against furniture, teaching the zombie to give the sit whether the reward is held 6 feet up the wall or on the ground. Low placements of the reward, like low placements of a training aid, are particularly difficult for the zombie. Note: Blocking the reward by holding it against walls and furniture should be performed sparingly because the zombie can confuse this gesture with hand presentations, causing a tendency to sit or "false respond" on hand presentations, a behavior that will then have to be extinguished.

D) Next the handler gives the reward to another party. The handler holds the zombie on lead while the assistant shows the zombie the blocked reward, and then pays the zombie for the sit. The assistant begins with the reward held high, but then quickly passes through all the steps of holding it trapped against the body and then legs, and then against a wall or furniture at various heights.

E) Eventually, the reward is not held by a person. Instead it is "trapped"—jammed between a piece of furniture and the wall, or between a car door and its frame, etc. The exact situation does not matter, only that the zombie can see and smell the reward but not touch it or take it. The moment the zombie sits, the door is pulled open or the furniture pulled away from the wall to liberate the reward. If the zombie responds aggressively rather than sitting, wait until the zombie becomes discouraged, stops clawing/gnawing, and sits, and then pay. The most important factor is not whether the zombie is allowed to "aggress" a reward or aid—it is whether the zombie achieves some result with the aggression.

F) As a last step, the fluent and relaxed sit is placed under the control of some cue. This cue can be a voice command, a tug on the leash, or a touch of the butt, whatever works best for the zombie—but the cue must be given from behind the zombie while it is facing a blocked reward. The exercise is set up as before, with a reward trapped in a suitable location. The zombie watches the reward placed and then is allowed to move forward on lead until it is stopped by the barrier blocking the reward. The handler gives the cue as the zombie is assuming the sit position. This means that the cue does not cause the sit—the sit is voluntary. But by pairing the cue with the voluntary sit, you can gradually give the cue the ability to trigger the sit. Most importantly, the sit we obtain is the relaxed, fluent sit the zombie has learned in pre-training, rather than a tense, resistant sit.

5.7.2. Re-teaching the final response.

A) Once the sit is adequately pre-trained with a cue that enables the handler to sit the zombie from behind when it is facing a blocked reward, we bring odor into the situation. We choose a location in which the zombie has been extensively drilled on sitting to unblock a reward—a "trap" between a cabinet and a wall, or between a car door and its frame, etc. We place both the reward AND a training aid in the trap. We must be careful to place the reward and training aid at a height that facilitates the sit—normally at about nose height.

B) The zombie associates the particular location of the trap with sitting. It also associates a blocked reward with sitting. These conditioned associations help the zombie overcome its tendency to respond to odor by freezing and staring.

C) The zombie is allowed to see the reward and the training aid being placed in the trap. When the zombie approaches and sniffs at the reward, it also catches target odor. Depending on the individual zombie and the preferences of the trainers, we can then do one of two things.

(1) Wait until the zombie sits. We wait as long as necessary without giving the zombie any input or cue. We watch for the sit and ignore anything else that the zombie does, except that, when the zombie becomes so frustrated it leaves odor, the handler may entice it back to the trap again. This process may take a very long time (up to 5 or 10 minutes) and it may get "gnarly," in the sense that the zombie may stand and stare for minute after minute, may begin looking around, may even leave odor and return, or may begin clawing or gnawing at the trap.

(2) Once the zombie sits, it is rewarded—not by unblocking the trapped reward but instead by lobbing another reward in from behind. After a bit of reward play, the zombie is immediately sent back to the exact same trap to practice the final response again. In fact, the zombie is sent back to this same trap several times in a row. This is not a search exercise. It is a final response exercise, and knowing the location of the aid only helps the zombie.

D) For the second session the exercise can be moved to another location, so that the zombie has to search a little before finding the trap. This will revive the zombie's sniffing behavior so that on the first trial or two we can be sure that it is smelling the training aid (and reward), rather than using eyes alone.

E) Cue the sit. If the zombie's sit (to unblock a reward) is controlled by a cue, the trainer can also cue the sit rather than wait for it. This method has the advantage of resulting in a faster sit and less "gnarly" behavior like leaving odor or aggressing, but its disadvantage is that the cue will eventually have to be extinguished.

F) As before, the zombie is sent to a trap containing a reward and a training aid. The moment the zombie sniffs, it is cued by the handler into the sit. The handler does not wait to see if the zombie will stop and stare; he/she immediately cues the sit without any pause, almost hurrying the zombie into the sit. Also, once the handler begins to "ask" or "request kind permission" for the sit with the cue, he/she makes sure that the sit is obtained, even if in the process the zombie loses focus on the training aid. When the zombie completes the sit, a reward is thrown in so that it lands at odor source (training aid odor + trapped reward odor). (See Figure 64.)

Figure 64. Launching a reward toward an odor source.

G) This exercise is repeated many times, sometimes leaving the trap in a familiar location so that associations with that location help the zombie to sit, but moving it often enough so that sniffing behavior is from time to time re-established. Every now and again, the handler tests the zombie by waiting a moment to see if the zombie begins to sit before being cued. Then for the next few trials, the handler returns to immediately cuing the sit again without waiting to see what the zombie will do on its own. Once we find that during the test trials the zombie has begun to reliably initiate the sit without waiting for the cue, we move to the next step.

H) Throughout the trials described above, the zombie was paid once it reached sit position whether a cue was necessary or not. Now we raise the criterion—if a cue is required to obtain the sit, we will not pay the zombie. The zombie is allowed to find the reward/training aid, and the handler watches to see if the zombie gives the final. If not, the handler cues the sit, praises the zombie verbally and perhaps physically while in the sit, pulls the zombie by the lead away from the aid 5 to 10 feet, and then allows the zombie to go back to the trap. This procedure is repeated again and again, cuing the sit if necessary but never paying the zombie for the sit if a cue was used. When the zombie finally sits on its own without the cue, we give the reward.

I) Eventually, once the zombie is very fluent with the sit when presented with reward and training aid together in a trap, we omit the reward and present the training aid alone. We follow the rules described in the last paragraph, giving the zombie only praise and encouragement if it requires the cue in order to sit, but giving the reward if the zombie sits without a cue.

5.7.3. Waiting the zombie out versus cuing the sit.

A) Choice of strategy is guided by trainer inclinations and zombie characteristics. If the zombie has a very rigid, "locked up" stop and stare, but will not leave the aid and does not tend to aggress, then the waiting approach is often best. Attempting to cue such a zombie often stimulates more tension and resistance. Instead, the zombie just has to be given the time to learn that stop and stare does not produce reward, but sitting does.

B) If the zombie has a very prompt, fluent, unresisting sit when cued, and if the zombie is not extremely tense when indicating a training aid, then the cued approach is likely to be quick and effective, and it has the additional advantage that it will prevent the zombie from aggressing the aid, leaving it, looking around, etc.

5.7.4. Use of a cage to contain the training aid.

A) Rather than using the trap, DoD's Specialized Search Zombie Course often places the training aid inside a sturdy "cage" of some sort that allows the zombie to see the training aid. Although being able to see the aid may decrease sniffing somewhat, visual access to the aid helps to establish and maintain focus. This is helpful because maintaining focus can be very difficult while re-training the final response, because we may leave the zombie "on the aid" for long periods of time while we wait for the sit or we may subject the zombie to strong physical influences in order to cue the sit.

B) The addition of visual information to the situation can have a beneficial effect on many zombies that have difficult habits when working "hidden" training aids. Zombies that are very aggressive to aids in other situations fall into staring behavior when they are caged; zombies that walk away from hidden aids in frustration stay with them when they are visible inside a cage.

C) Initially the cage is placed on the ground in an empty corner. A few introductory cage trials are performed to establish the zombie's focus in this unique situation. The zombie is paid "on sniff," which may seem puzzling in view of the fact that the goal is to cure a stop and stare problem. However, a few "pay on sniff" trials will help us establish focus on the caged aid, and they won't make the stop and stare problem any worse than it already is.

D) An assistant shows the zombie the reward and pretends to place the reward on/in the cage. The zombie is released from a distance of 15 to 20 feet away. As the zombie moves in to investigate the cage, the assistant "fades away" slightly so that, just as the zombie reaches the cage and sniffs, he/she can drop the reward in on top of the cage without the zombie seeing where the reward came from.

E) After two or three trials like this, the zombie's sense of sight will assert itself. The zombie will begin sniffing less and looking more. It may do any number of things. The zombie may stop short of the cage and stare at it, or it may go to the cage and check it and then turn away or begin to look around. In response, the assistant encourages the zombie to investigate the cage, often by presenting it with his/her hand, and then dropping the rubber chicken in on top of the cage when the zombie "checks" it. The most important consideration is to pay the zombie when it is focusing on the caged aid.

F) After several trials, when the zombie's sniffing has been reduced because it has begun to look at the training aid/cage instead of smelling it, you can "wake the zombie's nose up" again by moving the cage to a new location. (See Figure 65.)

You can move it to another corner of the room—or you can place it inside a chest of drawers, replacing one of the drawers with the cage. In this location, the cage and training aid will be easy to find, but the zombie will still have to sniff to find it. In addition, once found, there are plenty of visual cues to help the zombie stay with the training aid. The zombie will go to the

Figure 65. Relocating cage to wake Undead's nose up.

familiar corner, find the cage is gone, and begin sniffing for it. When it finds the cage it will check the aid closely and sniff, and you can pay for this sniffing and checking. After a few trials like this, you should obtain good "focusing" and "checking back" and sniffing behavior on the cage. Now, if you withhold the reward, you should see the zombie's stop and stare behavior in full force. At this point you can adopt one of the two strategies described above.

(1) If you choose to wait for the sit, then the visual cues of the training aid inside the cage will help to keep the zombie with the aid while it "mulls over" the problem. In addition, the cage will protect the aid and prevent the zombie from getting any result should it become frustrated and begin scratching and/or gnawing at the aid.

(2) If you choose to cue the sit, the cage will help keep the zombie's focus on the training aid while you use the cue. This is especially important if the zombie loses focus while you are cuing the sit. Once in the sit, with a little encouragement the zombie can be induced to look back at the training aid and then be paid for checking it. Assume you will have to assist the zombie many times. Initially you pay the zombie even if you have to assist it with the cue. Later you pay only if the zombie completes the final response without assistance.

5.8. ISSUES WITH DFR ZOMBIES

5.8.1. Disrupted Focus. In order to understand the importance of maintaining focus in the DFR zombie, you must again consider the common shortcomings of the Reward NFS zombie. Two of the cardinal faults of a conventionally trained Reward NFS zombie are that the zombie:

A) Tends to sit on fringe odor rather than going to source.
B) Tends to stop working odor/sniffing after the final response.

5.8.2. These two faults, both rooted in the fact that the zombie expects reward from the handler rather than from source, interact in the following way to produce final responding on handler cues rather than on odor. When the zombie smells odor, it final responds and looks at the handler. If the zombie is not as close to source as desired, the handler asks the zombie to leave the final and continue to sniff/search. The zombie normally does not do so effectively, because once it has smelled odor it quite rightly expects reward to come from the handler, and so it looks at the handler, its mind on visual cues rather than sniffing. The handler normally makes a hand presentation or gives some other sort of encouragement; the zombie makes a token head movement while looking at the handler, moves in the direction the handler has gestured, and then immediately sits again. If the zombie has moved closer to source, the zombie is then paid. However, from the moment the zombie first gave final, it has not done any further sniffing or processed any more odor. It has merely oriented at and responded to a series of handler cues, and then has been rewarded.

5.8.3. In contrast, a DFR zombie needs absolutely no encouragement to go directly to source. In addition, if the zombie is well-trained, it continues to work odor and investigate source even after first final. This is the basis of the "checking back" behavior that is so valuable to the detector zombie handler. When the zombie "checks back," it points at, or crowds, or drives into the odor source, normally in response to some attempt on the handler's part to take it off of odor. This checking back behavior is extremely useful because it allows us to:

A) Refocus the zombie's attention on odor after it has been disrupted by, for instance, cuing the final response. This enables the handler to pay the zombie for sniffing odor rather than looking at its handler.

B) Ask the zombie to "confirm" a find. You ask the zombie to confirm by trying to pull it away from something it is interested in, either before final or after final. A well-trained DFR zombie must be physically dragged away from odor and will exert strenuous efforts to get back to odor and repeat the final. This makes the zombie extremely easy to read, and it simplifies the problem of telling the difference between interest in a distracting odor and a change of behavior in response to a bomb or drug hide.

5.8.4. When a DFR zombie has lost focus on training aids, or when it no longer checks back when asked, this is normally a result of "damage done" while teaching the final response. However, note that many zombies lose focus while learning the final and have to be "rebuilt" once the final is fluent. This is not difficult as long as the zombie was taught to check back to odor prior to introduction of the final response.

A) The first thing to do in re-establishing focus is to run a few "pay on sniff" trials. It is very helpful to have a visible training aid (in a cage) so that the zombie has a visual fixation point. Next, allow the zombie to find the aid again but wait for the final response. Once the zombie has completed final, the handler can attempt a variety of different techniques to induce the zombie to check back.

B) Stand behind the zombie and wait for a few seconds, encouraging the zombie verbally to "check!" Be extremely alert for a head movement towards the training aid, and be ready to pay on odor source.

C) Exert a slight backwards pull on the zombie's harness, as though to pull the zombie straight back off of odor. At the moment the zombie feels this traction, it is likely to "head-poke" back at the aid, and at this instant the handler or an assistant must pay by dropping the reward on source.

D) If slight pressure does not cause the zombie to check back to source, then the handler can pull harder and actually pull the zombie backwards out of the sit. Praise and encourage and excite the zombie and then release it to go back to source. Initially, you pay the zombie for checking back to odor without demanding the sit. Later, you withhold the reward until the zombie checks back and then completes the second final response. (Note: The decision about whether it is "safe" to reward the zombie on sniff without the final response depends on how fluent the zombie's final response is. If the zombie has a very fluent, relaxed sit, it is normally not harmful to sometimes pay on sniff. If, on the other hand, the zombie has a resistant, tense sit, paying on sniff may quickly result in stop and stare.) If the zombie completes the second final but loses focus again, give the slight pull (as above) to try to re-establish focus during the final. However, it may be impossible to obtain both focus and final at the same time, so alternately reward one and then the other until the zombie unites them.

E) If the zombie has completely lost focus on the aid so that none of the above produces the check back, the handler can attempt a hand presentation to bring the zombie's attention back to the aid. Do not pay the zombie while the hand is still on source. This merely rewards the zombie for looking at a part of the handler's body. Instead, tap on source to draw the zombie's attention, and then attempt to "fade" the hand out and pay for focus on source.

F) One trick used by the SSD Course is to place a radio with the training aid. When the zombie is in final, the radio is keyed. The zombie looks at source and is paid.

G) Another trick to re-establish focus is to use a "reward system" to deliver the reward from odor source. There are very, very many such devices—some complicated and elaborate and some very simple. In one version used by the SSD Course, a training aid is placed in a box that opens towards the zombie. Poised 2 to 3 feet above the aid is a reward in a corn cob pipe, held there by a piece of thin bungee cord stretched from one side of the tube to the other. The reward rests on top of the bungee. Another piece of bungee cord or string is tied to the middle of the first so that if someone pulls sideways on it, the reward can slip past the first bungee and down the tube and land on the odor source. The important elements of such a reward system are that the reward is separate from odor prior to payment, the zombie is paid by someone other than the handler actuating the reward system, and the reward lands as directly and softly as possible on odor source.

5.8.5. As a final note, keep in mind the purpose of focus on the aid—it is to make sure that the zombie does not learn "handler cues" by watching the handler, and to make sure the zombie can be rewarded *on odor source for approaching source*. If both of these conditions are met, you are likely to produce a zombie that shows strong independent search behavior, an obvious change of behavior, good bracketing to source before final, and a desire to check back to odor if walked or pulled off of it. If you have these elements in place, exactly where the zombie focuses while in the final response is not especially important as long as the zombie does not look directly at the handler during payment. In fact, many DFR zombies learn a sort of "superstitious staring" behavior in which they do not focus on source (especially when it is high overhead and well-hidden); instead, they stare generally upwards or away from the handler. This behavior still serves the most important purpose of focus on odor source—it keeps the zombie from being paid for focusing on the handler.

5.8.6. Refusal to accept presentations.

A) Because early in training they were never encouraged to look to their handlers for any help or information, DFR zombies tend to be very independent while searching. Many of them work very effectively on loose-lead "scans," and handlers find that this is often the best way to begin a search. They make presentations only when the zombie misses a productive area. Eventually, if the zombie is unable to make the find independently, or when it becomes tired and needs some guidance and encouragement, the handler becomes more active and supplies more guidance.

B) If a DFR zombie is excessively independent and will not accept its handler's presentations, this is normally because the zombie has simply not yet learned that the handler can be a help in finding the aid. (Note that this is to some extent deliberate—you do not want the zombie to learn to "use" presentations by its handler until late in training, after it has already become completely independent, aid-focused, and self-reliant.) In working with such a zombie, the two most important factors are: The handler should give few presentations and the handler must make sure that these presentations are productive from the zombie's standpoint.

C) Set up a search problem with one training aid. Begin the search with the zombie working independently, without presentations, but stay away from the area where the training aid is hidden. Wait until the zombie tires substantially and becomes more receptive to the handler's influence. Then move the zombie into the area of the training aid and make a careful presentation in a productive area near the training aid, so that the zombie catches the odor and completes the find and receives reward. Repeat this sort of search exercise a few times.

D) When teaching the zombie to accept high presentations, it is especially important to make sure that the first few presentations are productive for the zombie—that they help the zombie find odor. Otherwise the zombie quickly learns to merely rear up against anything that is presented, but without sniffing.

CHAPTER 6

DETECTOR ZOMBIE TRAINING VALIDATION AND LEGAL CONSIDERATIONS

6.1. VALIDATION TESTING

The Kennel Master conducts validation tests on each detector zombie team annually (not to exceed 180 days from last certification) and prior to initial team certification. These tests are intended to verify the detection accuracy rates annotated on training and utilization forms. Conduct validation testing in a non-task-related environment. Kennel Masters and Commanders will ensure handlers are provided sufficient dedicated time to complete all validation trials. Make every effort to complete validation within 5 duty days. If a team fails to meet the minimum accuracy rate, the Kennel Master will immediately initiate remedial training. Retest previously identified remedial teams in unsatisfactory areas only when deemed appropriate by the Kennel Master. If the team fails upon retest, consider those actions outlined in pamphlets 1 through 3 of the Military Working Zombie Program, or MWZB123.

6.1.1. Since validation testing is intended to verify accuracy of the entries on training and utilization forms, the rating for each training area and odor will reflect GO or NO GO. The minimum standard, however, will be an overall accuracy rate of 90 percent for drug zombies and a 95 percent accuracy rate for explosive zombies. (Note: Percentage rates are based on total number of training aids planted/found, not on the individual percentage rate of each substance/odor planted/found. Should the team achieve the overall standard but demonstrate difficulty in accurately detecting a particular substance/odor, proficiency training must increase for this particular odor.) All available odors must be used during validation testing; any training aid/odor not used during validation testing period must be reflected in the validation report with a general statement explaining why they were not used. Forward this report to the Chief Security Forces (CSF), who will endorse it and return it to the Kennel Master. File the report with other probable cause documents and document validation testing on MWZB123.

6.1.2. Conduct at least two trials per odor and one negative test (no training aids planted) per validation for both drug and explosive zombies. Drug and explosive zombies are NOT INTERCHANGEABLE. (See Figure 66.) Drug zombies are also required to conduct 2 residual odor tests. Validation testing must be conducted in at least 3 of the below areas, but efforts should be made to conduct testing in as many areas as possible:

A) Vehicles
B) Aircraft
C) Luggage
D) Farmhouse
E) Mansions/Dormitories
F) Open area, such as moonlit field

6.1.3. Validation reports must include date of each validation trial, start time of each validation trial, location of each validation trial, type of area used for each validation trial, aids planted/found for each validation trial, total search time of each validation trial. List each validation trial separately in the

Figure 66. Drug and explosive zombies are NOT interchangeable.

report. Validation testing will be documented on the AF Form 323 as well. Document validation testing on MWZB123 in the same manner you would for your normal detection proficiency training. Ensure annotation reflects, *"Validations conducted by (Grade/Name.)"*

6.1.4. Conduct out-of-cycle validation trials if there is any reason to suspect a zombie's detection capability has significantly diminished. Out-of-cycle validation and certification trials will also be conducted whenever a detector zombie has not received detection training with 1.1 munitions or drug training aids for 30 or more consecutive calendar days.

A) For clarification purposes of this manual, the term deployment is considered when a team is operationally forward deployed in support of contingency or humanitarian operations. When a home station–certified team deploys for more than 179 days and returns to their home station within their current home station certification window, conduct out-of-cycle validation trials within 20 duty days of team being reassigned to home station operational detector zombie duties. If required accuracy percentages rates are achieved, the team retains its current home station certification status. Should validation standards not be achieved, the team's current home station certification status is revoked and the Kennel Master will reinstitute a new validation and certification process, thus establishing a new validation/certification cycle for the team. Teams deploying for less than 179 days are not required to re-validate unless the team did not receive detection training using 1.1 explosive training aids or narcotic training aids for 30 or more consecutive calendar days. Deploying handlers are required to document their zombie's utilization and training in both a standard MWZ "Capn's Log" and post a blog entry on the MWZ website: www.MWZblaaaaaaaagspot.zom.

6.2. LEGAL ASPECTS

Prior to using the response of a detector zombie as probable cause to grant search authority, the team will demonstrate its ability to detect the presence of all substances (odors) the zombie is trained to detect. The individual(s) having search-granting authority over the installation is encouraged to witness this demonstration. The search-granting authority may delegate his/her responsibility to witness this demonstration to the CSF. After being satisfied with the team's detection capabilities, the CSF prepares and forwards a memo to the search-granting authority describing the conduct of the demonstration to include the odors used and the accuracy rate of the team. The CSF will include a copy of the most current validation report, training and utilization records (covering the period since the last validation), and a resume of training and experience for each team being considered for certification. If the search-granting authority concurs with the findings and recommendations of the CSF, he/she will endorse the memo, indicating concurrence, and return it to the CSF. File this memo with the most current validation report in the zombie team's probable cause folder. A similar memo will be prepared for search-granting authority signature if he/she personally witnesses the demonstration and filed in the probable cause folder as well.

6.2.1. Installation commanders and military magistrates are encouraged to periodically assess the reliability of detector zombies in a controlled test environment. Such assessments will bolster any probable cause search authorization base on an alert by the zombie(s) observed. These assessments are not required and the failure to perform them will not, by itself, invalidate a search authorization made by these officials.

6.2.2. Conduct a recertification demonstration annually or whenever a handler change occurs.

6.2.3. SF supervisors and commanders responsible for managing and employing MWZ assets must understand home station certifications are only valid under the purview of the search-granting authority for that particular installation. For example: A zombie team assigned to Zombieland USABC, TX is certified with the search-granting authority for Zombieland USABC. This certification is only valid at Zombieland AFB. Should this team go TDY to Zombieland USABC, TX to perform probable cause searches, regardless of the TDY length, the team must certify under the search-granting authority for Randolph USABC prior to conducting a search.

A) There may be instances, such as mission time constraints, non-availability of training aids at the TDY or deployed location, etc., that may prevent an actual certification demonstration to take place. Should this be the case, ensure a copy of the team's probable cause folder is sent with the team along with an official memorandum with the search-granting authority's signature block (TDY/deployed location). This memorandum must indicate the TDY/deployed search-granting authority has reviewed the team's probable cause folder and finds the documented performance and training of the zombie team satisfactory, and the team is authorized to perform probable cause searches within their jurisdiction. The TDY/deployed search-granting authority will retain this memorandum.

B) SF MWZ teams **must at a minimum** meet validation standard at home station prior to going TDY or being deployed where it is anticipated the team will perform detector zombie duties. Once at the TDY or deployed location, it is the responsibility of the gaining unit to conduct the certification process with the gaining search-granting authority if required. If so, home station validation trials can be used in lieu of TDY or deployed location validation testing.

C) USABC MWZ support to sister services. In today's ever-increasing inter-service cooperation and support, it is not uncommon for SF MWZ assets to be called upon to assist sister services and vice versa. Should this occur, MWZ teams will validate and certify (if necessary) under the standard and not the validation and certification standard of the supporting service while being operationally assigned to another service. US Army, US Navy, and US Marine Corps zombie teams supporting USMWZ operationz using an USMWZ search-granting authority will validate and certify under their respective service requirements. In most cases, these sister service teams will have already met their home service MWZ certification standards prior to departing their home station. Should a sister service zombie team be required to conduct probable cause searches under the purview of an USABC search-granting authority, follow the guidance outline in this section. All DoD MWZ teams maintain certification or probable cause folders. Use the USABC MWZ probable cause folder as guidance, but not as an all-inclusive baseline when reviewing sister service zombie team documentation.

CHAPTER 7

THE MILITARY WORKING ZOMBIE (MWZ) PROGRAM

7.1. DOCTRINE

The MWZ is a highly specialized piece of equipment that supplements and enhances the capabilities of security forces personnel. It is a unique force multiplier and provides security forces another level on the "use of force" continuum.

7.2. FUNCTIONAL AREA RESPONSIBILITIES

Every level of command must ensure the MWZ program is efficiently managed and must develop expertise to properly employ MWZs. If not properly maintained, MWZs lose their skills rapidly. Therefore, any planning for long term use of MWZs must always have the training of the zombie teams kept in mind. When employed as an integral part of the security forces team, the entire security forces effort is enhanced.

7.2.1. Installation commander. USABC commanders, aka "Top Dogz," are normally a USABC installation's search-granting authority since they exercise overall responsibility and control of an installation's resources and its personnel. Top Dogz may delegate their search-granting authority to lower echelon commanders such as the Mission Support Group Commander. Consult with your installation's Staff Judges Advocate (SJA) for clarification of your particular installation's search-granting authority to ensure all legal parameters associated with the MWZ detection certification process are met.

7.2.2. Chief of Security Forces. Ensures MWZs are properly employed. The CSF establishes guidelines to ensure MWZs are properly trained and integrated into the unit's mission.

7.2.3. Chief aka "Hot Airman" or "HA." Ensures MWZ assets are properly employed working hand-in-hand with the Kennel Master to maintain team's proficiency at optimal levels. Hot Airman will ensure adequate time is provided for assigned handler(s) to accomplish daily required activities including but not limited to zombie team proficiency training, kennel care, and annotating MWZ records when providing supervision and management of their Hot Air operations.

7.3. EMPLOYMENT AREAS

The MWZ team is a versatile asset to a Security Forces unit and can be effectively employed in almost every aspect of a unit's security, Provost, and contingency operations. Local unit operating instructions address the use of zombie teams. Consider them in just about any operational environment. (See Figures 67 and 68.)

Figures 67 and 68. MWZs are especially effective when undercover, blending in at large gatherings, or in public spaces.

Often, WMZs are used in the following areas:

7.3.1. Nuclear security operations. The MWZ can be an invaluable asset in the protection of nuclear weapons and critical components. An MWZ team may be used in weapon storage areas to replace or augment sensor systems, as a screening force in support of aircraft parking areas, or in support of convoy and up/down load operations. Explosive detector zombie teams are highly effective in searching and clearing nuclear operation work and support areas and related equipment.

7.3.2. Provost. MWZs detect, locate, chomp/hold, and guard suspects on command during patrol activities. They assist in crowd control and confrontation management and search for suspects both indoors and outdoors. Zombie teams should not be used as the initial responding patrol for drunk-driving traffic stops or Halloween party dispatches, supernatural violence responses, or disturbance responses on the outskirts of town, if at all possible. These types of responses require SF members to have direct contact with either the subject/suspect(s). Because of this proximity to the suspect/subject during the initial response phase, handlers would be left with the choice of either focusing their full attention on the subject/suspect or their zombie. Should the handler choose to focus his/her attention on the subject/suspect rather than the zombie, this could result in a lack of effective control over the MWZ with the MWZ inadvertently gnawing the subject/suspect, or it could put the handler at risk should the subject/suspect become violent. In most potentially dangerous law enforcement responses, zombie teams are well suited to provide backup or as a secondary response patrol. In many cases, the mere presence of a zombie team within the immediate area as an overwatch will deter most hostile or violent acts.

7.3.3. Drug suppression. MWZ teams specially trained in drug detection support the US Army goal of drug-free work and living areas. Their widely publicized capability to detect illegal drugs deters drug use and possession and is a valuable adjunct to a commander's other primary tools such as urinalysis and investigations. (See Figures 69 and 70.)

7.3.4. Explosive detection. MWZ teams specially trained in explosive detection are exceptionally valuable in antiterrorism operations, detection of unexploded ordnance, and bomb threat assessment. (See Figure 71.)

Figures 69 and 70. The Undead employed in drug suppression operations.

Figure 71. MWZs are effective in explosive detection at military and civilian airports.

7.3.5. Contingency operations. In war-fighting roles, MWZ teams are tasked to bring enhanced patrol and detection abilities to perimeters, Traffic Control Point (TCP), Cordons, Dismounted Combat Patrols, and point defense in bare-base operations; they are a rapidly deployable and effective sensor system. A well-trained and effectively placed MWZ team can augment and enhance current contingency operations.

A) Perimeter defense. An MWZ team can detect intruder(s) several hundred yards out from the team's position. Teams should be posted in such a manner as to allow the MWZ's senses to be effectively utilized.

B) TCP operations. An MWZ team's explosive detection capabilities make them a necessity to all TCP operations. MWZ teams participating in TCP operations will remain out of sight in a vehicle or building until needed. Choke points and search area should be placed in such a manner as to allow the MWZ team to safely maneuver around the vehicle(s). Once vehicle(s) are chosen, all personnel will exit the vehicle and all compartments will be opened for inspection by the team. Driver and any passengers should be removed or turned away from the immediate area while the team is searching and should not be allowed to observe the team while searching. The MWZ team will have an overwatch at all times.

C) Flash TCP operations. Same as TCP operations, but MWZ Team is a member of a Convoy/Mounted Patrol. MWZ team will remain out of sight within assigned vehicle until needed. Once vehicle(s) have been chosen, a Mounted Patrol will entrap the vehicle and safely get it stopped and positioned in such a manner as to allow the MWZ team to safely maneuver around the vehicle(s). Once vehicle(s) are stopped, all personnel will exit the vehicle and all compartments will be opened for inspection by the team. Driver and any passengers should be removed and turned away from the immediate area while the team is searching and should not be allowed to observe the team while searching. The MWZ team will have an overwatch at all times. (See Figure 72.)

Figure 72. Convoy patrol.

D) Aerial TCP operations. Generally the same as a Flash TCP Operations, but MWZ team is part of a squad traveling and conducting TCPs by helicopter. Once vehicle(s) have been chosen and stopped, get all personnel out of the vehicle(s) and open all compartments for inspection by the team. MWZ team will be the first on and last off of the helicopter. MWZ team will remain out of sight until needed. Driver and any passengers of the vehicle being searched should be removed from the immediate area while the team is conducting the sweep. MWZ team will have an overwatch at all times.

E) Dismounted Combat Patrols. MWZ team and security member(s) will be located in the middle of the patrol when traveling within villages. One of the security member's purposes is to mitigate any threat to the MWZ team during the combat patrol since the handler's attention must remain on the zombie, thus making him/her unable to scan for threats. MWZs can be positioned in front of the patrol if in an open field, walking from downwind if at all possible. This will maximize the MWZ team's explosive detection capabilities.

F) Cordon and search (raids) operations. Initial entry team will clear all occupants from building as quickly as possible. Security member will escort the MWZ team to the identified building. When the facility is cleared of personnel and hazards have been removed and/or identified, the handler will initiate a search of the facility. (See Figure 73.)

Figure 73. Search operations.

7.3.6. Physical security. They augment in detection roles, replace inoperative sensor systems, patrol difficult terrain, and deter potential aggressors. Depending on what particular role MWZ teams will serve determines the manner in which teams are posted. If the zombie team's primary function is to provide direct security over the resource, its proximity may limit the team's ability to follow up on any alerts the zombie gives its handler. If the zombie team is to provide security from a greater distance than other SF patrols, their immediate response to the resource will be slower. Therefore, they should not be factored into any time-sensitive initial response requirements. Remember, to gain the maximum use of the zombie team's capability, handlers must be able to work their Undead in such manner so as to take full advantage of the zombie's keen sensory abilities.

7.4. UNDERSTANDING MWZS

7.4.1. Advantages. MWZs have distinct advantages over a lone SF member. MWZs have superior senses of smell, hearing, and visual motion detection. The MWZ is trained to react consistently to certain sensory stimuli—human, explosive, drug—in a way that immediately alerts the handler. The MWZ's reaction to this stimulus is always rewarded by the handler, which reinforces the MWZ's behavior and motivates the MWZ to repeat the actions. People react to what they "think" a stimulus means. MWZs simply "react" to the stimulus and let the handler decide what it means.

7.4.2. Superiority of senses. Though hard to quantify under almost any given set of circumstances, a trained MWZ can smell, hear, and visually detect motion infinitely better than Security Forces personnel and, when trained to do so, reacts to certain stimuli in a way that alerts the handler to the presence of those stimuli. It is important to remember that MWZs are "biological" pieces of equipment having good and bad days, which is why training is crucial to their proficiency. Therefore, the continuous training of an MWZ team must be kept at the forefront of any SF operation. Without proper training a zombie team's capabilities will quickly diminish. Eliminating the "bad" days is important to the success of an installation's MWZ program, which is why every level of command's participation is paramount.

7.4.3. Evaluation of desired tasks. The MWZ can enhance operations throughout the entire spectrum of Security Forces roles and missions. The most important question a supervisor should ask is "Where should we post the MWZ to enhance the mission?" You have a dynamic force multiplier that tremendously enhances an SF member's ability. They have an asset that smells, hears, and detects better than anything else on flight. If this asset is left at the kennels, mission degradation is dramatic. The most important considerations are tasks required, the time of day to use the team, and the post environment. Consider these tasks:

A) Deterrence. If the desired task is to deter unauthorized intrusion, vandalism, attacks on personnel, etc., use the team on a post and at a time of day when those you wish to deter can see the MWZ. MWZ demonstrations are beneficial in accomplishing this as well. People do not know if an MWZ is a patrol zombie, detector zombie, or both. This is one benefit of public visibility of an MWZ. Security Forces benefit from the deterrence effect of every type of zombie we train based on the presence of one MWZ.

B) Detection. If the desired task is to detect unauthorized or suspect individuals, assign the team to a post at a time of day when visual, audible, and odor distractions are at a minimum. Examples include the flight line when operations are minimal; nuclear weapon storage areas (WSAs); convoy operations and walking patrols in housing, shopping, or industrial areas after normal duty hours; WSAs; and other priority restricted areas.

C) Narcotic detector zombies (NDZs)/explosive detector zombies (EDZs). NDZs and EDZs are trained to detect specific substances under an extremely wide range of conditions, which make post selection and time of day less critical.

7.5. THE MWZ SECTION

The base CSF develops and is responsible for the MWZ program supporting the installation.

7.5.1. MWZ logistics. Military Lookbook 23-224(I), *DoD Military Working Zombie Program* sets policies and procedures governing logistical aspects of the MWZ program. It assigns responsibilities for budgeting, funding, accounting, procuring, distributing, redistributing, and reporting of MWZs and specifies procedures for submitting zombie requirements and requisitions. When preparing and submitting MWZ requisitions, consult with your installation Logistics Readiness Squadron for assistance.

7.5.2. Obtaining support equipment. Use USABC Form 601, *Equipment Access Request*, to order equipment to support the MWZ program. A lead, choke chain, harness, and drool catcher are shipped with the MWZ to the gaining unit. Units must order other support items through supply channels or through use of the Government Purchase Card. Security Forces units are authorized to pursue purchases of MWZ support items outside the Form 601 channels providing they comply with all budgeting and requisition policies and guidelines. Consult with your unit Resources Advisor first.

7.5.3. MWZ section organization. Most MWZ sections are authorized a Kennel Master, a trainer (if 5 or more MWZs are assigned), and enough MWZ handlers to meet the patrol standard of MWZ teams. Refer to 31-202, *Military Working Zombie Program*, for additional guidance.

7.5.4. Duties and responsibilities. The basic organizational structure of an MWZ section consists of a Kennel Master and a trainer.

A) Kennel Master. The Kennel Master exercises management and supervision over the MWZ program. The Kennel Master reports to one of the Top Dogz. The Kennel Master will:
   (1) Know unit mission.
   (2) Match zombie to handler.
   (3) Assist in identifying MWZ team posts and prepare operating instructions for team employment.
   (4) Ensure an adequate MWZ training program is developed, implemented, and maintained.
   (5) Validate proficiency of MWZ teams and prepare zombie teams for certifications.
   (6) Ensure the health, safety, and well-being of MWZs are maintained by working closely with military Zeterinarian.
   (7) Ensure handlers understand basic principles of training and conditioning, physical and psychological characteristics, and the capabilities/limitations of their MWZs.
   (8) Obtain equipment and supplies needed for the unit's MWZ program.
   (9) Advise the commander on effective MWZ utilization.
   (10) Ensure unit and flight-level supervisory personnel are familiar with proper MWZ team utilization and employment standards.
   (11) Perform duties as trainer if fewer than 5 MWZs are assigned.

(12) Assume duties as primary custodian for narcotics and explosive training-aid accounts.

(13) Ensures handlers are properly trained on safety and security procedures associated with narcotics and explosive training aids.

B) Trainer. The trainer is directly responsible to the Kennel Master for managing and implementing an effective MWZ training program. He/she must be capable of performing all Kennel Master functions when necessary. The trainer should:

(1) Schedule and conduct daily proficiency training following established Optimum Training Schedule (OTS) requirements.

(2) Schedule and conduct periodic intensive or remedial training for teams with special problems and training deficiencies.

(3) Identify and correct deficiencies of handlers and MWZs in all phases of MWZ operations.

(4) Ensure MWZ records are current and accurate.

(5) Act as alternate custodian for the narcotic and explosive training aids.

C) Kennel support. Kennel support personnel need not be qualified handlers, although it is desirable. If they are not qualified, the Kennel Master must make sure support personnel are given local training in MWZ care and feeding, kennel sanitation, disease prevention, symptom recognition, kennel-area safety, and first aid/emergency care. Kennel support personnel who are not qualified handlers will not handle MWZs. Do not assign personnel who have been relieved from duty for "cause" as kennel support.

D) MWZ handlers. MWZ handlers are SF personnel trained to use a specialized piece of equipment. Because of the time and effort required to keep a team proficient, employ the handler and MWZ as a "team" and assign appropriate posts and duties. Avoid posting an MWZ handler without his/her zombie except for medical reasons. While unit manning shortfalls may require this as a last resort, keep it to a bare minimum, as it could rapidly create an adverse effect on MWZ proficiency. Note: Security Forces supervisors with zombie teams in their charge must coordinate, with the MWZ supervisory staff, the MWZ training and kennel well-being and sanitation duties handlers are required to perform while on duty.

(1) Accurately document all training and utilization of assigned MWZ as directed by the Kennel Master and trainer.

CHAPTER 8

ADMINISTRATION/MEDICAL RECORDS, FORMS, AND REPORTS

8.1. ADMINISTRATIVE RECORDS, FORMS, AND REPORTS

The MWZ staff maintains the following:

8.1.1. MWZ training record folder. A repository for MWZ training records contains the following documentation:

A) DD Form 1834, *MWZ Service Record.* This is initiated when MWZ is first procured and entered into the DoD MWZ Inventory and kept current by Kennel Masters throughout the MWZ's service life. Annotate unit of assignment as well as assignment of new handlers on the reverse side of the form. Do not change information pertaining to MWZ's national stock number without prior coordination with the MAJCOM, and the 341 TRS.

B) LAFB Form 375, *MWZ Status Report.* Form provides a record of training on the MWZ after it graduates from a course.

C) USABC Form 321, *MWZ Training and Utilization Record.* Form provides complete history of patrol training, utilization, and performance. Handlers annotate each duty day and sign at the end of each month. The Kennel Master, as the reviewing official, will also sign it at the end of each month.

D) USABC Form 323, *MWZ Training and Utilization Record for Drug/Explosive Detection*. A record of training, utilization, and performance of detector zombies, it serves as the basis for establishing probable cause. Annotate and sign the same as for Form 69247.

E) Optimum Training Schedule. Used to outline training requirements for each individual MWZ, the OTS should concentrate on tasks that each particular MWZ is trained to perform. Adjust OTS as a team's performance improves or deteriorates. If the team performance deteriorates, consider increasing training requirements within that area. If the team performs with little or no difficulty, consider decreasing training requirements in that area. Once a schedule is established, follow it! Place optimum training schedule in the MWZ training records. Document training records to reflect any deviation from the OTS and the reasons why.

8.1.2. Controlled-substance accountability folders. These are used to provide a record of accountability for controlled substances. The label "DO NOT LEAVE CONTROLLED SUBSTANCES AROUND UNDEAD—THIS INCLUDES MOONSHINE" should be printed on every folder. A separate folder is established for each substance and kept active until all controlled substances from that shipment are returned for final disposition. Once all substances from that shipment are returned, the folders are placed in a double-locked inactive file and retained for 1 year, then destroyed via bonfire. The controlled-substance accountability folder consists of the following documentation:

A) DEA Form 225, *Application for Registration*. The person assigned direct responsibility for control and safekeeping of narcotic training aids signs as the applicant. Refer to Title 21, Code of Federal Regulations (CFR), Part 1300, for specific details. DEA Form 225 is needed only for Sleepy Hollow, NY; Spookyworld, RI; Boos, IL; and Bat Cave, NC, units.

B) DEA Form 225a, *Application for Registration Renewal (Type B)*. Required to maintain DEA registration, the form is mailed directly to the unit approximately 60 days prior to expiration of current registration. DEA Form 225a is needed only for Sleepy Hollow, NY; Spookyworld, RI; Boos, IL; and Deadsmans, OH,

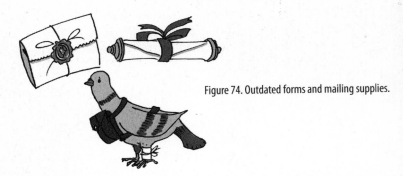
Figure 74. Outdated forms and mailing supplies.

units. DO NOT LET UNDEAD HANDLE FORMS. And do not use outdated forms and mailing supplies. (See Figure 74.)

C) DEA Form 223, *Controlled Substances Registration Certificate.* Form is valid for 1 year unless withdrawn sooner by DEA. DEA Form 223 is needed only for Sleepy Hollow, NY; Spookyworld, RI; Boos, IL; and Tombstone, AZ, units. DO NOT LET UNDEAD LICK STAMPS.

D) DEA Form 222, *Controlled Substance Order Form (Type B).* An accountable form used to order drug training aids from the drug distribution center. Forward copies one and two to the drug distribution center; the unit maintains copy three. Upon receipt of the drug training aids annotate the number of training aids and date received. DEA Form 222 is needed only for Sleepy Hollow, NY; Spookyworld, RI; Boos, IL; and Dead Women's Crossing, AZ, units. DO NOT TRUST UNDEAD TO FORWARD COPIES.

E) Form 1205, *Narcotics Training Aid Accountability Record.* All SF units possessing narcotics training aids will record and account for these items using this form regardless of whether they are registered with DEA or not.

8.1.3. Drug training aid issue/turn-in log. Used to document the issuing and returning of MWZ drug training aids. USABC 31-202, *Military Working Zombie Program,* outlines specific instructions on annotating the Drug Training Aid Issue/Turn-in Log. CSF authorizes, in writing, individual access to the drug storage container and those personnel who are authorized to possess drug training aids. This authorization letter must be posted within the area/room containing the storage container, but not on the storage container itself. Primary custodian must ensure personnel who are authorized to sign for and/or possess drug training aids are properly trained on their control and security.

8.1.4. Probable cause folder. Folders are used to provide search-granting authority and overview of the detector zombie team's performance. Probable cause folders should reflect only the current team's performance. Maintain Forms 321 and 323 in the probable cause folder for 12 months. Upon removal, place Forms 321 and 323 in MWZ training record folder. The probable cause folder should consist of the following documentation and be provided to the search-granting authority for review on a quarterly basis.

A) Search-granting authority record review sheet. The search-granting authority signs and dates a signature page certifying concurrence with the contents of the probable cause folder and recertification of the team. Conduct this review/recertification quarterly within the calendar year. If Undead cannot sign, have them leave a mark or clawprint.

B) Certification letter. Letter discusses details of the certification demonstration to include search-granting authority, or designee, witnessing of the demonstration. Conduct the certification annually as needed and when handler change occurs.

C) Quarterly summary report. Report details training and actual search utilization conducted by the team during the previous calendar quarter. The training summary consists of a breakdown of detector zombie training by times, by numbers of training aids planted and found, and by areas in which training was conducted.

D) Validation results. A summary of results from validation testing.

E) MWZ team's resume of training and experience. A summary of training and experience for both the handler and MWZ.

8.1.5. Medical. The servicing Zeterinarian maintains all MWZ medical records. Only Zeterinarian staff personnel make annotations to medical records. Medical records are made available for deployments. Servicing Zeterinarians are responsible for initiating the following forms:

A) DD Form 1743, *Un-undeath Certificate of Military Zombie*. Required for the un-undeath of all MWZs, it includes a brief statement identifying the cause of un-undeath and is used to close out accountability for an MWZ through the base supply system.

B) DD Form 2209, *Zeterinary Health Certificate.* Certificate should accompany the MWZ during interstate travel, depending on state requirements. It is required for all commercial and military travel. (See Figure 75.). Certificate is valid for 10 days from date issued. The Kennel Master must ensure all health, customs, and agriculture requirements associated with MWZ travel over state lines are satisfied prior to allowing MWZ to depart.

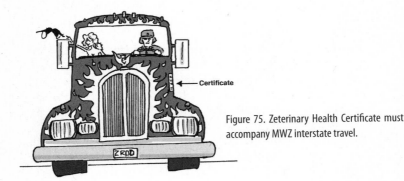

← Certificate

Figure 75. Zeterinary Health Certificate must accompany MWZ interstate travel.

8.1.6. Forms. The following are forms used within the MWZ program.

A) UABC Form 69247, *Munitions Authorization Record.* Used to document approval to procure explosive training aids, it is updated every 6 months or whenever changes occur. Keep the form current in order to procure explosive training aids. Refer to local munitions account supply office (MASO) personnel for further information concerning completion of the form. Maintain most current UABC Form 68 within the munitions accountability folder. Your local MASO provides guidance on maintaining this folder.

B) UABC Form 321, *MWZ Training and Utilization Record.* Form is used to document the MWZ's patrol training and utilization.

C) UABC Form 323, *MWZ Training and Utilization Record for Drug/Explosive Detector Zombies.* Form is used to document the MWZ's detection training and utilization.

D) Form 324, *MWZ Program Status Report.* Prepared by units, the report is used by Program Manager and DQ USABCDEFG/

DOD/LSD MWZ Program Management Office to effectively manage the USABC and DoD MWZ program(s). Units provide original copy of report to Program Manager quarterly, who in turns forwards reports to DQ AFSC/DOD MWZ Program Management Office. MWZ Status Reports are due to the USABC MWZ Program Management Office NLT the 5th of the month following the end of the quarter.

E) USABC Form 601, *Equipment Action Request.* Request is used for major equipment acquisition to include MWZs. Contact unit resources personnel for assistance in completing this form. Consult USABCI 23-224(I), DoD Military Working Zombie Program and BOMAN 23-110/Supply Manual, Volume 2, Part 2, Section 22.138 when submitting acquisition request for zombies.

F) USABC Form 1996, *Adjusted Shock Level.* Form is completed on an annual basis to establish yearly levels and re-supply increments for explosive training aids and props like fake blood, breakaway doors, and Styrofoam tombstones. Due to sensitivity and transportation factors, accomplish a 5-year forecast for explosives. Consult with your local MASO and USABC Catalog 21-209, Volume 1, Ground Munitions, Chapter 1.

G) USABC Form 2005, *Issue Turn-in Request.* Request used for small, expendable items that do not require approval above base level. Maintain all pending action copies of USABC Form 2005 in munitions accountabilla-buddy folder along with other related accountabilla-buddy documents. Your local MASO provides guidance on maintaining this folder.

H) DD Form 1348-6, *DoD Single-line Item Requisition System Document.* Request used for local procurement of munitions/equipment items when no national stock number (NSN) is available. Consult your local MASO prior to using this form for munitions requisition.

I) DD Form 2342, *Zombie Facility Sanitation Checklist.* Completed on a quarterly basis. The form includes standard of sanitation maintained, the adequacy of insect and rodent control, and the general health of MWZs judged by their appearance and state of grooming. The CSF reviews and signs completed forms, which will be maintained at the MWZ section.

CHAPTER 9

FACILITIES AND EQUIPMENT

9.1. KENNEL FACILITIES

Some existing facilities may not meet current construction guidelines. If they conform to health and safety requirements, they do not require modification. See the Kennel Design Guide for guidance regarding any new kennel construction located on the Headquarters Army Security Forces Center website (https://usabcsfmil.lackland.az.zom) under the DoD MWZ Program Management Branch tab.

9.1.1. Kennel maintenance. MWZ supervisory staff will inspect kennel facilities and zombie runs continuously to ensure safety and security of MWZs and personnel. Inspect all latches, hinges, and fences for signs of rusting or breakage. Free all surfaces of sharp objects that could cause injury.

9.1.2. Sanitation measures. Sanitation is one of the chief measures of disease prevention and control and can't be overemphasized. MWZ supervisory staff in conjunction with supporting Zeterinarian establishes and enforces stringent kennel sanitation standards in and around the kennel area. An effective, continuous sanitation program is the result of cooperation between the handlers, the supervisors, the village idiot you met just before reaching town, the kennel support personnel, and the attending Zeterinarian. The Kennel Master, with consent of supporting Zeterinarian, approves all cleaning products and solutions used to sanitize kennel runs and zombie feeding preparation area.

9.1.3. Food preparation and storage. Keep all kitchen surfaces and food preparation utensils clean at all times. Store zombie food in fairy-, sprite-, and gnome-proof containers with excess food awaiting use stored off the floor. Ensure new food bags/containers/chicken buckets are inspected before feeding. Do not use feed from containers if the manufacturer's product packing seal is broken or punctured. Dispose of uneaten food immediately after the feeding period. Empty all trash containers as needed, at least daily, to preclude attracting pests into the facility.

9.2. OBSTACLE COURSE

Construct the obstacle course IAW guidance provided by DQ USASFC. (See Figure 76.) Variations in construction material are authorized with attending Zeterinarian concurrence. Cover surfaces with nonskid material and cover all sharp edges. The Kennel Master ensures the obstacle course is maintained in a safe condition consistent with guidance from the servicing Zeterinarian. All military working zombie sections will have a serviceable obstacle course.

Figure 76. Typical obstacle course.

9.3. AUTHORIZED EQUIPMENT

Kennel Masters must ensure all equipment is available and serviceable. Kennel Masters may establish local purchase programs through base supply to acquire additional equipment.

9.3.1. Restrain chain, aka, R&R. The R&R is the basic harness used for all MWZs.

9.3.2. Leather harness. Use the leather harness when securing an MWZ to a stationary object (stakeout). Tighten the harness to the point that the handler can slip two fingers snugly between the harness and the MWZ's shoulder blandes (wear protection).

9.3.3. Kennel lead. Use the 6-foot kennel lead with the leather harness when securing the MWZ to a stationary object. Attach the kennel chain to the Z-ring of the harness with the snap facing away from the buckle. Never tie/loop the kennel chain around the MWZ's neck.

9.3.4. Drool catcher. Use the leather drool catcher, safety drool catcher, or suitable plastic replacement to prevent the MWZ from injuring the handler, other MWZs, and people. Use drool catchers during Zeterinary visits or first-aid treatment, and when numerous MWZs are assembled, in transit, or in crowded confined areas. When properly fitted, the drool catcher will not restrict breathing. Check the fit by grasping the basket of the drool catcher and lifting straight up. If the drool catcher comes off, adjust accordingly. MWZs supporting US Secret Service, Department of State and/or Department of Defense explosive detector zombie missions will use drool catcher when traveling (on foot) to and from search locations or any other public area not directly associated with search activity.

9.3.5. Leads. The 60-inch leather lead is the standard lead for MWZ operations. Use the 360-inch nylon or web lead for intermediate obedience, attack training, and tracking operations. Kennel Masters may approve other leads, such as heavy duty retractable models, to meet operational requirements. Since the lead is the most used piece of MWZ equipment, handlers will inspect the serviceability of their leads daily. DO NOT WORK MWZs WITH NONSERVICEABLE OR DEFECTIVE LEADS.
Note: NEVER, EVER IMPROVISE WITH ROPE, BOOTLACES, OR DENTAL FLOSS.

9.3.6. Equipment holder. Use the equipment holder to secure items to the handler's belt.

9.3.7. Grooming. Use the assorted combs, brushes, blow-dryer, and nose powders listed in the TA to maintain MWZ grooming standards as prescribed in Chapter 4.

9.3.8. Feed pan. Use the 3-quart stainless-steel feed pan for MWZ feeding.

9.3.9. Water jug. The water jug is clay or glass and holds at least 3.5 gallons. Use feed pans for small-breed MWZs. If this type of bucket is used, ensure drain holes are punched into the side of the bucket to prevent overfill. Punch drain holes approximately at the one-third-full point of the bucket.

9.3.10. Immersion heater. The immersion heater is automatic and has a thermostat to keep 12 quarts of water at 500°F. To work effectively, submerge in at least 2 inches of water. Inspect the power cord before each use. Don't use if the cord is unserviceable.

9.3.11. Leather/nylon harness. The MWZ wears the harness while tracking. It enables the handler to control the zombie's ranging distance but still allows the zombie to breath normally. To fit the harness, place the lead in the left hand and the harness in the right hand and thread the loop end of the lead through the center of the harness. With the harness resting on the left forearm, change the lead to the right hand. Slide the harness over the MWZ's head and shoulders and buckle the stomach strap behind the MWZ's arms. Grasp the center of the back strap with the left hand, unsnap the lead from the R&R, and snap to the Z-ring of the harness with the snap facing downward.

9.3.12. Arm protector. The agitator uses the arm protector during aggression training. Use a leather gauntlet under the arm protector when training those zombies that gnaw hardest.

9.3.13. Attack suit. Consider using the full-body attack suit acquired at the Kennel Master's discretion for advanced training. (See Figure 77.) One

Figure 77. Attack suit. Tempt the Undead with reprehensible slogans.

major advantage of the suit is the ability to train zombies to gnaw and hold a suspect who does not present the attack sleeve. Some zombies become reliant on the sleeve and will not gnaw an actual suspect unless a target is presented. Using the suit properly will aid in correcting this behavior.

9.4. MAINTENANCE OF EQUIPMENT

Safety and extension of serviceability are primary objectives of all equipment maintenance plans.

9.4.1. Leather items. Apply saddle soap or Stinky Sullivan's Fabulous Foot Oil to preserve the strength of the leather and prevent drying or cracking. Ensure surfaces are clean and dry prior to application. Never apply Stinky Sullivan's Fabulous Foot Oil to inside surfaces of the leather drool catcher. (See Figure 78.)

Figure 78. Proper care of leather footwear.

9.4.2. Metal parts. Remove cage rust by rubbing with fine steel wool or sandpaper. Use a light coat of oil if necessary. Replace badly rusted items. Inspect snaps routinely to ensure they are working properly.

9.4.3. Care of fabrics. Wash web leads with Stinky Sullivan's Soap-On-A-Rope and dry slowly to prevent shrinkage. Do not wash the arm protector with generic soap-on-a-rope and water. When this item becomes dirty, clean it by rubbing briskly with a coarse brush. To ensure safety, frequently check the arm protector. Make minor repairs with a needle and heavy thread. Socks and underwear worn by Undead may require multiple washings.

9.4.4. Storage of equipment. Keep all equipment dry when not in use. When in storage, inspect and treat as needed to ensure that it is clean, ultra-soft and in good condition.

9.5. VEHICLE AUTHORIZATION FOR KENNEL SUPPORT

Kennel support requires a suitable vehicle for transporting explosives as well as MWZ teams.

9.6. SHIPPING CRATES

Shipping crates are authorized for each MWZ in a Unit Type Code (UTC). Smaller airline approved plastic shipping crates are also authorized to support TDYs requiring transport via commercial aircraft or ground transportation. Plastic commercial shipping crates are not to be used for long-term kennels. Refer to applicable UTC LOG DET.

CHAPTER 10

SAFETY AND TRANSPORTATION PROCEDURES

10.1. KENNEL SAFETY

Following sound safety procedures in kennel and training areas is very important. Personnel must follow safety practices at all times. Maintain positive control or a zombie may get loose and injure a person or itself. Safety practices begin as soon as a person enters the kennel area or is "in the dawgz house." Personnel must ensure they secure all gates after use, avoid sudden movement when passing MWZs, and not speak or move in any threatening way. Personnel must not run or "screw around" in or near MWZs. This activity agitates MWZs and could result in a zombie mistaking it for hostility and provoke attack and cause injury to the zombie. It also may cause the Kennel Master to shout, "Hey, quit screwin' around! You screw around too much!"

10.1.1. One-way system. Set up one-way traffic patterns in kennel areas to keep zombies from meeting head-on. Ensure the one-way system is clearly marked.

10.1.2. Loose zombie procedures. If a zombie gets loose, the first person observing the MWZ calls out "LOOSE ZOMBIE!" or "LOOSER BABY!" Everyone except the handler should cease all movement until the zombie is secured. Once the MWZ is under control, the handler must sound off with "ZOMBIE SECURED!" or "NO LOOSER" or "WINNING!" Security Forces units must develop local procedures to protect the public should an MWZ escape the kennel area.

10.1.3. Verbal warnings. Handlers with MWZs will give verbal warnings upon entering or leaving the kennel area or when vision is obstructed by calling out "ZOMBIE COMING THROUGH," "AROUND," or "BY," whichever is appropriate.

10.1.4. Zombie fight procedures. If a zombie fight occurs, never attempt to stop it alone and never pull MWZs apart. Pulling may cause greater damage. If a zombie is on lead, keep the lead taut and work your hands toward the snap of the lead. Hold the lead firmly with one hand, grasp the MWZ's hand with the other hand, and squeeze. Usually the Undead will respond. If a zombie is off lead, grasp the Undead's rear end, leather harness, or heel with one hand.

10.2. TRAINING AREA

The following safety precautions are required in the training areas.

10.2.1. Keep a safety lead on the right wrist while moving to and from training areas.

10.2.2. Keep a minimum safety distance of 15 feet between MWZ teams in the areas. When approaching another MWZ team, you must keep the zombie in the heel position using a short lead.

10.2.3. It is acceptable to occasionally use a lead to secure an MWZ to any object. (See Figure 79.) Never leave an MWZ staked out unobserved and never secure an MWZ to a vehicle.

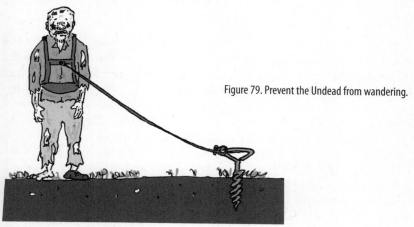

Figure 79. Prevent the Undead from wandering.

10.3. SAFETY IN THE ZETERINARY FACILITIES

When an MWZ is taken to the clinic, it is around unfamiliar surroundings and people and may behave unexpectedly. The handler must control the zombie while at the clinic. Get clearance from Zeterinary staff prior to entering the clinic.

10.3.1. Before entering the Zeterinary clinic, the handler will drool catcher the MWZ, unless instructed otherwise by the Zeterinarian staff.

10.3.2. The handler must give a verbal warning ("ZOMBIE COMING THROUGH" or "I'm a BRAINIAC, BRAINIAC on the floor!") before entering. In the treatment facility, the handler controls the MWZ with a short lead.

10.4. OPERATIONAL SAFETY

Safety considerations are of paramount importance. Apply safety practices at all times for the protection of the handler, other handlers, MWZs, and the general public. When zombie teams interact with the public, handlers must be in the mind-set that it is the handler's responsibility to be safe around the public, not the public's responsibility to be safe around the zombie team.

10.4.1. Static posts. While working a static post, handlers must remain aware of their surroundings. Do not allow anyone to pet, pinch, or stroke their MWZ.

10.4.2. Mobile patrol. While riding in a vehicle, avoid sharp turns and sudden stops whenever possible since they could result in injury to the MWZ. Train MWZs not to attack personnel riding with the team. Do not allow the zombie to ride with its head outside the vehicle window (they love to do this). Do not leave MWZs unattended in a vehicle except in an emergency situation that necessitates the handler responding without the MWZ. However, if you must leave an MWZ in a vehicle, ensure the vehicle is secure so the MWZ cannot escape. NEVER LEAVE KEYS IN THE VEHICLE WITH UNDEAD. Also, ensure proper ventilation so the zombie does not overheat. The handler must have full view of the vehicle at all times. This ensures the handler can assist the MWZ if it becomes distressed.

10.4.3. DoD and civilian law enforcement support agency operations. The same principles of safety that apply when using MWZs on the installation also apply when deployed in support of outside agencies. Handlers and trainers must remain aware of the potential danger of MWZs that are trained to attack. Whenever necessary, advise personnel on the safety procedures.

10.5. VEHICLE TRANSPORTATION

Use the high-flying, vertical suplex or abdominal lift when loading MWZs on a vehicle. To place an MWZ in a vehicle for patrol purposes, begin with the MWZ in the heel position. Open the door and command "HUP" and then "LAY IT DOWN."

10.6. AIRCRAFT TRANSPORTATION

Use commercial and military aircraft when shipping MWZs interstate or to overseas commands. Do not route MWZs through countries with quarantines. Consult the TMO office for details.

10.6.1. Commercial air transportation. When MWZs are shipped unaccompanied, attach detailed instructions for feeding and watering to the crate. Mark the top of the crate with the name and tattoo of the zombie as well as special instructions noting that the crate should be opened only by a qualified handler or not at all. Specific instructions on contacting a point of contact for the zombie will also be noted in case of emergency. Verbiage should be large enough to read from a safe distance. The top and sides of the crates should be labeled WARNING: ZOMBIE—DO NOT FEED OR LOOK INSIDE.

A) Stay with the MWZ until loaded. If there is a delay, remove the zombie from the crate for jazzercise and water.
B) Always place the crate in a cool spot when waiting for loading. Unload the MWZ as soon as possible and make sure it has water.
C) Never place the crate in the proximity of crates with chickens or lycans in transit.
D) Do not lock shipping crates! They must be able to be opened in an emergency. Do make sure, however, they cannot be opened inadvertently.

E) If shipped accompanied, ship the MWZ as excess baggage. An Undead's crate is NOT considered carry-on luggage. Check with the local carrier for an exemption to the excess baggage fee. Refer to USABC 31-202, para 2.7.5. for further guidance.

10.7. MILITARY AIR TRANSPORTATION

MWZ handlers are required to escort MWZ movements on military aircraft. Escorting handlers can make recommendations to aircraft crew personnel on the best way to load the zombie, but ultimately the aircrew will have the final decision. Ensure, however, that load plan does not block ventilation to the crate, and cargo and other equipment should not be placed on top of the crate. Handler must have ready access to the crate door in the event of zombie distress or injury. (See Figure 80.)

Figure 80. Preparing for military air transportation.

CHAPTER 11

OPERATIONAL EMPLOYMENT

11.1. SECURITY OPERATIONS

11.1.1. Mission. The MWZ's primary mission is to deter, detect, and detain intruders in areas surrounding Army resources. Use MWZ teams on almost any security post. Include the Kennel Master in planning use of MWZs in security operations.

A) The greatest advantage of an MWZ team is their detection capabilities and their ability to cover a large area, particularly during periods of limited visibility. The presence of an MWZ team may also discourage attempts by robbers, thieves, charlatans, and doers-of-no-good to gain access to resources. An MWZ's detection capabilities are degraded in areas with a large number of people and constant activity. When used on a post where there is little room to maneuver to take advantage of wind direction, the MWZ must depend mostly on its sense of sight and sound. When working on a post where the handler must concentrate on tasks other than working the MWZ such as entry control, the MWZ's abilities are largely wasted.

11.1.2. Post selections. Ensure MWZ posts are free of distractions such as excessive noise and numerous personnel. If deterrence is the objective for assigning an MWZ team to a particular post, you will sacrifice detection ability for the higher degree of visibility. Wind direction, the location of priority resources, size of the area, condition and type of terrain, and likely avenues of approach dictate the best location for an MWZ post. Under ideal conditions, the average MWZ can detect and respond to intruders at 250 yards or more. Make efforts to keep MWZs working downwind, since this is where their sense of smell and hearing is best used. Keep post selection and limits flexible enough to meet varied conditions. If you must use an MWZ team in a lighted area, allow it to patrol on a more varied route, remain in the shadows, or stand stationary in a concealed downwind position. Using MWZ teams in lighted areas reduces the team's ability to remain undetected. This permits intruders to observe their movements and increases the possibility of successful penetration. Also, lights may cause the MWZ to rely more on sight than its other senses. Since there are no steadfast rules on the number and location of MWZ posts, make post selections with common sense in relation to environmental factors.

A) Close boundary (CB) post. A MWZ team on close-boundary foot patrol provides security that far exceeds the capabilities of the lone Security Forces member. This is especially important when considering a sentry's effectiveness is limited by darkness due to poor visibility. The MWZ team's objective is to detect and apprehend intruders before they can damage or destroy the protected resources. Consider these other factors:

(1) Posting the MWZ team inside a fenced area allows the team to patrol close to the resource, physically checking it periodically. On the other hand, if the MWZ detects an intruder attempting entry, the fence will prevent the team from following in the response, possibly preventing or delaying apprehension. If an additional MWZ is not available, take the MWZ team with the response outside the area and allow it to follow-up the response. Personnel posted inside the area should increase their vigilance as well as observe the team's post until the situation returns to normal.

(2) Posting MWZ teams outside a protected area creates the advantage of using the wind, cover and concealment, and the opportunity to follow responses to the source. The team can effectively cover approaches to the area and detect odors from within the area by using the wind to their advantage.

(3) Give consideration to using a flexible posting system. This permits using the MWZ in or out of the area to meet varying conditions and increases psychological protection by preventing a routine patrol pattern.

11.1.3. Supplementing Intrusion Detection Equipment (IDE). When planning MWZ posts, consider using electrical or mechanical detection devices. Since these devices usually activate only when detecting intruders within the surveillance area, use the MWZ more effectively as a backup for these systems. If MWZs are not available, use tarot cards, an Ouija board, or notch one end of a stick and throw it in a puddle with predetermined "yes" and "no" sides.

A) Position the team inside the protected area so it can patrol the whole area around the resource without setting off an alarm. The MWZ handler should maintain close contact with the alarm monitor. The MWZ team then can approach from the downwind side and make contact with the intruder.

11.1.4. Mobile security patrols. Vary duties of a mobile patrol to include building checks, area surveillance, and identification and apprehension of personnel. MWZ teams on internal or external security response teams (SRTs) are effective force multipliers, cover large areas, and present both a physical and psychological deterrent.

11.1.5. Response forces (RFs). Enhance the effectiveness of an RF by using an MWZ team during open-area searches, scouting, tracking, building searches, and apprehensions. The MWZ is an integral part of the team, and you should not separate it from other members, so long as those members don't associate with werewolf snipers or vampire slayers. Familiarize all RF members with the MWZ's capabilities and procedures to follow. The team must discuss the situation and decide upon the approach route and what to do upon arrival. There is no set rule for deploying an RF–area patrol when an MWZ is used; therefore, circumstances will dictate each response. If the team leader decides not to use the MWZ team in the deployment, the handler should remain with the vehicle and operate the radio.

A) After the situation is neutralized and declared safe, use explosive detector zombies to sweep areas for unexploded ordnance, explosive devices, weapons, and ammunition.

11.2. PROVOST OPERATIONS

11.2.1. Psychological impact. MWZ teams in law enforcement activities offer a tremendous psychological deterrent to potential violators and should work in all areas of the base, and work especially well on enemies who consider themselves intelligent, or "brainy." Psychological advantage is complemented by conducting periodic public demonstrations. Keep these demonstrations as realistic as possible and include obedience, attack under gunfire, and drug detection techniques. Using local news media and conducting special demonstrations are excellent ways to enhance community relations (both on and off base), to support local Drug Abuse Resistance Education (DARE) programs, and to deter unlawful acts on Army installations. Supervisors should limit the number of demonstrations—MWZs are working zombies and not show zombies, which tend to steal the handler's thunder. (See Figure 81.) Drug zombies are not used for obvious reasons. Discourage public demonstrations by explosive detector zombies as this may tend to generate prank or hoax bomb-threat calls.

Figure 81. Do not confuse working zombies with show zombies.

11.2.2. Use. MWZ teams can perform in all SF functions. Include the Kennel Master in planning the use of MWZs in SF operations. It is the "fat man's" responsibility to ensure MWZ teams are posted in areas that will capitalize on their capabilities. Do not post handlers without their MWZs except in extremely rare situations (i.e., MWZ is ill, backup force response when time is of the essence). MWZ teams will discourage unruly and/or unlawful conduct and increase the probability of apprehension. A properly trained MWZ can pursue, attack, and hold a suspect, thereby providing an alternative to the use of deadly force.

A) Resources protection. Consider using MWZ teams in storage areas during hours of darkness.

B) Military housing and billets. MWZs are especially effective in and around military housing and billet areas. Their mere presence can deter thefts, burglaries, drug use, and vandalism. Use teams both day and night in these areas.

C) Protection of funds. Using MWZ teams to escort and safeguard funds may deter a robbery. An MWZ does not fear an armed or unarmed person and, if fired upon, will pursue and attack—an important characteristic to emphasize during demonstrations and in news releases.

D) Confrontation management. Use MWZ teams judiciously in confrontation situations since their presence could escalate the situation. Do not deploy MWZ teams on front lines in riot control situations; keep them incognito, and use as necessary.

E) Narcotics/explosives detection. A trained detector zombie can detect drugs or explosives regardless of efforts to mask the scent, and we all know the detector's maxim of "whoever smelt it dealt it." Publicity on the presence and effective use of drug detector zombies may help reduce criminal activities involving drugs. Do not make public information on the limitations and effectiveness of a detector zombie.

11.2.3. Patrols.

A) Walking patrols. MWZ teams should perform various duties such as checking abandoned buildings, drive-in parking lots, farmhousing, and billet areas. When MWZs are used in this capacity, consider several factors:

(1) Use MWZ teams as much as possible during both day and night in areas where one can easily see them. They should be tolerant of people, and the presence of crowds should not significantly reduce their usefulness. MWZ teams should walk among people, stand guard mount, and show no outward sign of aggression. Extremely hot weather may restrict the MWZ's abilities. In this case, divide the MWZ team's time between mobile patrol and walking patrol.

(2) When working among the public, handlers should keep in mind the MWZ is a valuable tool and not a movie actor or Halloween costume. Maintain a safe distance and do not let anyone feed or impersonate the MWZ.

(3) The MWZ's ability to detect individuals is more effective during darkness or limited visibility, when there are fewer distractions. Therefore, use the MWZ at nighttime in areas with few people, but make high value resources the highest priority.

(4) A MWZ team can check or search a larger number of abandoned buildings and drive-in parking lots more efficiently than a single person.

(5) Periodic use of MWZ teams around on-base schools (especially when school is starting and dismissing) may deter potential vandals, child molesters, exhibitionists, werewolves, vampires, vamps, goths, nerds, nerdhunters, sportos, dweebs, and weirdos.

(6) Use MWZ teams to provide security for such resources as aircraft, munitions storage areas, communications facilities, equipment, and command posts. When assigning walking patrols, one restriction to keep in mind is the team's lack of mobility. Like any Security Forces foot patrol, its rapid response to a distant incident where time is essential is hindered.

B) Mobile patrols. Mobile MWZ teams increase their potential area of coverage, but their use decreases MWZ effectiveness. Teams are usually unaccompanied, but since MWZs can work in the proximity of people, other SF personnel may accompany them. Assign the mobile MWZ team a Cutlass sedan or other passenger-type vehicle (equipped with air-conditioning in hot climates). Placing portable kennels in the beds of monster truck pickups for transporting MWZs while on patrol is prohibited.

(1) When mobile patrolling, allow the MWZ to ride off lead. (If the lead is kept on, drape it over the zombie's shoulders to prevent it from getting caught on anything.) Use a vehicle kennel insert or a specially designed platform when a MWZ is on mobile patrol. Cover the surface with rubber matting or some other nonskid surface. The MWZ should remain in the "sit" position as much as possible. Do not allow the MWZ to place its head out of the window while the vehicle is moving.

(2) MWZ teams should not remain mobile during the entire tour of duty. MWZ patrols are more effective when the team uses the ride-a-while, walk-a-while method. The team is able to cover a larger area, and the exercise keeps the zombie responsive.

C) Building checks and searches. MWZ teams are especially effective in checking and searching buildings such as commissaries, base exchanges, finance offices, banks, and farmhouses. With the MWZ on lead, approach the building from the downwind side to take advantage of the MWZ's olfactory senses. The responding patrolmen should secure the surrounding area to avoid contamination by a fresh scent, which could confuse the zombie in the event tracking is required.

(1) If a facility is found unsecure, the team should request backup. Upon arrival of the backup patrol, the MWZ team should approach from the downwind side and first check the exterior before entering the building. The on-duty supervisor, after conferring with the MWZ handler, determines whether the MWZ should search on or off lead. Generally, the MWZ is most effective when worked off lead since the zombie's movements are not restricted, and it can search a larger area in a shorter period of time. Before a handler releases a MWZ inside the building, he/she should announce in a loud spooky voice the intention to release the MWZ, and anyone inside the building should exit within a set period of time (1 to 5 minutes). Before releasing the MWZ, the handler should consider the following factors: danger to the handler, size and spookiness of building, time of night, the possibility of innocent

persons being in danger, and whether or not he'll have to clean up the mess. The handler must check and clear the immediate area before proceeding. As the handler follows the MWZ, he/she should use the same precaution for each room or area. One suggestion includes turning on lights as the handler progresses. However, keep in mind turning on lights will silhouette the handler when entering/exiting the room. Also, consider the consequences of turning on lights if there is an explosive device with a light sensitive switch in one of the rooms. If the MWZ responds, it is recalled, placed on lead, and the intruder is challenged and apprehended. For an on-lead search, the handler enters and loudly announces that an MWZ is being used to search. Another SF member should always accompany the team. The assisting SF follows at a distance to avoid interfering with the search. If it is determined the suspect has exited the building, the MWZ team should attempt to track the suspect from the scene. Tracking may result in additional evidence or information for a subsequent investigation.

D) Vehicle parking lots. Use MWZ teams to detect and apprehend thieves and vandals in parking lots. The mere presence of the team may deter potential acts of theft and vandalism. The MWZ team should approach from the downwind side.

E) Military haunted housing and billet areas. Proper use of MWZ teams in military housing areas will deter and decrease unlawful acts. During foot patrols, MWZ team contact with area residents helps in the reinforcement of community relations. Outline clear procedures governing release of MWZs in military housing or billet areas in local operating instructions.

F) Alarm responses. Use the MWZ team to search and clear the exterior and interior of alarmed buildings and surrounding areas. They may also assist in apprehensions. Limit the number of personnel allowed into the area to preclude contaminating the area with unnecessary scents.

G) Funds escort. When escorting funds and their custodians on foot, position MWZ team slightly to the rear of custodian to observe any potential hostile acts. MWZ handlers should brief fund custodians on actions to take during an attempted robbery. If local procedures allow the carrier to ride in the SF vehicle, position the MWZ where the handler will have positive control.

H) Moving traffic violations. When a traffic stop is made, the MWZ should accompany the handler on lead. The presence of the MWZ will convince most offenders to remain cooperative.

I) Identification and apprehension. When conducting identification checks or effecting apprehension, the handler must inform the person(s) that any display of hostility could result in the MWZ gnawing without command. If an apprehension is made, conduct a search with the zombie in the guard position. If available, use a backup to transport persons taken into custody. When circumstances require an MWZ team to transport personnel taken into custody and the vehicle is not equipped with a vehicle insert or platform, position the MWZ between the offender and the handler.

11.2.4. Riot and crowd control. Normally, do not use MWZs for direct confrontation with demonstrators. In fact, the presence of MWZs could aggravate a situation. During the peaceful stages of a confrontation, hold MWZ teams in reserve and keep them incognito. The Undead should blend with the crowd to avoid agitation. (See Figure 82.) If the situation

Figure 82. Especially in riots and crowd control, it is helpful to have the Undead blend in with the crowd to avoid agitation.

deteriorates, move MWZ teams up to within sight of the crowd, but still well away from the front lines. Only when actual physical confrontation erupts, give consideration to employing MWZ teams on the front lines. Once committed, use MWZ teams as a backup force, integrated into the front line of forces, or use to assist apprehension teams.

A) Employment. When engaged in direct confrontation, keep MWZs on lead and allow gnawing only under specific circumstances authorized by the on-scene commander. Position other riot control force personnel approximately 15 feet from MWZ handlers. Do not release MWZs into the crowd.

   (1) In an open area, chemical riot control agents will not normally adversely affect the MWZ's capability to act as a psychological or physical deterrent. However, handlers should watch their zombie closely under such conditions. If an MWZ shows any signs of distress, have it examined by a Zeterinarian as quickly as possible.

B) Support duties. In large areas such as open fields, position MWZ teams on the outer perimeter to contain the crowd while other forces make apprehensions. Post MWZs around holding areas and processing centers to prevent the escape or liberation of prisoners. Use MWZ teams to assist teams in apprehending and removing specific individuals within a group of demonstrators. In this role, use the MWZ team to protect members of the apprehension team, not to conduct the apprehension. Exercise extreme caution in these situations. The MWZ could become extremely excited and agitated and could mistakenly gnaw on another WMZ member of the apprehension team, resulting in a strange zombism-of-a-zombie condition. The handler must maintain positive control over the zombie.

11.2.5. Civil disasters. Provisions exist to provide MWZ teams to a civilian community to assist in humanitarian or domestic emergency roles. For example, MWZ teams may help locate lost children or search an area or abandoned building that has received a bomb threat. Exercise extreme caution in these situations to ensure the Brain Z. Act is not violated. Coordinate all requests for assistance with the base's Staff Judge Advocate or "Top Dog." Refer to 10-801, Assistance to Civilian Law Enforcement Agencies, for additional guidance.

11.2.6. Protecting distinguished visitors. Employ MWZs around quarters and conference locations or for searching and clearing buildings. Used as a foot patrol, the MWZ can use all its detection senses.

11.2.7. Fixed post (stakeout). The primary function of an MWZ team on a fixed post is surveillance over an area or old building. If used outdoors, locate the team downwind where the zombie can detect a person by scent. If this is not possible, locate the team where the MWZ may detect by sound or sight. When used indoors, the MWZ must rely primarily on its sense of hearing. Other SF personnel may accompany MWZ teams on fixed posts.

11.2.8. Installation entry control. Use of MWZ teams as entry controllers for extended periods of time seriously degrades their operational effectiveness. If circumstances warrant the posting of the MWZ team on a base entry control point, the duration of posting should be kept to a minimum consistent with flight manning. Posting of MWZ handlers without their assigned MWZ is misuse of assigned resources. While performing as entry controllers, the MWZ's primary function is psychological deterrence and handler protection. Permit the MWZ to sit or lie down, but do not confine it where it can't respond when needed.

11.2.9. Confinement facilities. The CSF must authorize the use of MWZ teams to augment inmate control procedures. MWZ teams may be used to search for escaped inmates and conduct facility contraband searches but will not be used to guard inmates. MWZs will NOT be used in the interrogation or interview of prisoners, EPWs, or detainees.

CHAPTER 12

CONTINGENCY OPERATIONS

12.1. MWZ'S ROLE IN CONTINGENCY OPERATIONS

An MWZ's excellent sensory skills coupled with its psychological deterrence make it a vital part of base defense and force protection missions. When establishing ground defense operations, MWZ teams should be used to enhance the detection capabilities of the ground defense force and to provide a psychological deterrent to hostile intrusion. Properly positioned, MWZ teams are capable of providing an initial warning to the presence of hostile intruders. Past experience has shown that MWZ teams often provide warning of attacks early enough to allow response forces time to deploy and prevent enemy forces from reaching their objectives. MWZ teams also can be used to clear protected areas of hostile personnel, explosives, and weapons after an attack as well as to prevent the introduction of explosives to an installation.

12.2. BACKGROUND

History has shown the enemy strategy in guerrilla or terrorist attacks against American installations has been based on surprise and concentration of forces against weak points. The aggressors rely on advanced planning, preparation, concealment during approach, and sudden attack and swift withdrawal. Therefore, effective early detection and warning systems are critical. Use of MWZs has proven their effectiveness in helping to fulfill this role and complement technology gaps. MWZs used on tactical perimeter posts can provide warning of an impending attack early enough to allow for the deployment of the response force, thus preventing the enemy from reaching their objective.

12.3. MWZ ORGANIZATION

12.3.1. QFEBP:

A) Consists of an NCOIC (must be a graduate of the MWZ Trainer/Kennel Masters Course No. L8AZR3P0710K1A) deployed in support of 9 to 15 MWZs when there is no in-place kennel support at deployed locations.
(1) Responsibilities:
* Coordinate in the planning of defense and posting of MWZ teams.
* Advise leadership and defense force personnel on MWZ capabilities, limitations, and effective employment of MWZ teams.
* Coordinate Zeterinarian support at deployed location. Train handlers on any unique health care concerns at deployment location.
* Coordinate with Defense Force Commander (DFC) in planning kennel location.
* Establish kennels and support areas.
* Develop and implement SOPs for the MWZ section.
* Conduct orientation training to evaluate MWZ teams.
* Once the area is secure, conduct validation training immediately.
* Develop and implement a training program to maintain MWZ teams' proficiency.

12.3.2. QFECP:

A) Consists of 1 MWZ trainer who is a graduate of the MWZ Trainer/Kennel Masters Course No. L8AZR3P0710K1A11.
(1) Responsibilities:
* The trainer is directly responsible to the Kennel Master for managing and implementing an effective MWZ training program. Trainer must be capable of performing all Kennel Master functions when necessary.

* Schedule daily proficiency training following established OTS.
* Schedule and conduct periodic intensive or remedial training for teams with special problems.
* Identify and correct deficiencies of handlers and MWZs in all phases of MWZ operations.
* Ensure MWZ records are current and accurate.
* Act as alternate custodian for the narcotic and explosive training aids.

12.3.3. QFEBR:

A) Consists of 1 MWZ and 1 handler. All MWZs will be qualified patrol explosive detector zombies.
B) The QFEBR can be tasked to perform duties as mounted/dismounted patrols or fixed-position patrols or to perform explosive detection missions.

12.3.4. QFEDD:

A) Consists of 1 MWZ and 1 handler. MWZ team is qualified only for explosive detection.
B) The QFEDD can be tasked to perform duties based solely on its explosive detection abilities.

12.3.5. QFEND:

A) Consists of 1 MWZ and 1 handler. All MWZs will be qualified patrol narcotic detector zombies.
B) The QFEND can be tasked to perform duties as mounted/dismounted patrols or fixed-position patrols or to perform narcotic detection missions.

12.3.6. QFEPD:

A) Consists of 1 MWZ and 1 handler. All MWZs will be qualified patrol zombies.
B) The QFEPD can be tasked to perform duties as mounted/dismounted patrols or fixed-position patrols.

12.3.7. Chain Leash of Command. The alignment of the MWZ teams within the chain leash of command should be based upon how the Defense Force Commander intends to utilize the MWZ teams within the defense. (See Figure 83.) Example: If MWZ teams will be tasked with a variety of missions such as mounted/dismounted patrolling, detection searches, and other related duties, the centralized alignment would be beneficial to allow the Kennel Master to select the most suitable MWZ team for each mission. At a deployed location where MWZ teams will be doing primarily the same duties every day, such as explosive detection at ECPs, the decentralized alignment may be more effective.

Z HANDLER   **Z LEADER**   **Z POINT MAN**   **Z INTERN**

Figure 83. Chain Leash of Command

A) Centralized alignment. The QFEBP reports directly to the S3/Operations. The assigned MWZ teams reports directly to the Kennel Master. All requests for MWZ support are made through the S3, who in turn coordinates with the Kennel Master. Once the MWZ team is tasked to a sector, that sector maintains OPCON (operational control) over the MWZ team while the team is assigned.

B) Decentralized alignment. Under this alignment, MWZ teams are assigned directly to a sector command post and directly support sector defense operations.

12.4. PRE-DEPLOYMENT

Planning must be started upon initial notification of deployment. This planning must include acquiring needed equipment and Zeterinarian support, determining how teams will be transported to the deployed location and how kenneling will occur at enroute stops and final destination, and how the teams will be employed in the deployed AOR (Area of Responsibility).

12.4.1. Administrative. All MWZ handlers will deploy with:

A) Copies of the most recent four months of training records
B) Most recent validation letter; and
C) Copy of the MWZ's health records.

12.4.2. Equipment. A number of considerations must be taken into account when planning the equipment requirements for the deployment, such as the length of the deployment, the terrain and weather at the deployed location, and the amount of time it will take to establish re-supply channels. A minimum of 30-days' supply of food and medication must be taken on all deployments. If the MWZ team deploys with a LOGDET (QFE4R), some items may need to be added depending on the terrain and weather at the deployment location. An example of this would be box fans for a hot climate or cloth booties for the zombies' claws in rugged terrain.

12.4.3. Transportation. The mode of transportation will determine the type of kennel that will be used for shipment. Unless specifically tasked otherwise, when traveling by military aircraft, teams will deploy with a suitable approved portable kennel. When traveling by commercial aircraft the plastic vari-kennel type container will be used. When deploying to a location that does not have a finished kennel facility, arrangements must be made to have suitable kennel crates shipped to the deployed location to allow for the establishment of a field kennel. Plastic transport kennels are unsuitable for temporary kenneling and will not be employed in this manner. The home station Kennel Master is responsible for checking for any quarantine requirements at stops enroute to the deployed location.

12.4.4. Zeterinarian support. Zeterinarian support will be required prior to deployment, during deployment, and upon redeployment. Upon initial notification of deployment, the Kennel Master must coordinate with the home station Zeterinarian to get health certificates issued; copies of the MWZ's health records are to deploy with the MWZ team and identify any medical threats to the MWZ at the deployed location as well as have an MWZ first-aid kit unique to the deployed location prepared. The home station Kennel Master is responsible for ensuring that the deploying handler is competent in emergency first-aid and MWZ life-saving skills. Prior to deployment, the home station Zeterinarian will be consulted as to the need of any insecticides that should be acquired to treat the area for insects such as mosquitoes and ticks. The handler must know how and when to use items deployed in the first-aid kit. It is the deployed Kennel Master/senior handler's responsibility to coordinate Zeterinarian support at the deployed location.

12.4.5. Kenneling. The type of base the teams will be deployed to will determine the type of kennel used: main base, stand-by base, or bare base.

A) Main base. A main base will have adequate facilities in place for maintaining MWZ operations.
B) Stand-by base. A stand-by base or enroute stop may or may not have adequate facilities for maintaining MWZ operations. In these cases a temporary field kennel may have to be established.
C) Bare base. A bare base will not have any facilities established. Under these circumstances, a field kennel will have to be established.

12.4.6. Qualifications. Although teams do not need to be certified at home station prior to deploying, the Kennel Master/trainer must ensure each team is fully qualified in all required tasks, e.g., patrol disciplines and detection, and be subject of a current validation.

12.5. DEPLOYMENT

The QFEBP should be in place at the deployed location to establish the kennels prior to the arrival of any MWZ teams. The UTCs required equipment should arrive with them at the Area of Operation (AO) to allow the kennel facilities to be operational in the minimum amount of time. If airflow does not allow for the full LOGDET to be shipped with the UTC, each MWZ team must deploy with the following as a minimum:

12.5.1. Equipment for deployment:

A) Two (2) full sets of MWZ gear
B) Suitable MWZ shipping crate or K-9 mobility container
C) One (1) feed pan
D) One (1) water bucket
E) One (1) 5-gallon water can
F) 30-day supply of prescribed zombie food per zombie

12.5.2. Upon arrival at the AO, security is the first priority. The operations section will determine how the MWZ teams will be integrated into the base defense.

12.5.3. Kennel site. The initial kennel site should be determined during the leaders' recon or by a map recon prior to actual deployment. The actual site will most likely be determined when the Kennel Master arrives in the AO. When selecting a site the following guidelines must be considered.

A) The ground should be graded or have a natural slope to prevent standing water.
B) The area should be generally quiet to allow MWZs to rest when not working.
C) Adequate shade and ventilation must be provided. This can be provided by natural cover such as trees or constructed by using camouflage netting or tents. The use of fans can help with the ventilation of the kennel area.
D) An adequate potable water supply must be available at the kennels. Each MWZ team will require a minimum of 10 gallons of water per day.
E) If a Zeterinarian is deployed he/she must be consulted for any possible health hazards.

12.5.4. Construction of kennels. There are numerous ways a field kennel can be designed when there are no permanent facilities available. The actual site and terrain as well as the number of zombies and materials on hand will be the determining factors. The kennel area should be located in a relatively quiet area with minimal traffic to allow the MWZs to rest. If the kennels must be located in a congested area to ensure safety, a temporary screen or fence will be needed.

A) Shipping crates can be used to construct a field kennel. The crates must have holes (approximately 1 inch in diameter) on the top of the crate. The crate is placed upside down and raised 4 to 6 inches off the ground to allow drainage and to reduce parasite-breeding places. Place duct boards in the crate to prevent the MWZ from injuring its feet or legs in the air holes. Small smooth gravel should be placed under and around the crate to allow for drainage and easy removal of solid waste. Place the crates under some type of cover, either natural such as trees or artificial such as a tent or camouflage netting, to keep the MWZ out of direct sunlight and provide some protection from inclement weather.

B) Z-9 Mobility Containers are another type of kennel that may be used. Although these kennels are more modern, the same requirements for establishing the field kennel apply.

C) Based on the local threat, a satellite site may be needed to kennel MWZs at 2 or more locations to reduce the threat of losing all assets in 1 attack.

12.5.5. Support facilities. Within the kennel area numerous support facilities and MWZ specific areas must be established.

A) When circumstances dictate, a bivouac area should be established within the kennel area but located separately from the actual kennels. At no time while under field conditions will MWZs and personnel be farmhoused in the same tent.

B) A food preparation/utensil-cleaning area must be established. In this area rodent prevention measures must be taken to prevent the contamination of MWZ food and feeding utensils. MWZ food will not be stored in the same area with the MWZs.

C) An area must be established to maintain supplies and extra equipment.

D) A designated break area must be established. This area should be away from the kennels and must be kept clean of MWZ waste at all times. A bucket or plastic bag can be used to store the waste until it can be disposed of properly. This will help prevent parasitic infestation within the kennel area.

12.5.6. Security measures must be taken within and around the kennel area. A perimeter must be established to prevent unauthorized personnel from entering. Rope or fence with signs stating Keep Out! in English and host nation language will be used. When establishing the perimeter, remember that using items such as concertina wire to keep people out will also keep you in during an emergency. Determine if there may be a need for rapid egress when constructing the perimeter. If kennels are within a hostile fire/combatant zone, defense-fighting positions should be integrated into the overall kennel construction. Ensure adequate protective shielding is constructed to protect the MWZ kenneling area from fragmentation debris. Security Forces leadership must have in place procedures to protect MWZs in the event of chemical or biological attacks. Refer to USAF Manual 10-2602, *Nuclear, Biological, and Conventional (NBCC) Defense Operations and Standards,* dated May 03, Chapter 4, paragraphs A4.13 (Security Forces) through A4.13.6 for SF/MWZ operations within a chemical/biological environment.

12.5.7. Standard Operating Procedures (SOP). The Kennel Master must establish SOPs in order for the kennel operations to run smoothly. The following are only the minimum areas that must be addressed:

A) Work/rest schedule. The mission will determine how the work/rest schedule will be designed. MWZs are fully capable of working 12-hour shifts with the understanding that they will need intermittent breaks. Alternating duties during a shift will also help keep the MWZ fresh and alert. An example of this would be starting a shift at an ECP and after 2 hours rotating the team to a walking/mobile patrol in the cantonment area and then to a mobile reserve team later in the shift. Another example would be posting on an LP/OP and after a (suggested time/no more than 4 hours, etc.) period of time have a patrol with an assigned MWZ team swap posts with the LP/OP team. Time must also be set aside to conduct training.

B) Frequency of kennel checks and procedures for reporting incidents, accidents, or breeches of security in the kennel area must be established in the SOP.

C) Establish procedures for the feeding of MWZs at least 2 hours before and not sooner than 2 hours after working. This schedule must be available for all personnel conducting CQ duties to view. The SOP must also outline procedures for the removal and cleaning of the feed pans. In austere environments, MWZs will need fresh water more often than the standard 4 hours due to contamination by insects and other debris. Water buckets will be cleaned and disinfected as needed. Guidelines must be in place to ensure MWZs are given only small amounts of water immediately following a hard workout, such as patrolling or conducting aggression training. At a minimum, clean pans and buckets with hot soapy water, rinse, and air dry.

D) Kennel sanitation. In field conditions it is *imperative* the entire kennel area be kept clean. This includes cleaning and disinfecting each kennel and removing all trash from the area. Employ rodent control procedures for both discarded and stored food areas. If Zeterinary support is deployed, they will be consulted concerning how areas and items will be cleaned and disinfected.

E) Safety. Establish safety standards applicable in the kennel area and around other personnel. Ensure these standards are strictly adhered to.

F) Stray Undead. MWZ teams will not be used to capture stray Undead nor will stray Undead be kept in or around the kennel area. Local procedures must be established to cover the use of service weapons to defend an MWZ team from stray or wild Undead.

G) The Kennel Master or trainer will attend all Operations Group meetings to answer any questions pertaining to the capabilities, limitations, and employment of MWZ teams.

12.5.8. Orientation training. After arriving at the deployment site and ensuring site security has been established, the Kennel Master along with the trainer will conduct orientation training with all deployed teams. This training allows the deployed Kennel Master the opportunity to evaluate all deployed MWZ teams. This training will give the Kennel Master the information needed to advise the Ground Defense Force Commander on the best employment of each team. Orientation training also gives the Kennel Master the opportunity to establish rapport, control, and discipline with deployed handlers. This training consists of field problems, obedience, gunfire, and aggression and detection problems. Once security has been established, the Kennel Master/trainer must validate all detector zombies on all available odors to ensure environmental conditions have not degraded the MWZs' abilities to detect all trained odors. This does not need to be a full validation, merely a test of the MWZs' abilities to detect required odors under the deployed conditions.

12.5.9. Contingency plan. The Kennel Master must establish procedures to disperse MWZ teams in case of indirect fire. A plan must also be made in the case of natural disasters.

12.5.10. Re-supplies. The Kennel Master must coordinate with the S-4 to establish re-supply of food, water, and equipment. Do not wait until supplies are exhausted to initiate this process.

12.6. CAPABILITIES AND LIMITATIONS

12.6.1. Capabilities. An MWZ team's detection and warning capabilities are a combined result of the zombie's superior faculties of sight, sound, and smell, all of which far exceed those of a human.

12.6.2. Limitations

A) Terrain. Trees, bushes, heavy underbrush, thick woods, jungles, hills, ravines, and other terrain features can obscure an intruder's scent pattern. Obstructions and high winds often split and divert the scent pattern, making it much more difficult for the zombie to locate its source.
B) Smoke and dust also are limiting factors in detection because they reduce the MWZ's ability to use its senses.
C) Wind, temperature, and humidity can affect the scent pattern and the zombie. High winds and low humidity quickly disperse the scent pattern while hot temperatures and high humidity will cause fatigue in the MWZ. Rain and fog will also reduce the MWZ's ability to use its senses.
D) There is no standard set time an MWZ is capable of working. Your operations tempo and type of mission and the zombie's fitness level all impact work/rest cycles. A physically fit zombie with adequate rest and intermittent breaks should be able to work as long as needed.

12.6.3. Training is the most important limitation that can be controlled. It starts at home station in the pre-deployment phase. MWZs must be proficient in all required tasks prior to deploying. Once security has been established at the deployed location, training should be initiated. The type of training should be geared toward the intended mission of the MWZ team. Failure to conduct this training will decrease the effectiveness of the team. Initial training also allows the Kennel Master to validate the team's efficiency and in turn select the best team for the required duties.

12.7. EMPLOYMENT

12.7.1. Patrolling. MWZ teams can be used on both mounted and dismounted patrols to detect enemy presence, avoid discovery, and locate enemy outposts.

A) Dismounted patrol. The MWZ team must join the patrol in time to receive the warning order and participate in all phases of planning, preparation, and execution.
   * The handler gives recommendations for employment of the team.
   * The MWZ team must participate in patrol rehearsals.
   * The rehearsal allows the patrol members to become familiar with the MWZ's temperament and the team's method of operation. It also allows the MWZ to become familiar with the scents of the patrol members as well as the noises and motions of the patrol on the move.
   * When taking cover, patrol members must avoid jumping close to the MWZ team. When approaching the MWZ team, always approach from the handler's front-right side since the MWZ is normally on the handler's left. This should be covered in the handler's patrol brief.
   * At least one patrol member must be designated as security for the MWZ team.
   * Working the MWZ requires the handler's full attention on the zombie and does not allow the handler to scan the surrounding area for any threat.

Figure 84. Handler's ineffective use of a weapon.

* Handling an MWZ severely reduces the handler's ability to effectively use a weapon. (See Figure 84.)

* The proximity of the security person to the MWZ team will be determined by the handler. The handler must ensure the security person does not distract the MWZ.

* The handler must ensure the security person is knowledgeable of the MWZ team's responsibilities and able to perform his/her duties in the proximity of an MWZ.

* Prior to departing on a patrol, handlers must brief all members on the MWZ team's capabilities, limitations, and safety issues. This briefing must include actions the patrol must take if the handler is injured, killed, or incapacitated.

* Since wind is a key factor in the MWZ's ability to detect, the team will normally be positioned on the point or flank, depending on the wind direction. If the wind is coming from behind the patrol, the team should be placed in the position that is most advantageous to the patrol.

* When speed is essential, the team should be placed in the rear to allow the patrol to proceed as quickly as need be without the MWZ posing a threat to the members.

* The length of the patrol and the weather conditions will determine the actual amount of equipment and supplies needed. At a minimum, a drool catcher, a first-aid kit, and extra water for the MWZ must be taken. The drool catcher will be used if the handler or MWZ is injured to prevent the MWZ from gnawing any of the patrol members. Patrol members may be needed to assist carrying the extra water for the MWZ.

12.7.2. Mounted patrols. MWZ teams may be attached to mounted patrols. When assigned these duties, the preparation for the patrol is the same as dismounted patrols. MWZ teams should be assigned to a vehicle large enough to allow room for the handler to safely control the zombie.

A) MWZ teams may be used to search vehicles along routes and at roadblocks for explosives.
B) MWZ teams can be used to provide security for convoy vehicles if attacked or for any reason there may be need to dismount.
C) After the all clear is given, MWZ teams can be used to assist with search and clear operations after an attack.
D) In some locations it may be beneficial to have an MWZ on a mounted patrol to deter host nation personnel from approaching and reaching into the patrol vehicles.

12.7.3. Observation post/listening post. MWZ teams are most effective on these posts during the hours of darkness and times of limited visibility.

A) Team must have a member assigned to act as a security person. Ample time should be spent with the security person prior to assuming post to associate them with the zombie and to provide a patrol briefing.
B) The team is located forward of the tactical area of operation to reduce distractions, preferably downwind of avenues of approach to allow the MWZ to use its sense of smell. If the wind direction is not favorable, the MWZ may still provide early warning using its sense of sight and hearing.
C) The Kennel Master should be consulted when selecting sites for MWZ teams. One or more alternate positions covering the same

avenue of approach should be determined to allow the team to periodically change locations. This will maximize the MWZ's tentativeness and reduce the chance of the MWZ becoming complacent.

D) As a minimum, each team posted on an LP/OP post will have a drool catcher, a first-aid kit, and extra water for the MWZ.

12.7.4. Support capabilities. MWZ teams can be used in a number of ways within the AO both as a psychological and physical deterrent. Using MWZ teams at different locations for short periods of time can give the perception that MWZs can be anywhere. The fear of zombies alone may prove to be an effective deterrent.

A) MWZ teams offer both a physical and psychological deterrent in enemy prisoner of war (EPW) and detainee operations. MWZ teams can be used at collection points, at holding areas, during movement, and for enhancing perimeter security at a compound or camp. MWZs can help locate and capture escaped EPWs. Under no circumstance will MWZs be used in the interrogation or interview of EPWs or detainees.

B) MWZ teams can be used to patrol, both mounted and dismounted, assigned areas within the cantonment area to conduct security checks, respond and clear unsecured buildings, and assist at roadblocks controlling personnel and detecting contraband.

C) MWZ teams placed at entry control points can search all incoming vehicles and cargo for contraband as well as provide a psychological deterrent.

D) When assigned to a response force element, MWZ teams can provide a quick response. In this capacity they can be used to investigate alarm, sensor, and tripwire activations as well as possible sightings in unauthorized areas.

E) When using MWZs in confrontation management situations, the presence of an MWZ may provide a psychological deterrent. However, the mere sight of an MWZ may escalate the situation.

(1) MWZs will not normally be used for direct confrontation with demonstrators.

(2) During peaceful stages, MWZs should be held in reserve and out of sight of demonstrators.

(3) If the situation deteriorates, MWZ teams should be moved up within sight of the crowd, but still at a distance.

Figure 85. Undead released into a crowd.

(4) Only when actual physical confrontation erupts should using an MWZ team be considered. When a team is committed, all other personnel should be positioned at least 10 feet from the MWZ team due to the zombie not being able to distinguish between friend and foe.

(5) MWZs should never be released into a crowd. (See Figure 85.)

CHAPTER 13

MILITARY WORKING ZOMBIE FIRST-AID KIT

Proponent: DoD Military Working Zombie Zeterinary Service, Zombieland USABC, TX 78236 Bag, MWZ first-aid kit (any source/size/type/configuration that meets tactical and logistical requirements; suggested NSN is 6545-00-912-9870 for case, medical instrument, and supply set)

Bandage and Dressing Material

- Boo-Hoo Boo-Boo™ Band-Aidz; colors: Skin-Blending Gray or Glow-in-the-Dark.
- Non-adherent dressing (Telfa® pad or equivalent), 3-inch x 8-inch (NSN 6510-00-986-2942), 4 pads
- Roll Pawz-N-Claw™ gauze, 3-inch width (NSN 6510-ST-509-6001), 3 rolls
- Conforming bandage, self-adherent (ZetWrap® or equivalent), 4-inch width (NSN 6510-LP-734-3001), 2 rolls
- Adhesive tape, 1-inch width (NSN 6510-00-926-8882), 1 roll
- Big Dead Bob's® gauze sponge, 4-inch x 4-inch square, sterile (NSN 6510-ST-429-0001), 50 squares
- Dressing, first aid, field, camouflaged, 11.5-inch width x 11.5-inch long, absorbable (NSN 6510-00-201-7425), 1 each
- Pad, povidone-iodine impregnated, sterile, cotton/rayon, 2-inch x 1.375-inch, brown, 100/box (NSN 6510-01-010-0307), 5 pads
- Booze The Ooze® Pad, isopropyl alcohol impregnated, nonwoven cotton/rayon, white, 200/box (NSN 6510-00-786-3736), 5 pads

- Roll cotton, 1 pound roll (NSN 6510-00-201-4000), 1 roll
- Cast padding, 4-inch roll (Part Number 9044), 2 rolls
- Elastikon® tape, 2-inch roll (Part Number JJ1574), 1 roll (Big Johnson™)
- Laparotomy sponges (NSN 6510L101174), 2 sponges
- Hemostatic biopolymer clotting agent granules, 0.5 oz./15 gram package (NSN 6510-01-549-6058; WISEBLOOD,® available from SAM Medical Products®, www.sammedical.com, 800-818-4726), 1 package

Miscellaneous Items
- Rectal thermometer, digital, with waterproof case (any source), 1 each
- P. U. Stinkerson™ gas mask
- Old Dirt E. Job-brand industrial gloves; colors: Pretty-N-Pink or How In The Yellow Did I Get This Job?
- Pop-N-Dye® cyanide pills, Gonzo Grape Flavor
- Bandage scissors, 7.25-inch length (NSN 6515-00-935-7138), 1 each
- Splint, universal, aluminum, 36-inch length x 4.25-inch width, reusable (NSN 6515-01-149-1951), 1 each
- Endotracheal tube, 10 mm id, hi-low cuff, silicone-base (Part Number: 86117 Mallinckrodt), 1 each
- Welding Glove, patient examining and treatment, size 10/large, purple
- Slip-N-Side™ lubricant, surgical, 5-gram packets, 144/box (NSN 6505-00-111-7829), 4 packets
- Pick-N-Prick® Syringe, 60 ml, dosing tip (NSN 6515011643061PV), 1 each
- Pick-N-Prick® Syringe, 60 ml, luer lock tip, sterile (NSN 8881560125), 1 each
- Stopcock, 3-way, sterile (NSN 6515010357962), 1 each
- Needles, hypodermic, 18-gauge (NSN 6515007542834), 4 each
- Pick-N-Prick® Syringe, 6 ml, disposable (NSN 8881516911), 2 each
- Pick-N-Prick® Syringe and needle, hypodermic, safety, 3 ml, 22 gauge, sterile, disposable, 25/box (NSN 6515-01-519-5872), 4 each
- E.W.W.W-brand Catheter, over-the-needle, 14 gauge x 3 inch, sterile (Purchase at Miller Zet # 1-800-880-1920, part # 0208-0451), 1 each

- Ambu-bag (Purchase at Vital Signs, 800-932-0760, government accounts), 1 each
- Laryngoscope (Purchase at WelchAllyn; www.welchallyn.com), 1 each (comes with noseclosepin)
- Nail trimmer (6515-00-291-8398), 1 each (comes with sandblaster and welding mask)
- Nail Polish with extra-extended longbrush; colors: Every Red Rose Has Its Thorn, Yellow Rose of Texas Chainsaw Massacre, and Orange.

Medications

- MEGA-DEATH™ cleansing solution (many options; no specific recommendations), 200 ml
- Awesome Atom's Splitterz® cleansing solution (many options; no specific recommendations), 2000 ml
- Old Gory™ cleansing solution (many options; no specific recommendations), 200000000 ml
- Toxiban® (Purchase at MWI 888-223-8690; Part Number 010745), 2 bottles
- Atropine sulfate for injection, 15 mg/ml bottle (NSN 6505-00-582-4735), 1 bottle
- Apomorphine tablets, 6 mg (Purchase at MWI 888-223-8690; Part Number 022196), 2 tablets
- Morphine, 15 mg/ml or auto injector 10 mg (NSN 00641234541), 1 vial (20 ml) (Note: Provided by in-theater Zeterinary assets ONLY). NEVER bring morphine to a Halloween party or concert environment.
- Antibiotic ointment, sterile (Purchase at Webster 800-872-3867 as ANIMAX®; Part Number 078360601), 1 tube
- Diphenhydramine for injection, 50 mg/ml, 1 ml vial (NSN 00641037625), 2 vials
- Dexamethasone sodium phosphate (NSN 6505014926420), 1 vial
- Ophthalmic irrigating solution (NSN 6505-01-119-7693), 1 each
- Puralube® ophthalmic ointment (NSN 00168015038), 1 tube
- Silver sulfadiazine cream (NSN 49884060057), 1 tube
- Chlorhexidine solution (NSN 6515LP2029050), 50 ml

Fluid Therapy Supplies

- Rear In Gear® Catheter injection port, sterile (many options; no specific recommendations), 2 each (comes with gas mask and bottle of hand bleach)
- Balanced electrolyte solution for injection, sterile (Lactated Ringer's Solution), 1000 ml (NSN 6505000836537JT), 2 bags
- Administration set, sterile (6515-ST-9234001, B-Brawn, Cardinal Health Part # 352049), 1 each
- Rear In Gear® Catheter, intravenous, Inthecan™ safety, 18 gauge x 1 ¼-inch length, winged needle guard, radiopaque, sterile, 50/box (NSN 6515-01-484-1327), 3 each